Philosophy & Political Action

Philosophy
& Political Action

Essays edited for the New York Group of the
Society for Philosophy and Public Affairs

VIRGINIA HELD ❧ **KAI NIELSEN**
CHARLES PARSONS

New York
OXFORD UNIVERSITY PRESS
London 1972 Toronto

Preface

There is now apparent among philosophers, students, and the public at large a growing interest in philosophical consideration of the fundamental moral and political problems confronting any responsible individual in contemporary American society. This book, and the organization which gave rise to it, are reflections of that interest. The essays that follow attempt to deal philosophically but in non-technical language with a number of the issues involved. They indicate, we think, a new concern among philosophers for what might be called specialized moral problems, problems which lie in a region between philosophy and the social and natural sciences, but which have, as yet, no recognizable scholarly fields in which to receive responsible discussion.

The Society for Philosophy and Public Affairs (originally Society for Philosophy and Public Policy) was founded in May 1969, by Sidney Morgenbesser, Thomas Nagel, and others. Its aims can best be indicated by quoting from its statement of purpose:

> The Society for Philosophy and Public Affairs seeks to promote the application of philosophical techniques to the consideration of public issues, and to give substantive political

and social questions a central place in the professional concern of philosophers. The subject is not political philosophy or ethics in the abstract but rather concrete contemporary problems like conscription, police power, methods and occasions of warfare, treatment of individuals charged with crimes, population control, compensation for social disadvantages, eugenics, and so forth.

The Society is intended not especially for political philosophers, but for anyone who thinks it worth while to bring to bear on concrete social problems the general critical and theoretical abilities demanded in all areas of philosophy. One of its immediate aims is to organize discussion of public issues at a high level of technicality. If valuable ideas emerge, the participating philosophers will be able to present them in broader discussions of public issues in their universities and communities or in courses which might benefit from the introduction of such substantive material. It is time to make these concerns a part of the professional activity of philosophers, and to encourage those entering the profession to feel that an interest in public affairs can be an important aspect of their vocation.

The Society initiated the organization of local groups. A New York Group was established in October 1969 and met regularly during that academic year and since. In the spring of 1970, the possibility was raised of publishing a volume of papers along some lines that seemed to be emerging in the discussions and in the thinking of various members of the group. The undersigned editors, who were, respectively, executive board member, chairman, and secretary of the group during its first year, invited the submission of papers from all our members. From the resulting collection of essays they have chosen a limited number on some of the most pressing issues, and added a small number of essays from periodicals. Some excellent papers could unfortunately not be included. Decisions have been made jointly, but Mrs. Held has had primary responsibility for Part I, Mr. Nielsen for Part II, and Mr. Parsons for Part III. All monies received through the sale or use of this book go directly to the New York Group of the Society.

Stuart Hampshire's essay appeared in *The New York Review of Books,* October 8, 1970, and is reprinted by permission. Mr. Hampshire was the speaker at our first meeting in October 1969.

Noam Chomsky's essay appeared in *Ethics,* vol. 79, no. 1 (October 1968) and is reprinted by permission of the author and the University of Chicago Press. Although Chomsky has not participated in the activity of the New York Group, his essay is included not only because of its intrinsic interest and relevance to the others, but because Chomsky's writing and activity in recent years have served as an inspiring example of what might be accomplished in the area of 'philosophy and public affairs' by a man whose specialty is apparently quite remote from social and political philosophy.

We wish to express our gratitude to all those who submitted papers for this project, and to our authors for revising their manuscripts in response to our suggestions. Each editor would like to thank the other editors for helpful criticism of his own contribution. We should like to thank Sidney Morgenbesser and Thomas Nagel for valuable advice at various points, and James Anderson and Stephanie Golden of Oxford University Press for their helpful editorial guidance.

V. H.
K. N.
C. P.
Fall, 1971

Contents

Introduction

CHARLES PARSONS   3

One   REFORM, REVOLUTION, AND
      VIOLENCE   13

      1. On the Choice Between Reform
         and Revolution

         KAI NIELSEN   17

      2. On the Ethical Defense of Violence and
         Destruction

         JOSEPH MARGOLIS   52

      3. Reform and Revolution

         PETER CAWS   72

Two   DEFIANCE OF THE STATE   105

      4. On Understanding Political Strikes

         VIRGINIA HELD   109

      5. Military Service and Moral Obligation

         HUGO ADAM BEDAU   129

6. Governmental Toleration of Civil
Disobedience
SIDNEY GENDIN 160

7. The Morality of Resisting the Penalty
GORDON J. SCHOCHET 175

Three THE RESPONSIBILITIES OF
PHILOSOPHERS 197

8. Philosophers and Public Policy
NOAM CHOMSKY 201

9. The Concept of a Politically Neutral
University
ROBERT L. SIMON 217

10. The Responsibilities of Universities
LEWIS M. SCHWARTZ 234

11. Russell, Radicalism, and Reason
STUART HAMPSHIRE 258

Notes on Contributors 275
Index 279

Philosophy & Political Action

Introduction

CHARLES PARSONS

That Philosophy and Political Action should be the subject of a book in these times is no doubt a reflection of the climate of political activism which in recent years has gripped large parts of American society, particularly university communities. Professional philosophers as citizens of the republic would naturally participate in this movement or at least take some stance toward it. But in addition there are circumstances, some relating to professional groups in the contemporary world, others relating to philosophy as such, that might give philosophers a special concern or a special role.

Philosophy has from its beginnings been concerned with social and political matters, and any discussion of them which reaches the most general principles or the most fundamental problems of justification will be philosophical. It is often thought that such discussion is best carried on at some remove from the most pressing current practical concerns. There is much truth in this, but it is also true that in politics as well as in other things critical situations often bring to light the most serious difficulties of principle. Although few of the great political philosophers were professional politicians, they all participated in some way in the struggles of their own times and wrote with the contemporary situation in mind.

One of the great issues of political philosophy is that of legitimacy and political obligation: What conditions must a state satisfy in order to merit the allegiance of its citizens? Why is the citizen obligated (if indeed he is) to obey the laws and other enactments of the state? When is this obligation suspended or even replaced by a duty to disobey or even to overthrow the government?

The general question what conditions a state or government must satisfy to be legitimate, so that this obligation exists prima facie, and the more general question of the foundations of legitimate government are likely to be most pressing where a change in the basic political structure (e.g. the constitution) is vital to realizing the aspirations of important parts of the population, and where such a change is feasible; in other words in actually or potentially revolutionary situations. Whether America is now in such a situation is a matter of controversy. At least until very recently the dominant opinion was that it is not. Political discussion proceeded on the assumption that it was neither possible nor desirable to rewrite the American constitution *ab initio* and that the more subtle subversion of it which either was taking place or might take place in the near future was to be deplored. Even where the legitimacy of the American government seemed to be denied, as in the title of the 1967 manifesto *A Call To Resist Illegitimate Authority,* the purpose was to justify and encourage a limited range of acts of resistance against the Vietnam war and the military establishment.[1] This dominant opinion is reflected, though subjected to challenge, in the essays below on the question of reform and revolution.

1. The *Call To Resist* was printed as an advertisement in the *New York Review of Books,* vol. 9, no. 6 (October 12, 1967), and elsewhere, by a group called *Resist,* organized mainly to support draft resistance.

The example of the *Call To Resist* shows the practical situation which the theoretical concerns of philosophers reflect: the most acute discontents lead to acts of a limited nature, of 'civil disobedience' or 'resistance,' either because the state is felt to be impregnable or because the discontents are focused on a specific area of the government's functioning.[2] The intent of such acts is not to overthrow the government but to limit its power and to make it change its course. It is in relation to the problems of such acts that the topical concerns of philosophers interact with the tradition of political philosophy.

A man might regard his government as on the whole legitimate and therefore accept an obligation to obey it, and yet feel morally compelled to disobey some of its laws and enactments for one of two reasons: he might find certain situations which the government tolerates or promotes morally intolerable and yet find legal means of action against them insufficient, or he might find that some enactment commands *him* to do something he considers immoral, or to refrain from doing something he considers his right. It seems clear that unless the standard of legitimacy is set so high that no real government meets it, the obligation to obey a legitimate government is not so absolute that it cannot be overridden by the above-mentioned sorts of considerations. Nonetheless, the 'law-abiding' citizen is faced in such situations with a moral conflict which can be very serious. And given that it is *sometimes* right to disobey the law, the question what kinds of disobedience are justified under what circumstances can

2. Some disobedience to law might be justified in situations whose moral significance is much less than in the typical cases of civil disobedience, and where no one would hold that he morally *must* disobey. It is certainly not wrong simply to disobey, without fanfare and even secretly, a silly or irresponsible law or regulation which encroaches on one's interest in a serious way.

be difficult, both theoretically and practically.[3] This question and related questions arising from it have given rise in recent years to a considerable literature, which has been perhaps the principal contribution of political philosophy to current political discussion; the essays on these matters (see Part II) should be seen as part of an ongoing discussion. Many other subjects of current interest have a certain philosophical tradition behind them, and philosophers have written about them in recent times. Of these revolution (see Part I) is only one, and therefore a whole range of current philosophical concern is unrepresented in this volume.[4]

That philosophers should seek to bring their professional

3. The category of civil disobedience presumably covers only a limited range of the possible actions in disobedience to law which fall short of overthrowing the government. Some objections to narrow definitions of civil disobedience seem to presuppose that it should cover *all* such acts which are justifiable. This seems to me a poor choice of terminology. But it reflects the fact that not enough has been done to define those types of acts short of revolution which might be justified but which do not fit in with the traditional types of civil disobedience. Civil disobedience is usually understood as presupposing the general legitimacy of the government against which it is directed. Much of the discussion of 'resistance' in recent years seems based on the assumption that the government is illegitimate but that overthrowing it is either impossible or too costly. But the general illegitimacy of the government may not be a necessary condition for the moral justification for acts which go beyond the limitations traditionally associated with civil disobedience. For example, much of the actual resistance to government in the world takes the form of evasions of various sorts. This is not normally classified as civil disobedience, for a number of reasons which seem to me good: for example, it does not have the character of a demonstration or an attempt at forceful persuasion of the authorities; it is not necessarily motivated by conscience. But it does not seem to me that acts of evasion are necessarily wrong or politically insignificant. Consider Prohibition; part of the case against it is that it made acts *seem* justified which encouraged genuine criminality.

4. The writings of legal philosophers such as H. L. A. Hart have for some years provided examples of the kind of philosophical discussion we seek to encourage. Among the subjects treated more recently are abortion, war, and violence. A new journal, *Philosophy and Public Affairs,* edited by Marshall Cohen, began publication in 1971.

resources to bear on current issues, however, is not distinctive of philosophers in these times but rather exemplifies a movement characteristic of professional groups generally. In practically every academic field, and in other professions such as law and medicine, people, and especially younger people, have felt not only a concern with public matters and an urge toward political action but a great discontent with the separation of their professional roles from their political or other public roles. They want not just to act about public matters but to act in their capacities as scholars, scientists, doctors, or lawyers.

Hence we find a proliferation of organizations of professionals of different types 'for peace' or 'for social and political action' (of which our Society is a modest example); the development of radical schools in academic fields such as political science and history; the intrusion of political struggle into the affairs of professional associations through such efforts as attempts to get meetings to pass political resolutions;[5] the growth of the more politically relevant sides of many fields; the new encouragement given in medicine and law to alternative careers outside the normal pattern of professional advancement; and especially many activities within universities, intended to alter their politically relevant commitments and to introduce new ones, some alien to traditional conceptions of what kinds of activity it is proper for a university to undertake.

It ought to be observed that some of these activities fall within the normal range of activity of the profession in question: for scholars, research and writing, though motivated by social and political concerns; for lawyers, defending clients

5. In the American Philosophical Association, this has been quite successful. The Eastern Division meeting in December 1970 passed resolutions which were more radical in tone than the average member would be likely to endorse. (See *Journal of Philosophy*, vol. 68 (1971), pp. 22-24.) A counterattack is developing.

in prosecutions of a political character or where civil liberties issues are at stake, or pressing lawsuits on behalf of some cause; for doctors, working to bring medical care to deprived groups or into situations of confrontation. Other such activities are more direct political action and efforts to involve the institutions of the profession in such action.

This drive has met with great resistance in universities, professional associations, and other professional institutions. This was to be expected on obvious *political* grounds: the political commitments expressed are almost entirely directed against established powers and interests. However, the resistance has stood not just on the substance of the issues at stake (in our major universities today, hardly anyone, least of all a high administrator, will publicly defend the American war effort in Indochina) but on values calling for a certain political neutrality on the part of the institutions involved. Just what these values are is not easy to define (but see the paper by Simon below), and those who have introduced them into these disputes may have had ulterior motives. In part, the call for neutrality may be merely an expression of a desire to stay out of disputes in which one might get hurt (just as in international affairs) or of pessimism about what substantive political positions will triumph if neutrality is abandoned.

It seems to me that this social phenomenon is not just an interesting problem for sociological explanation[6] but a more

6. About this problem I have only speculation to offer. It seems that professions (and very likely occupations generally) provide a more important and basic source of personal and collective identification for middle-class people today than in the past, at the expense of family, religion, region, and even nation. If being a doctor or a physicist is not just a way of making a living but defines who one is and what sort of community one relates to, one will not want the role to be isolated from one's most morally serious commitments. About the academic world, it ought also to be remarked that universities are more total communities than most places of work and now they are larger and apparently more significant for the society as a whole than before. In the

or less necessary response to the realities of modern society. The professions are the institutions which maintain, advance, and apply organized knowledge, and everybody knows that the role of such knowledge is greatly enlarged in today's world. The professions are larger and more important than in the past, and the consequences of their actions are more visible, more serious, and more likely to cause conflict.

The invention of nuclear weapons dramatized what should have been clear all along: even quite abstruse researches in the sciences can prove to have applications with bad or even catastrophic consequences. A scientist who puts his work at the service of such applications has moral responsibility for the consequences. A responsible practitioner of any branch of knowledge would be concerned about the consequences of applying it. He would naturally want his profession to have *institutions* which watched over its application, to promote the good and to guard against the bad.

In the more theoretical branches of knowledge, the development of such institutions has been quite one-sided, at least since the decline of theological censorship: science and its application have been promoted with very little attempt, before the nuclear era, to develop the kind of restraints which the enormous power of technology requires. And recent times have seen an enormous increase in the promotion of technological power, so that although the effort devoted to restraint has increased, the situation may be more unbalanced than ever.

The practical relevance of branches of theoretical knowledge other than natural science has not been so dramatically demonstrated. Social scientists have served government and

---

Columbia crisis of 1968, it was remarkable how the participants viewed the university as a political society of which students, faculty, administrators, and employees were different classes of *citizens*. (The Columbia University Senate, instituted in 1969, is based on that conception.)

other institutions and movements as 'technicians,' and the
nature of this service is one of the prime issues around which
unrest in universities has revolved. But in the social sciences
and humanities there is another problem: the relevance of
the theories to ideology, not only in the sense (which arises
in natural science also) that ideologies may have committed
themselves to propositions which can be refuted by science,
but in the sense that the theories themselves may be ideological and rest partly on faith or commitment. There is great
temptation for intellectuals to be enlisted as apologists for
one or another regime or movement.

All of these considerations show, I think, that there is no
lack of an objective basis for a scholar in an academic field
(and, I should argue, even more so in another profession) to
find in the content of his field much that is relevant to his
political concerns, and to believe that his professional status carries political responsibilities. It is a serious question
whether these responsibilities are discharged by devoting a
certain amount of time to 'concerned' professional practice,
or whether they require full entry into the political arena.
What the answer is clearly depends on the professional field
and on the abilities and circumstances of the individual. A
physicist concerned about nuclear weapons is almost bound
to do something to bring the issues to the attention of laymen,
whether in government or the public at large, and therefore
to do something quite different from the normal activities of
physicists. A philosopher, on the other hand, may step outside his professional role almost completely when he does
things other than research, writing, teaching, and perhaps
certain political activities within universities. Only the most
exceptional philosopher, such as perhaps Bertrand Russell,
possesses an authority with the public or with government
comparable to what being a scientist confers. The value of
political pronouncements by philosophical organizations is

for this reason very limited. But philosophy carries with it no special knowledge of or experience in practical politics. What philosophers *as such* can do to influence public life is principally to influence the general climate of opinion by ideas and arguments.[7]

In closing, I shall try to indicate briefly the more essential values which underlie resistance to the intrusion of politics into professional life. Invasion of academic life and equally of the more 'practical' professions by politics has familiar dangers. What criticism of the political neutrality of many institutions often succeeds in showing is that they are not totally free of political influence or bias, particularly those which pervade the whole society and constitute the 'established order.' One may concede this and still distinguish this situation from one of much more overt politicization, where an institution becomes a direct arena of political struggle and decisions are made for the purpose of enhancing the position of one or another faction, or where other normally autonomous considerations become subordinated to political ones. As a practical matter, the doctrine of political neutrality seems designed to guard against this, and insofar as it does it serves an essential function. Perhaps it would serve this function better if it were better defined so as not to commit institutions to a neutrality they barely even pretend to observe.

But this consideration is not just one of institutional peace; it rests on values intrinsic to the nature of knowledge: knowledge rests on the autonomy of reason, which in turn requires that judgments about matters of objective truth, which are at the core of the function of any profession, no matter how practical, be made on objective grounds, independent both of coercion and of the biases of the person

7. The reader may compare this view with those expressed by Chomsky and Schwartz in this volume and by Earle in the article referred to by Schwartz.

judging. This represents a norm which is not refuted if it is shown not to be observed in some particular case or even if it cannot be shown *ever* to have been observed. The same autonomy must apply also to decisions about furthering any branch of knowledge—about the competence of personnel, about the organization in other respects of institutions for the furtherance and dissemination of knowledge. Every genuine profession must be in certain essentials self-governing, because it institutionalizes the kind of knowledge on which decisions about its government must be based. This much is certainly agreed by those who have written about the matter in the present volume.

We have seen that concern for the morally responsible use of knowledge calls for a certain engagement on the part of professionals, which is bound to affect the institutions of the profession. We have also seen that autonomy of judgment and investigation requires strongly limiting the effect of politics on professional activity and the government of professional institutions. The use of knowledge in a morally responsible manner requires a reconciliation of the conflicts which arise between these tendencies. It seems to me that we do not know the principles on which such a reconciliation must be based. On the other hand we must proceed on the assumption that a responsible use of knowledge is possible. The search for such principles is a serious theoretical task. Because of its practical relevance, philosophers will not be the only ones to engage in it.[8]

8. I should like to thank Miss Nadya Nemikin for typing the Preface and Introduction and for other services in the work on this book.

One
REFORM, REVOLUTION, AND VIOLENCE

Introduction

Can revolution be justified? Can reform bring about an equivalent improvement in the social condition? Do those in positions of unwarranted privilege yield to reform without the threat of revolution in the background? Do the bad consequences of violence predictably outweigh the good? Must revolution be violent? And to what extent, if indeed violence must occur, are the amount and kind of violence crucially relevant?

The seriousness, the inescapability, the meaningfulness of moral evaluations of political and social choices have contributed in recent years to a decline in noncognitivist ethical approaches among philosophers. The noncognitivist position so influential among writers in the social sciences has maintained that fundamental moral judgments and indeed whole normative ethical theories cannot be validated and cannot, accordingly, be components of knowledge. On this view, moral justification of choices with regard to the central, principled questions of reform and revolution is impossible.

Developments in ethical theory putting such a view clearly on the defensive are discussed by Kai Nielsen in the paper that follows. Moreover, as the papers by Nielsen and by Peter Caws in Part I illustrate, philosophers dealing today with normative political and social issues are frequently willing to maintain that moral justification of alternative positions is indeed sometimes possible, and must often be at least attempted. By supporting either continuation or change in any given social system or in any of its components, we cannot escape acting as if one position is more justifiable than another.

These papers seek to provide reasonable answers to some of the most fundamental questions concerning revolution and reform. Conceptual clarification of these terms is a necessary beginning, but the authors proceed, beyond this, to specify various aspects of society which can and ought to be transformed, and to offer reasoned judgments about the justifiability of alternative courses of action open to citizens and philosophers. They discuss issues directly relevant to us at the present time, as well as basic questions relevant to other contexts.

The older noncognitivist position in ethics is still maintained by various philosophers, among them Joseph Margolis, who has contributed the second paper in Part I. However, Margolis employs this approach in such a way that it has, itself, normative implications. Since no existing set of established attitudes or institutions can be morally justified, the "radical equality of ethical visions" he discerns yields the advocate of gradual reform and accepted procedures no superior moral position over the advocate of revolutionary violence.

There are, in any case, kinds of revolution and kinds of reform. To act reasonably under some conditions may require us to choose either revolution or reform. Or it may require that, in some senses at least, we choose both.

1

On the Choice Between Reform and Revolution

KAI NIELSEN

I

Given the history of this century it is understandable that there should be both an extensive fear of revolution and a distrust of the efficacy of reform. Yet when one considers such countries as the United States, Rhodesia and South Africa (not to mention the poorer and savagely exploited parts of the world), it is also becoming increasingly obvious to any tolerably well-informed person who is also humane that a fundamental social transformation of these societies is, humanly speaking, imperative. And this, of course, thrusts one back on the suspect ideas of revolution and far-reaching social reform. This in turn raises questions about what one is committed to in believing in the moral necessity of radical social transformation. Is one committed to revolution or only to some form of very fundamental social reform? And this in turn naturally provokes the question what exactly is the difference between them and what is one asking for when one advocates a progressive fundamental or radical social transformation?

A revised version of an essay first published in *Inquiry*, vol. 14, no. 3 (1971), Universitetsforlaget, Oslo, Norway. Reprinted with revisions, by permission.

Such questions were debated by Kautsky, Bernstein, Lenin and Luxemburg in another context, but without even remotely suggesting that what they had to say is irrelevant for us today, I want to look at this cluster of questions afresh. Is the assumed distinction between revolution and fundamental or radical reform a distinction concerning only the means, the instrumentalities, of social change, or does it refer to what is aimed at as well, e.g. *the kind* of change and the extent of change? Is the putative distinction between fundamental or radical reform and revolution a spurious one? And if the distinction is a genuine one, are they on a continuum? And more fundamentally still, is it necessary, if one is committed to seeking and advocating a fundamental social transformation, to be for revolution? Or, is the working for reform the only reasonable alternative for a humane person? This cluster of questions in turn raises a bevy of more specific questions including such overtly conceptual questions as what is meant by 'revolution' and 'reform.'

To gain some purchase on these issues, it is well to begin by asking: what are we asking for in asking for a fundamental social transformation or a transformation of society?

In asking for a fundamental social transformation or transformation of society, we are surely asking—if we are committed to a progressive transformation—for an end to human oppression and exploitation. Even if this is only a heuristic ideal and we can actually only hope, realistically, to diminish the extent and severity of oppression and human degradation, it still remains a fundamental guiding ideal: it tells us what we are aiming to approximate as much as possible in any progressive transformation of society. To achieve this transformation all forms of racism, ethnocentrism, chauvinism (including male chauvinism) and rigid social stratification, with its built-in privileges, must come to an end. Class divi-

sions and alienated labor would have to disappear.[1] This
would involve the abolition of the bourgeoisie; that is to say,
there could no longer be a capitalist or any other kind of corporate ruling class, an unresponsive and privileged bureaucratic or technocratic elite, or even an establishment with extensive privileges and advantages. The modes of production
in the society would have to be thoroughly socialized so that
their underlying rationale would be to serve the interests of
everyone alike. To be morally acceptable, specific privileges,
when they are necessary at all, must be such that they further
this underlying ideal.

This above characterization of what is involved in a progressive transformation of society is for the most part negative. Positively our characterization will be vaguer. As we
know from Dante, evil is much easier to characterize than
positive good. It is difficult, in talking about such a transformation, to say anything general which is not vague or
platitudinous or (what is more likely) both. A progressively
transformed society would give men and women a fuller and
more human life. This quasi-tautology unpacks into the claim

1. I do not even suggest here, much less assert, that there could in any society
be a complete end to social stratification. To take as a goal the end of all social stratification is an idle fantasy. Indeed Ralf Dahrendorf has given us good
reasons for believing that a society without any social stratification at all is a
conceptual impossibility. See Ralf Dahrendorf, *Essays in the Theory of Society* (Stanford, Calif.: Stanford University Press, 1968), pp. 151-78. In working
for the achievement of a classless society and for an end to alienated labor,
one need not and indeed should not deny that some social stratification will
remain. But to say that is one thing, to say there must remain something like
a capitalist class or party elite exploiting workers or a bureaucratic elite controlling the destinies of people is quite another. That such class divisions
shall come to an end within the foreseeable future may be very problematic
indeed, but such a goal is not an idle fantasy; it is not an impossible ideal.
For an analysis of the central importance of the concept of alienated labor
see István Mészáros, *Marx's Theory of Alienation* (London: Merlin Press,
1970).

that people in such a transformed society would attain a
liberation in which their full human powers and their creative capacities would be developed in many directions. They
would not be one-sided, emotionally or intellectually stunted,
or academic *Fachidioten,* but would be capable of managing
their affairs, helping in the management of society in the
interests of everyone alike and capable of a wide range of
enjoyments and creative activities. And they would not only
have these capabilities, they would be anxious to exercise
them. In addition, there would be an end to possessive individualism and a commodity accumulation which goes beyond
what humans need and would want if their wants were not
artificially stimulated to enhance capitalist enterprise. Rather
there would be a commitment to social equality and to a fair
and nearly equal distribution of the available goods and
services. In different concrete situations these different notions, positive and negative, will of course take different
specifications and amplifications. But the elasticity of these
specifications is not endless, since they are bounded by these
general but non-formal conceptions. In transforming society
our aim should be human freedom (the liberation of human
creativity), equality, the enhancement of human happiness
and the avoidance of misery. In our present historical circumstances this is best achieved in (a) a society founded upon
common ownership of the means of production and (b) a
society in whose running all persons participate. To fully
exercise our human agency, we need a common culture with
a maximum of human participation. Here we have the
Leitmotiv for a progressive transformation of society.

For societies to be transformed so that this would be a
reality, we would need, even in the most progressive societies,
a very considerable institutional change; and in advanced
industrial societies such as the United States, Japan and West
Germany, the changes would have to be structural and very

profound indeed. Could such a transformation be achieved without a revolution? Before trying to answer this we need to clarify what is meant by 'revolution,' how it contrasts with 'reform' and what the conceptual links are between revolution and violence, for on *some* employments of 'revolution' our question would be nearly as silly as 'Are all emerald things green?' That is to say, on some readings of 'revolution' it may be true by definition or at least in some sense necessarily true that to be committed to seeking and advocating a fundamental progressive social transformation is to be for revolution.

II

So let us first try to see what is meant by 'revolution' and by 'reform.' In doing this it is important to keep in mind that only against the background of a belief in progress does it make sense to speak of either revolution or reform. To reform is to convert into another and better form; it is, as the *Oxford English Dictionary* puts it, "to free from previous faults or imperfections." In speaking of reforming institutions and social arrangements we take it to be the case that we are correcting or improving them by amending or altering them through removing faults, abuses, malpractices and the like. This gives to understand that one social arrangement or set of social arrangements or a practice or institution or set of practices or institutions can be an advance or improvement over another. But this is to believe that progress is possible within a limited time span at least, though this is not sufficient to commit one to the full-fledged conceptions of progress found in Condorcet, Hegel or Marx. A belief in the viability of revolutionary activity, as is well known and frequently remarked on, is even more obviously linked to a belief in progress. And if a belief in progress was one of the great and persistent illusions of the nineteenth century, then belief in either reform or revolution is belief in an illusion.[2]

We must remember that in addition to informational content terms have an emotive force, i.e. a tendency to express and evoke emotions. Compare, to see that there is such a feature of language, four-letter words with their genteel equivalents. Keeping this in mind, if we focus on the usage recorded in current dictionaries, it is evident that 'revolution' and 'revolutionary' have a negative emotive force while 'reform' and 'reformer' have a positive emotive force, though we must not forget that for some subgroups of native speakers the usage is changing and the terms come to have a different force for them. (After all, in the present pop culture, 'revolution' is in and 'reform' is out.) Given the conventional criteria for synonyms and near synonyms, 'remodel,' 'reconstruct,' 'reclaim,' 'redeem,' 'regenerate,' 'correct,' 'improve,' 'restore' and 'better' (all in certain types of sentences) count as synonyms or near synonyms for 'reform' when 'reform' is a verb; when 'reform' is a noun, 'correction,' 'progress,' 'reconstruction' and 'reformation' count as synonyms. Here we clearly see that by definition 'to reform' is to do something which at least the reformer takes to be desirable, and more generally, in many (perhaps most) contexts 'reform' is so employed that something would not as a rule be said within a society to be a reform unless it is thought to be desirable; though 'stupid and undesirable reforms' is not a contradiction in terms. But undesirable reforms are reforms which have somehow misfired, and misfired *as reforms*. Furthermore, if the word 'reform' is to continue to have an employment, reforms taken to be stupid or undesirable must be the exception and not the rule. If I assert that I have made a reform, I give you to understand that I have done something good.

2. I have tried to give a kind of minimal and de-mythologized defense of the idea of progress in my "Progress," *The Lock Haven Review*, no. 7 (1965).

There is in short for most speakers a pronounced pro-emotive force to 'reform.' Only on some uses of 'reformer,' where a reformer is equated with a zealot, crusader or do-gooder, does 'reform' have a negative emotive force. By contrast, given the usages assembled in dictionaries, it is evident enough that 'revolution' and 'revolutionary' typically have a negative emotive force. I shall come at this in an indirect way.

We are interested in revolution as a socio-political concept, but the word 'revolution' has other uses too; in attempting a very general characterization of 'revolution,' one dictionary tells us that we are talking about "a complete or drastic change of any kind." And when we keep in mind that 'revolution' has this wide range of employments, it is worth noting that sometimes 'revolution' is equated with 'spasm,' 'convulsion,' 'revulsion,' 'cataclysm.' Here we have words which have a negative emotive force. This emotive force is evident again in those contexts where 'revolution' is equated with 'rebellion,' 'insurrection,' 'subversion,' 'destruction' or 'breakup'; and we have adjectives such as 'radical,' 'extreme,' 'catastrophic' and 'intransigent' linked with 'revolution' and 'revolutionary.' And while it is true that the meanings of 'revolution' and 'reform' are not hobbled to their emotive force, this force is such that, unless we take pains to account for it and neutralize it in arguments about the justification of revolution, we are at an initial disadvantage in defending revolution.

In order to know what the actual substantive claims of the reformers are, we must consider what their criteria for 'improvement,' 'bettering,' and the like are. Socio-political reform involves legal, educational, economic and generally institutional correction or improvements. Faults and abuses are corrected. What is critical here is to be clear about the actual criteria for improvement, correction, amendment or making better. In speaking of reforming West Germany's archaic university system, for example, are we talking about altering it so that it will respond more efficiently to the needs of a modern industrial state or do we primarily have in mind altering it so as to extend, sharpen and systematize critical awareness among the West German population, or do we mean something else again? What in such a situation is the amplification of 'reform'? But whatever we may mean, we are also saying, when we defend educational reform, that we are for improvement in the educational structures and not for sweeping them away and replacing them by utterly new structures of a radically different nature. In talking more generally of socio-political reform, which typically would include as one of its crucial components educational reform, we are talking of amending or improving the fundamental institutions, practices and social arrangements of a society so as to correct and remove, as far as possible, its faults, abuses or malpractices.

Very typically, in speaking of reform we have in mind changes which apply to specific amendments or alterations of existing social arrangements. They are the type of reforms, aimed as they are only at the elimination of specific ills, that Karl Popper regards as the only admissible reforms. They can be handled by intelligent piecemeal social engineering without a challenge to the basic ideology of a culture and they do not require argument about fundamental human ends or Utopian blueprints for the improvement of the human condition. Commitment to reform here makes a ready contrast with revolution. But when we speak, as we do, of 'far-reaching socio-political reforms,' 'fundamental reforms,' or 'radical reforms,' the contrast with revolutionary change is not so clear. I shall return to this point after I have characterized revolution.

Political theorists have given us typologies of revolution and many have stressed that there is a single type, socio-political revolution, which is of the greatest critical interest when we ask about revolution and reform and about the justification of revolution.[3] This conception of a socio-political revolution is a more specific characterization than the related characterization given in the dictionaries, where the characterization of the relevant sense of 'revolution' is that a revolution is a complete overthrow of a government or social system by those previously subject to it and the substitution of a new government or social system. Paradigms of revolutions are the expulsion of the Stuart dynasty and the transfer of sovereignty to William and Mary, the overthrow of the French monarchy and the establishment of republican government during the French Revolution, and the American, Russian, Chinese and Cuban revolutions. But it is of some consequence to see that this is a mixed bag of examples. In particular the French, Russian, Chinese and Cuban revolutions are very different—and indeed particularly different in at least one important respect—from the American revolution and the English revolution of 1688. The former revolutions —those sometimes called 'the Great Revolutions'—are distinguished from the others in that these revolutions *altered in a profound sense the social structure of the societies in which the revolution occurred.* When these revolutions were consolidated, the social structures of the societies which were so revolutionized (and sometimes some others as well) were radically altered. But this was not so when the Stuart dynasty was overthrown and William and Mary became the English

3. See Eugen Rosenstock-Hüssy, *Out of Revolution* (1938), Crane Brinton, *The Anatomy of Revolution* (New York: Vintage Books, 1952), George S. Pettee, *The Process of Revolution* (New York: Harper and Bros., 1938), and "Revolution—Typology and Process," in Carl J. Friedrich, ed., *Revolution* (New York: Atherton Press, 1966). See also the essays by C. B. Macpherson, "Revolution and Ideology in the Late Twentieth Century," Eugene Kamenka, "The Concept of a Political Revolution," and Richard A. Falk, "World Revolution and International Order," all in Friedrich, ed., *Revolution*. See also Peter A. R. Calvert, "Revolution: The Politics of Violence," *Political Studies*, vol. XV, no. 1 (February 1967).

sovereigns, and it was not true of the American Revolution. In the last example there was an overthrow of a government and of colonial rule, but the rebellious colonists only established a government of a slightly different sort. There was no change in basic social structure. The change was quite unlike the change from Batista's Cuba to present-day Cuba. With so-called great revolutions there is what has been called a "shock to the foundations of society."[4] Such revolutions, as Karl Kautsky has pointed out, do not come from nowhere. They are like births, sudden in occurring but only possible after a complex development. When they occur there is "a sharp, sudden change in the social location of power," but this change is not one that can occur without certain tolerably determinate conditions obtaining.[5] For there to be a revolution, it is often claimed, there must be widespread misery, deprivation and exploitation following a brief period of rising expectations which, after some minor improvements in the oppressed people's condition, are in turn dashed by a turn of events for the worse. When there is a despair over the system coupled with a sense that things could be better, the ground for revolutionary activity is being broken; where there is widespread, despairing dissatisfaction with the present social order linked with a conception—often nebulous—of a new social order, where, in Fanon's phrase, we "set afoot a new man," we have conditions—though indeed not sufficient conditions—for revolution.

Where under these conditions a revolution is actually sustained so that a government topples and a new social order is brought into being, we have the type of revolution—a social and political revolution—that is relevant to our discussions of revolution and reform. This sense of 'revolution' is prop-

4. Paul Schrecker, "Revolution as a Problem in the Philosophy of History," in Friedrich, ed., *Revolution*, p. 35.
5. Kamenka, op. cit., p. 124.

erly caught by two political theorists on the Left: C. B. Macpherson and Herbert Mercuse. Macpherson characterizes a revolution as

> a transfer of state power by means involving the use or threat of organized unauthorized force, and the subsequent consolidation of that transferred power, with a view to bringing about a fundamental change in social, economic and political institutions.[6]

In a similar vein Marcuse writes that a revolution is

> the overthrow of a legally established government and constitution by a social class or movement with the aim of altering the social as well as the political structure.[7]

If we mark the distinction between violent and nonviolent radical activity by the refusal of the nonviolent radical to injure or (where he can help it) tolerate injury to his antagonists, we can see that there is no *conceptual* reason why a revolution must be violent, though there may very well be substantial empirical justification for believing that all revolutions of the type characterized above by Macpherson and Marcuse will *in fact* be violent. (It is important to remember that there are degrees of violence. Revolutions can and do vary.) On these terms it is a mistake to characterize a social and political revolution in such a way as to make 'a nonviolent revolution' a contradiction in terms and thus it is a mistake to define 'revolution,' as Carl Friedrich does, as "a sudden and violent overthrow of an established political order."[8]

6. Macpherson, op. cit., p. 140.
7. Herbert Marcuse, "Ethics and Revolution," in Richard T. De George, ed., *Ethics and Society* (Garden City, N.Y.: Anchor Books, 1966), p. 134.
8. Carl J. Friedrich, "An Introductory Note on Revolution," in Friedrich, ed., *Revolution*.

In the extant typologies the kind of revolution Macpherson and Marcuse have characterized is contrasted with (1) *private palace revolutions,* e.g. the murder of Duncan by Macbeth followed by Macbeth's succession to the throne; (2) *public palace revolutions,* e.g. a *coup d'état* such as the typical South American revolution; (3) systemic revolutions, i.e. a change, usually through a series of civil wars, in the system of state organization (e.g. a city-state system), affecting a wide-ranging cultural community, for example the change in the state system of the time of Pericles to that of the time of Augustus and the fall of the Roman Empire; and (4) *colonial revolutions* (rebellions) against rule by the government of another country. The American Revolution is a good example of the fourth kind. But when, as in the Algerian revolution, there is also a considerable alteration of social structure, we have not only a colonial revolution but a socio-political revolution. It is this latter kind of revolution—the socio-political revolution—that I am interested in when I ask about the contrast between reform and revolution. It clearly marks off revolutions from military coups, palace revolutions, colonial rebellions and preventative counterrevolutions. It in effect limits 'true revolutions' by a reasonable *persuasive* definition to the great social upheavals which bring about lasting and extensive socio-political change.

III

Given this construal, what exactly is the difference between revolution and radical reform? Typical reforms seek to amend, correct and improve what we already have; they do not seek to destroy it and replace it with something new. In the United States redistricting, lowering the voting age, a guaranteed annual income, and a weakening of the filibuster rule would be reforms, though certainly not sweeping reforms. What would count as radical reform? Suppose—to take a fanciful but instructive example—through the normal channels the constitution of the United States were to be so changed that (1) the United States like England and Canada went on a parliamentary system; (2) the division between federal and state government was abolished and newly drawn federally administered districts were created; (3) capitalism was abolished and all the major means of production came to be socially owned; and finally (4) the new government, together with the educational apparatus of the state, officially declared its support for atheism and socialism. Would such a set of changes in the United States constitute a radical reform or a peaceful revolution?

Surely such a change would be like reform in that it would be accomplished by 'going through channels' and by using the legal and political apparatus of a state that was subsequently to be radically transformed. But it is unlike reform in that, rather than simply improving or correcting the extant institutions and social arrangements, something quite new and different would be brought into being. Moreover, it would be like a revolution in that there would result a "radical transformation of the process of government, of the official foundations of sovereignty or legitimacy and of the conception of social order." [9] Yet here we have something which admits of degrees, for in the hypothesized change in the form of the government of the United States, we still have a parliamentary system with political parties and the like. *From a certain point of view,* the change could be said not to be very deep—certainly not deep enough to constitute a radical transformation of the official foundations of sovereignty or legitimacy. At this point we have something which is so essentially contested that there is no objectively correct thing to say. There are paradigms of revolutions and revolutionary

9. Kamenka, op. cit., p. 124.

acts which could not properly be called 'radical reforms,' e.g.
the Chinese revolution and the Cuban revolution. But, as with
so many quite useful concepts, there is no exact cutoff point.
There is no precise point where we can show that reformist
activity ends and revolutionary activity starts. As Wittgenstein in effect points out, we could by stipulation *set up* such
a conceptual boundary, but this would settle nothing, for
others with equal legitimacy could set up boundaries at other
points.

Someone might resist at this juncture and assert that my
above example is plainly only an example of radical reform,
because there is in it no use or threat of organized unauthorized force, and the use or threatened use of such force is a
necessary condition for revolutionary change. There is—it
might be claimed—a natural boundary; we need not just draw
one. But so to argue is in effect to emasculate the concept of
radical reform, for surely what would naturally be characterized as radical reform would typically—in actual fact
perhaps always—involve, through strikes (illegal or otherwise), demonstrations, disruptions, the seizure of factories, or
riots, unauthorized pressure to bring about such a change.
The radical reform would come about under the threat of
the use of unauthorized force. Such deep structural changes
as those in my example never in fact occur without the threat
of force or extreme social disruption. Logically speaking, it
could be otherwise, but it isn't. So it still remains true that
my hypothesized change in the state apparatus and social
structure of the United States could with equal legitimacy
be called 'a radical or fundamental reform' or 'a revolution'
or both. We have a *continuum* here and not a clearly de-
marcated boundary.

In turn it might be replied that there actually is a qualitative and important difference showing itself in my example,
namely that with revolution in contrast to radical reform

there is and indeed must be an overthrow of a legally established government. And since this cannot be so with a radical
reform, it is a mistake to claim that there is no principled
difference between radical reform and revolution. But it
should be replied that where there is extensive breakdown
in the functioning of institutions and established ways of
doing things, and where a government under the dire threat
of violence and total social chaos so fundamentally alters itself
that we have a radically different government and set of social
arrangements, it is hardly a deviation from linguistic regu-
larity to say that the legally established government has been
overthrown. With Nixon out under such extreme pressures,
the power of state governments and (consequently) of the
South broken, and a self-consciously atheistic and socialistic
group of ideologists firmly in control, with federal adminis-
trative districts rather than states, it would not be unnatural
to speak of 'the overthrow of the United States government.'
At the very least, the distinction between 'an orderly but
radical change in government' and an 'overthrow of the government' would not in such circumstances be a clear one.

IV

What I have been concerned to establish so far is that reform
and revolution are on a continuum and that, while there is
an evident difference between typical reformist activities and
revolutionary activities, there is no principled difference between a commitment to a set of radical reforms and a commitment to a socio-political revolution. (I say nothing here
of the weaker notion of 'a systemic revolution'; the difference
between it and at least some types of radical reform is even
less pronounced.)

It is the rather pervasive but mistaken assumption that 'a
violent revolution' is a pleonasm that is the principal cause

of the belief that there is a principled difference between radical reform and revolution and that if one is committed to one, one cannot consistently also be committed to the other. Moreover, to maintain that 'a violent revolution' is not a redundancy is not to use 'revolution'—as indeed is often done in current political discussions—loosely.

Having said this, I do not mean to leave the impression that I believe the question 'revolution or reform?' is a pseudo-question. What is sensibly at issue when such a question is raised is whether it is more reasonable to adopt the moderate and piecemeal reformist tatics of liberal reformers or whether a commitment to a more radical political stance is in order. Among present-day politial theorists—to give this question an amplification into a local habitation and name—is it more reasonable to adopt the general strategies of a Karl Popper, Ralf Dahrendorf or Isaiah Berlin, or are the more radical positions of a Herbert Marcuse, Jürgen Habermas or Alasdair MacIntyre more plausible? Note that within this liberal/radical division there is considerable room for technical philosophical differences, which are yoked together by practical and theoretical political affinities. Surely MacIntyre is closer to Berlin philosophically than he is to Marcuse, but in political orientation he is closer to Marcuse. What I want to do now is compare and assess some arguments of Popper and Marcuse which, I believe, sharply and paradigmatically bring out many of the substantive core issues that should be argued out when we ask about the justification of an allegiance to either revolution or reform. Both Popper and Marcuse have a considerable corpus of influential theory and both have been widely commented upon. But I want to focus on a single short but typical essay by each which, particularly when they are juxtaposed, dramatically and succinctly bring out what I take to be some of the central issues in the some-times choice: reform or revolution. The essays in question are Popper's "Utopia and Violence" and Marcuse's "Ethics and Revolution." [10]

Popper stresses that besides disagreements in factual belief —in opinion about what is the case—people also disagree because "their interests differ." Where interests clash there is, Popper maintains, no way—where the clash is a fundamental one—of proving or establishing that one interest or set of interests is right and the other or others mistaken. Where there is such a clash an agent must either seek a reasonable compromise or attempt to destroy or at least undermine the opposing interest. (p. 357) Popper is convinced we should always resort to compromise here rather than to violence. Over questions of fact, by contrast, we must be guided by the weight of empirical evidence, and where there is a divergence concerning the assessment of that evidence, we must all be open-minded fallibilists prepared to listen to argument and prepared to be convinced by an argument that goes contrary to our beliefs. We must eschew all intellectual imperialism and dogmatism. Violence in human affairs can be avoided if people develop and practice an attitude of reasonableness. That is to say, in coming to decisions, we must be willing to hear both sides, to realize and take into consideration that one is not likely to make a good judge if one is party to the case, to avoid claims of self-evidence, and to be willing, where interests conflict, to make reasonable compromises.

In adopting this attitude of reasonableness, we must give up all Utopianism, which Popper takes to be a persistent and disastrous rationalistic attitude found again and again in political theory from Plato to Marx.

We should not forget that Popper means something rather

10. Karl Popper, *Conjectures and Refutations*, 3rd ed. (London: Routledge & Kegan Paul, 1969), pp. 355-63, and Marcuse, op. cit., pp. 133-47. Subsequent reference to these two works are given in the text.

special by 'a Utopian.' A Utopian believes that an action is rational if it takes the best means available to achieve a certain end and that we can only judge an action to be rational relative to some given end. Thus to determine whether a political action is rational, we must ascertain the final ends of the political change the actor intends to bring about. His political actions will be rational only relative to his ruling ideas of what the state ought to be like. For this reason, as a preliminary to any rational political action, "we must [the Utopian believes] first attempt to become as clear as possible about our ultimate political ends. . . ." (p. 358) The Utopian then plausibly but (on Popper's view) mistakenly concludes that to act reasonably we need first to determine the state or society we consider the best and then determine the means by which we can most efficiently realize or at least approximate that situation. The rationally mandatory thing to do is first to get clear about our fundamental political ideals. Only in this way, the Utopian believes, can we be reasonable about political actions. We must have, if we would act rationally, "a more or less clear and detailed description or blueprint of our ideal state" as well as "a plan or blueprint of the historical path that leads toward this goal." (p. 358) But Popper believes that it is this political rationalism of Utopianism that we must decisively reject, if we would avoid irrationality and violence in human affairs.

We must reject it because we have, Popper would have us believe, no way of rationally ascertaining which set of these focal ends is the most reasonable or even which to choose reasonably, "for it is impossible to determine ends scientifically." (pp. 358-59) This means, according to Popper, that there is no rational way of choosing between Utopian blueprints for a truly human society. Because of this, a reasonable person will abandon all forms of Utopianism and will avoid "choosing ideal ends of this kind." Such a person will not have any Utopian blueprint—any conception of a truly human society—at all. It is not that Popper is criticizing particular political ideals *as such,* but that he is criticizing the kind of political theorizing and organization that would lead to the holding of any ideals of this type at all. They are to be avoided (1) because they cannot be decided on rationally and (2) because the holding of them leads to violence and tyranny and not, as their proponents believe, to human happiness. Thus Popper in effect argues for an end to all ideology and Utopianism. And he counterposes against this a reformism which takes as its procedural rationale: "Work for the elimination of concrete evils rather than for the realization of abstract goods. Do not aim at establishing happiness by political means. Rather aim at the elimination of concrete miseries." (p. 361) Do not try to construct systematic normative blueprints for human liberation, but engage instead, without articulating ultimate social and political ideals, in practical piecemeal social engineering. "Choose what you consider the most urgent evil of the society in which you live, and try patiently to convince people that we can get rid of it." This means that we should fight for the elimination of hunger, disease, the exploitation of women, racism and the like by direct means, e.g. by improved distribution of farm produce, by establishing socialized medicine, by voter registration in the South and by establishing nondiscriminatory practices in housing and employment. We should work at these problems directly and forget about trying "to realize these aims indirectly by designing and working for a distant ideal of a society which is wholly good." (p. 361) We can reach agreement "on what are the most intolerable evils of our society and on what are the most urgent social reforms," but we cannot reach agreement about Utopian ideals for the radical transformation of our society. (p. 361) We must steadfastly recognize and take to heart the poignant fact that "we cannot

make heaven on earth" though we can, if we put aside Utopianism and reason realistically, reasonably hope "to make
life a little less terrible and a little less unjust in each generation." (p. 362) We must accept man as he is and not try to
set a new man afoot.

Marcuse, in Popper's terms, is an arch-Utopian. Unlike
Popper, Marcuse believes that objective moral assessments
can be made of what Popper calls Utopian blueprints for
society, and he argues for an overall normative conception
of society. Marcuse believes that the governing criteria are
whether or not a given set of social arrangements makes for
the greatest possible freedom and greatest possible happiness
for people. And it is important to note, vis-à-vis Popper, that
in talking of happiness in political contexts, Marcuse has in
mind primarily the task of the avoidance of misery. He takes
it to be the case that the role of government in the advancement of human welfare and happiness should be primarily
to insure "a life without fear and misery, and a life in peace."
(p. 134) So in terms of what should be aimed at, the difference
between Popper and Marcuse is verbal rather than substantive. Marcuse is also one with Popper in believing that such
a radical change as would be involved in a socio-political
revolution would bring with it violence, but Popper denies
that this revolutionary violence is ever justified, while Marcuse argues that it is *sometimes* justified and asks about the
conditions under which it is justified. In this context it should
first be noted, so as not to raise spurious issues, that Marcuse,
like any sane and humane person, shares Popper's detestation
of violence and with him takes it as one of the foremost human tasks to work for "its reduction and, if possible, for its
elimination from human life." (p. 355). This attitude toward
violence is or at least ought to be a commonplace in the
moral life. Radicals and liberals, revolutionaries and reformers, are not divided on this issue. They are not always or even

typically divided over the use of violence in settling social issues. Popper, it should be noted, sanctions the use of counterviolence against the threat of revolutionary violence. So it isn't the case that Marcuse is for violence and Popper against it. Nothing as simple as that will do at all. What does divide them is the issue of whether violence is ever justified "as a means for establishing or promoting human freedom and happiness." Popper denies that it is, while Maruse argues that it is justified when and if certain conditions prevail. (He also argues that as a matter of fact they sometimes do prevail.)

While socio-political revolutions of the type we have been describing have almost invariably involved violence, and while they permit and, as Marcuse puts it, sometimes even demand "deception cunning, suppression, destruction of life and property and so on," it is likely to be forgotten that if there is a demand, *prior* to a revolution, for fundamental reforms to substantially increase equality and alleviate misery and degradation through a substantial redistribution of wealth and privileges, this peaceful demand for fundamental reforms, if it shows promise of gaining momentum, will be met by the privileged classes with violence and attempted suppression. But without persistent advocacy and pressure for such basic reforms, we would continue to have the day-to-day and year-to-year, rather unspectacular, yet extensive and persistent violence of any exploitative and repressive society. Such a pervasive form of violence does not make headlines, as do terrorist bombings, but it is more persistent, threatening, destructive and pernicious. We surely should join with Popper in his detestation of violence, but the issue he fails to face, which Marcuse squarely faces, is that in such situations violence cannot be avoided. The central relevant question is whether the use of revolutionary violence will, rather than the available alternatives, make for less misery and human degradation all around. The alternatives to violent revolution are: (1) pressure for radical reforms or even revolution—since it is not a conceptual truth that a socio-political revolution must be violent—which deliberately always stops short of using violence as a *policy;* (2) trying to stick with the *status quo;* or (3) advocating and seeking to implement the type of mild, small-scale reforms that are not likely to offend or threaten the bureaucratic establishment sufficiently so as to provoke counterrevolutionary violence.[11] We certainly, at least on the general ground he appeals to, cannot rightly claim, as Popper in effect does, that revolutionary violence is never justified or indeed never something that reasonable and moral persons ought to advocate and defend. We must go case by case and look at each situation as it comes before us. It may very well be that in some situations the use of violence as a political instrument will minimize misery and injustice and thus be morally mandatory or at least morally in order.

A standard counter here is that while sometimes revolutionary violence is justified, it is never justified in a democracy, because in a democracy we have fair procedural means for making the needed social transformation through elections, lobbying, uncoerced public advocacy and the like. But such a response reflects an extraordinarily idealized and naive picture of how bourgeois democracies work. The realistic and indeed the most reasonable moral stance is again (1) to keep to the above principle, i.e. the underlying rationale for political action should be to seek a society which will most likely

11. For a defense of a revolutionary but principled nonviolent stand, see Barbara Deming, "Revolution and Equilibrium," in *Philosophy in the Age of Crisis,* Eleanor Kuykendall, ed. (New York: Harper and Row, 1970). For a detailing of some contemporary forms of counterrevolutionary violence, see Noam Chomsky, *American Power and the New Mandarins* (New York: Pantheon, 1969) and *At War With Asia* (New York: Pantheon, 1970). For a detailing of some older forms of counterrevolutionary violence, see E. J. Hobsbawm, *The Age of Revolution: 1789-1848* (New York: Mentor Books, 1962), particularly chap. 11.

enable all persons to achieve the fullest "possible satisfaction of needs under the priority of vital needs and with a minimum of toil, misery and injustice" (p. 145), and (2) to go case by case. We need to ask whether in the long run less misery, degradation and injustice will result by going through channels, by playing the game according to the rules the bourgeois democracy sets, rather than by using revolutionary violence. If the answer is yes or probably yes, then revolutionary violence should not be used, but if resort to revolutionary violence will lessen the total misery, degradation and injustice, then revolutionary violence is justified and ought to be advocated. There are, as far as I can see, no conceptual barriers or moral barriers which turn this last prima facie possibility into either a conceptual or moral impossibility. And it might very well actually be something which we are morally required to do. Much would depend on the particular bourgeois democracy. What should be said about Sweden might very well not hold for the United States. Much depends on the present level of social equality and justice, on corruption in the society, on ruling class intransigence and on the extent to which the democratic procedures actually work or can, by reasonable effort on the part of the oppressed, be made to work, so as to enhance social equality, help achieve liberation for everyone and lessen misery and injustice.

It is fairly obvious that in capitalist countries such as the United States, the United Kingdom and West Germany, the outlook for such a transformation by going through channels and working within the system is very bleak indeed. But it is also true, loud alarms to the contrary notwithstanding, that at present (1971) these countries are hardly in a revolutionary situation, though in some segments of the population there has been a rise in class consciousness. What the revolutionary situation will be like in a decade or two, and generally what the outlook for progressive change in society is can hardly be settled in a philosopher's armchair; but once this is recognized, and if my above arguments are sound, it should also be recognized that it is equally arbitrary to rule out on general and aprioristic grounds, as Popper and many others do, the use of revolutionary violence as something which cannot be justified. Moreover, it is not always or even typically the case that it is irresponsible to be a revolutionary when the time is not ripe for revolution. Revolutions need to be nurtured into being; the groundwork for them must be laid, including, as Lenin stressed, careful revolutionary organization. To claim that revolutionary preparation in our period is morally irresponsible is probably in effect, if not in intention, little more than pacificatory counterrevolutionary propaganda—another example of the frequent counterrevolutionary subordination of liberal intellectuals, so well exposed by Conor Cruise O'Brien and Noam Chomsky.[12] It may very well even be the case, as Leszek Kolakowski has argued, that a revolution is not achievable if it is not proclaimed when it is impossible.[13] A certain kind of social consciousness is one of the necessary conditions for the attainment of a revolutionary situation. But this requires a radical tradition with a thoroughly radical consciousness and a will to make a revolution. To attain this, revolutionary demands must sometimes be made even when the time is unripe for revolution.

Marcuse wishes to show not only that in certain circumstances revolutionary violence is justified, but that in certain of the great revolutions in the past it was justified. He be-

12. Conor Cruise O'Brien, "Politics and the Morality of Scholarship," in Max Black, ed., *The Morality of Scholarship* (Ithaca, N.Y.: Cornell University Press, 1967); Noam Chomsky, *American Power and the New Mandarins*, particularly pp. 23-158, and "Knowledge and Power," in *The New Left: A Collection of Essays*, Priscilla Long, ed. (Boston: Porter Sargent, Publisher, 1969).
13. Leszek Kolakowski, *Marxism and Beyond*, trans. Jane Zielonko Peel (London: Pall Mall Press, 1968), pp. 90-91.

lieves, as Popper does not, that "there are rational criteria for determining the possibilities of human freedom and happiness available to a society in a specific historical situation." (p. 135) Marcuse argues that what constitutes human freedom and the possibilities of human freedom and happiness vary with the historical epoch. "Obviously," Marcuse remarks, "the possibilities of human freedom and happiness in advanced industrial society today are in no way comparable with those available, even theoretically available, at preceding stages of history." (p. 139) But, given this partial historical relativity of what the particular fettering and degrading conditions are from which people need liberation, it remains the case, according to Marcuse, that the great revolutions have, everything considered, reduced toil, misery and injustice and thus, since none of the historically possible alternatives could match this, these revolutions are on the whole justified.

In thinking about the justification of revolution, we are forced into admittedly rough historical calculations. On the one hand, we must take into account both the likelihood of Bonapartism or Stalinism in the successor state after a successful revolution and the likelihood that this state, whether Stalinist or not, will be brutal and authoritarian and actually harm human liberation more than it helps. On the other hand, we must "take into account the sacrifices exacted from the living generations on behalf of the established society, the established law and order, the number of victims made in defense of this society in war and peace, in the struggle for existence individual and national." (p. 140) In addition, we need to ask questions about the intellectual and material resources available to the society and the chances of the revolutionary group being able to utilize them in reducing the sacrifices and the number of victims. Finally, we must keep in mind the very value of the professed values originating in revolutions, e.g. the conception of the inalienable rights of man coming out of the American and French revolutions and the conception of the value of tolerance emerging from the English revolutions.

Popper makes utilitarian calculations too, but he limits them to the more immediate and palpable sources of misery and injustice and deliberately resists taking into account more distant and less easily calculable phenomena. This surely has the advantage of giving us more manageable materials, but it also cuts off morally relevant data which, to the extent that they are determinable at all, should be taken into consideration. In our calculations concerning what we ought to do, we should take it as a relevant consideration that some phenomena are less readily determinable than others, but this does not justify us in ignoring the less easily assessable data. By skewing what is to be taken as relevant material in the way he does, Popper cuts off the very possibility of discovering (1) systematic interconnections between human ills and (2) any deeper causal conditions (if indeed there are such) of the ills he would alleviate. Thus his theory unwittingly plays into the hands of conservative defenders of the *status quo* with whom Popper himself would not wish to be aligned. Marcuse's wider ranging utilitarian calculations are perfectly capable of taking into account and giving due stress to the phenomena Popper would account for, but they also hold out promise for attaining a more complete, and thus a more adequate, account of the relative harm and relative human advantages accruing to different social arrangements.

For Marcuse and for the revolutionary tradition generally, when violence is justified it is justified by reason in accordance with the overarching end of revolutionary activity, namely "greater freedom for the greater number of people." Popper, in spite of his distaste for Utopian blueprints, holds this as a guiding rationale as well, but he never establishes that violence can never be the means to its attainment or that the great revolutions did not extend and enhance human freedom.

It should not be forgotten that the English and French revolutions attained "a demonstrable enlargement of the range of human freedom." There is, Marcuse points out, a general agreement among historians that the English and French revolutions brought about an extensive redistribution of social wealth "so that previously less privileged or unprivileged classes were the beneficiaries of this change, economically and/or politically." (p. 143) Even when we count in the subsequent periods of reaction and restoration, it remains true that these revolutions brought about "more liberal governments, a gradual democratization of society and technical progress." When the extent and permanency of these changes are taken into consideration in our historical calculations, they outweigh the terror and the excesses of these revolutions. That is, there is a sound ethical justification for these revolutions, though to say this is not to condone all the actions carried out in their name, for it is a correct grammatical remark with moral overtones to say, as Marcuse does, that "arbitrary violence and cruelty and indiscriminate terror" cannot possibly be justified by any revolutionary situation. (pp. 140-41)

To the argument that the same changes would have come about more gradually but without all that terror and violence, it should be replied that while this is an empirical *possibility,* it is also only an unfounded speculation. We do not have comparable situations, in which the ruling elite of an *ancien régime* voluntarily gave up its privileges and desisted from exploitation and repression, where it was not true that there were no previous successful revolutions in similarly situated countries to serve as a warning prod that extensive reforms must be made. What we can say with confidence is this: there is the fact of the moral advance for humanity brought on by these great revolutions, and no adequate grounds have been given for believing that in those circumstances—those great turning points of history—advances would have occurred in anything like a comparable way without the use of force against the old order.

V

What we can conclude from our discussion so far is that there have been circumstances in the past and there will no doubt be circumstances in the future in which violence is a morally legitimate instrumentality in promoting transformations in society toward a greater degree of human freedom and happiness. It is toward this conclusion that a critical comparison of Popper and Marcuse leads us.

If what I have argued in the previous section has been for the most part sound, Popper could only defend himself by laying very considerable stress on, and indeed by establishing the soundness of, what I shall call 'the sceptical side' of his thought. Marcuse assumes, and I do as well, the correctness of what should be the truisms that human freedom and human happiness are very great goods and that misery and injustice are plain evils. Popper indeed makes the same assumptions; his passionate rejection of Utopianism is fueled by emotions rooted in these assumptions. But he does not believe that such value judgments are rationally supportable, since they are not scientific claims. (This note is perfectly general: it applies to any fundamental value judgment simply by virtue of its being a value judgment.) Thus, on Popper's view, if someone has a Utopian blueprint in which human freedom and happiness are not held to be very great goods, or misery and injustice to be manifest evils, there is no way of showing that that blueprint is mistaken or unreasonable, and that a blueprint in which these considerations have the weight Marcuse, Popper and I give them is right in this regard—or at least is more reasonable from a moral point of view than one which rejects or ignores them.

This is hardly the place to argue the general question of moral scepticism and/or some kind of radical noncognitivism in metaethics. However, it should be said that Popper is running very much against the stream of contemporary ethical theory and that he has not provided arguments to meet the many careful critiques of noncognitivism which are now well known. Noncognitivism is very much on the defensive; and while there is much conceptual work to be done in giving a thoroughly perspicuous cognitivist account of moral reasoning, the work of such astute and careful moral philosophers as Foot, Rawls, Winch, von Wright, Baier, Warnock and Griffiths has made it evident that noncognitivism will not wash and that it is utterly unwarranted to claim that we have no knowledge of good and evil.[14]

Moreover, as MacIntyre has pointed out, *in practice* Popper assumes the objectivity and rationality of certain ideals—general moral ideals very close to Marcuse's and my own—

14. A brief but brilliant defense of cognitivism occurs in A. Phillips Griffiths, "Ultimate Moral Principles: Their Justification," in *Encyclopedia of Philosophy*, Paul Edwards, ed., pp. 177-82. See also his "Justifying Moral Principles," in *Proceedings of the Aristotelian Society*, n.s., vol. LVIII (1957/8). Peter Winch has ably defended cognitivism with specific reference to Popper in his "Nature and Convention," in *Proceedings of the Aristotelian Society*, n.s., vol. XX (1960). See also John Rawls, "Outline of a Decision Procedure for Ethics," *Philosophical Review*, vol. LX (1951) and "Justice as Fairness," *The Philosophical Review*, vol. LXVIII; P. R. Foot, "Goodness and Choice," *Proceedings of the Aristotelian Society*, n.s., vol. LIX (1958/9), and "The Philosopher's Defense of Morality," *Philosophy*, vol. XXVII (1952); G. H. von Wright, *The Varieties of Goodness* (London: Routledge & Kegan Paul, 1963), and *Norm and Action* (London: Routledge & Kegan Paul, 1963); Kurt Baier, *The Moral Point of View* (Ithaca, N.Y.: Cornell University Press, 1958); and G. Warnock, *Contemporary Moral Philosophy* (New York: St. Martins Press, 1967). I have tried to articulate and defend a version of cognitivism myself in my "Moral Truth," in *Studies in Moral Philosophy*, Nicholas Rescher, ed. (Oxford: Basil Blackwell, 1968), and in my *Reason and Practice* (New York: Harper and Row, 1971).

which, if he would consistently apply them, would hardly allow him to back off all ideology in the way he does.[15] That is to say, for Popper the importance of relieving misery and developing the reasonable attitudes of human give and take, and the stress on freedom and on the equal right of "every man . . . to arrange his life himeslf so far as this is compatible with the equal rights of others" are leading moral ideas which inform many of his political judgments; together they commit him to a general set of political and moral ideals in accordance with which particular practices, institutions, governments and societies can and indeed should (if these principles are to mean anything) be appraised. But this is precisely to utilize a Utopian blueprint, and it is just this that Popper would avoid. Moreover, if he sticks with this blueprint, the Marcusean arguments for the rational justification of revolution seem at least to be inescapable; and if he rejects reasoning in accordance with these general moral principles and sticks steadfastly to an 'end of ideology approach,' he gets himself into the position where he could have no grounds for rejecting as barbarous and irrational ideologies which he indeed rightly believes to be barbarous and irrational, namely Nazi and other Fascist ideologies.[16]

Surely this is a conclusion that Popper does not wish to embrace; and his grounds for not accepting such ideologies turn on some commitment to something very like a form of negative utilitarianism—a theory according to which the ultimate test for the morality of acts or practices is whether they prevent misery or at least minimize it as much as possible. But this saddles him with a set of abstract moral principles which he in consistency should regard with distaste as Utopian.

15. Alasdair MacIntyre, "Breaking the Chains of Reason," in *Out of Apathy*, E. P. Thompson, ed. (London: Stevens & Sons, 1960).
16. For a masterful analysis of such ideologies see Georg Lukács, *Die Zerstörung der Vernunft* (Neuwied am Rhein, Berlin-Spandau: Herman Luchterhand, 1962).

Some tougher 'end of ideology' political theorist may really take this 'moral-scepticism side' to heart and argue that even if avoidance of misery and attainment of happiness are great goods, he sees no rational grounds for adopting some principle of equality or fairness and extending such teleological considerations to all men. Whether, he reasons, we should opt for such a universalistic ethic as underlies both Marcuse's and Popper's thinking, is an utterly nonrational matter resting on human preference.

If such a moral scepticism is rationally mandatory, then the very assumptions of progress essential for even Popper's commitment to mild reform are undermined. There can be no justification of reform or revolution or any normative principles. It may indeed not be easy to defend any system of overall normative principles, but if it is not possible to do so, the whole program of moderate reform and a commitment to reasonableness is undermined. It is only beause Popper himself has an unacknowledged but reasonable set of general moral political principles that his 'end of ideology approach' does not straight out appear to be an abandonment of any kind of reasoned defense of a set of normative standards or even of the taking of any principled stand at all.

Popper aside, what can we conclude about reform or revolution? There plainly is much injustice and unnecessary misery in the world and the level of human liberation is hardly what it could be. Without even remotely assuming we can make a kingdom of heaven on earth, a perfectly good society or anything of that fanciful Utopian order, it is not quixotic to hope and rationally work for a transformation of society in which these ills are greatly lessened and perhaps some of them are even utterly obliterated. Such a social order may never come into being, but there is nothing unreasonable about struggling for its achievement.

I have suggested that there can be no reasonable, unequiv-

ocal, non-contextual answer to the question: in struggling
for a better social order should we be reformers or revolutionaries? In the Scandinavian countries the needed transformation might very well come about gradually through a cluster of small reforms which, taken together, might add up in
time to a considerable transformation. In Brazil, the United
States and Argentina, to take some striking examples, this
hope would seem to be unrealistic. And while there is a
moral need for and a considerable material base for revolution in Brazil, the United States—the lynchpin imperialist
power in the Western social system—is at present hardly a
country in which there is a material base for a revolution,
though, as I remarked earlier, this is not to say anything about what the situation in the United States may be in
a decade or two. But morally speaking the United States
surely is in dire need of radical transformation; whether this
should be in the form of radial reforms or revolution is, if my
earlier arguments are sound, an empty question, more a
matter of political rhetoric than anything else. What is evident is that it becomes, the closer one looks, increasingly obvious, particularly when one considers the United States in
relation to the rest of the world, that very deep structural
changes need to be made. It is surely better, everything else
being equal, if they can be attained without a violent revolution. But if one considers Vietnam, the Blacks and America's
imperialist policies in the poorer parts of the world, the level
of violence is already very high. It is also true, however, that
actions which would trigger off or even risk a nuclear war are
insane. And to work to bring about in a decade or so a revolution which would involve in America something comparable
to the Russian or Spanish civil wars is also morally equiv-
ocal; but, as we have seen, there are revolutions and revolutions, and there are various levels of violence. What Marcuse
has given us are general criteria in accordance with which we

can reasonably answer when, humanly speaking, revolutionary violence of a certain kind and at a certain level is justified and when it is not. In many situations it is difficult to tell, though in others (present-day Angola, Mozambique, South Africa and South Vietnam, for example) it is quite evident that, when revolution has a reasonable chance of success, it is morally justified.

We have also seen that reform and revolution are on a continuum and that there are contexts in which the choice of labels for description of the transformation in question is—ideology and expediency aside—quite immaterial. Moreover, it is important to see, as Rosa Luxemburg did and stressed in the opening paragraphs of her *Reform or Revolution,* that a revolutionary should not oppose piecemeal reforms, though he should seek to give them a direction which will lead to a socialist transformation of society.[17] But a vital means for the attainment of a socialist revolution is the attainment of reforms. Reforms have indeed bought off the working class, but they have also raised its level of expectation and given people of working-class and peasant origins the education and consciousness to escape the bondage of prejudice and ignorance. Together with the alteration of the working force through technology, reforms have gradually given the rising new working class the know-how to govern themselves.[18] Moreover, since I lack the orthodox faith that history must be on the side of socialism, it seems to me that where it is evident that certain reforms will appreciably improve human conditions, they should be welcomed. They are, at least, small gains in an uncertain world, though this should not freeze us

17. Rosa Luxemburg, *Politische Schriften* (Leipzig: Philipp Reclam, 1970), pp. 7-125. English trans., *Reform or Revolution* (New York: Pathfinder Press, Inc., 1970).
18. Serge Mallet, *La Nouvelle classe ouvrière* (Paris: Seuil, 1962) and Norman Birnbaum, "Is There a Post-Industrial Revolution?" *Social Policy*, vol. 1, no. 2 (July/August 1970).

into being satisfied with them. Apocalyptic and quasi-apoca-
lyptic political programs are dramatic but rarely politically or
morally sound. An incautious and wholesale adoption of the
nach-Hitler-wir attitude is to be avoided. Working for Hitler's
victory over the Social Democrats, even granting they were
ersatz socialists, was a suicidal way to try to build socialism and
a truly human society. The similarly rationalized tactic of
working for the victory of Reagan—to turn to a much lesser
villain—while not suicidal, was counterproductive for progressive forces. Our ability to make long-range social predictions is so slight that it is irrational to develop any considerable confidence concerning claims about how things must be;
thus it is irrational and indeed morally irresponsible to accept,
where they might be avoided, extensive human ills in the
hope of realizing long-range social achievements. Noam
Chomsky was being realistic and responsible when he remarked: "Surely our understanding of the nature of man or
of the range of workable social forms is so rudimentary that
any far-reaching doctrine must be treated with great scepticism."[19] This does not at all mean that revolutionary hopes
should be abandoned as an opiate of intellectuals, but it
should warn a reasonable and humane person of the extensive
dangers inherent in aiding or even welcoming reaction to help
produce revolution. Sometimes extremism on the Left paves
the way for the achievement of moderate reforms and even
helps build socialism, but victories for reaction seldom pave
the way for socialist revolution. The thing to do is to work
persistently for a socialist transformation of society. Day by
day this means welcoming all genuinely progressive reforms,
even in those contexts in which it will strengthen liberals
against conservatives, while working for a broader structural
transformation of society by *radical* structural reforms where

19. Noam Chomsky, "Notes on Anarchism," *The New York Review of Books*,
vol. XIV, no. 10 (May 21, 1970), p. 32.

possible and by violent revolution where it is necessary and where the cure is not likely to produce worse ills than the disease. The rub, of course, is to tell in a particular historical situation whether the cure is worse than the disease. This surely takes more than philosophical sophistication and moral sensitivity for it takes as well, and in depth, a historical, sociological and economic understanding of the situation one is up against.

2

On the Ethical Defense of Violence and Destruction

JOSEPH MARGOLIS

The most touching instances in which academic questions of
ethical theory collide with the realities of intentional violence and destruction concern the pursuit of so-called just
wars (apart from indisputable cases of defense against attack)
and of revolutionary movements promoting social changes
thought to be of the highest or of extremely high value and
thought to be otherwise impossible to achieve or highly im-
probable or perhaps even risked by default of action. The
reason, if we assume sincerity of conviction, is that the partisans of such commitments must be divided within themselves by what they take to be the humane benefits of their
action and by what is palpably destructive of the life and interests of a significant population. Doubtless, ingenuity and
sincerity have a means of resolving such conflicts in ways that
are compatible with moral conviction—whether in the face
of wars, like the Nigerian-Biafran war or the Arab-Israeli
war, that are not easily construed primarily or exclusively in
terms of self-defense, or in the face of revolutions, like the
French and the Russian, in which the considerable membership of particular social classes was thought eligible for ex-
tinction or extremely severe penalty on grounds of personal
conviction or accident of birth or non-conformity or ideolog-

ical deviation or the like, grounds which have seemed, at other times, to be frivolous or manifestly unfair or merely partisan or expedient or draconian.

Deliberate violence directed against another raises, in a respect noticeably different from the puzzles of suicide, self-mutilation, disregard of one's own talents, and the like, certain profound ethical issues. For, to act thus against *another* is, at the very least, to act contrary to his presumed prudential interests (as, for instance, survival, reduction of pain, gratification of desires, a measure of stable personal power and security relative to pursuing one's interests effectively, and the like). It is not that men, by nature (whatever the implied claim may be made to mean), have such prudential interests but that, given the extensive experience of the race, it is statistically most probable that, in confronting another human being, one is confronting a creature that has such interests. These putative interests may be taken, then, to impose a formal and minimal condition on the behavior of men vis-à-vis one another. We can say that a man is not an ethically responsible agent if he deliberately acts in ways affecting the lives of others, that bear on their putative prudential interests, without attempting to assess the justification for so acting. The reason is instructive. For, surely, no specification of what it is to be ethically concerned would be plausible that did not include, centrally, the appraisal of the actions of men vis-à-vis one another; and the least quarrelsome sense in which the scope of such appraisal may be fixed would include the relevance of a threat to life or to the characteristic interests of men. What could be said to be an ethical issue, if acting so as to disorder another's life or whatever another's career is devoted to is not, as such, ethically significant? I confess I can see no remotely promising alternative. But the claim does not entail any substantive ethical principle or rule or judgment except a purely formal precept regarding (ethically) responsible behavior: no one may be said to behave responsibly if, on minimal considerations, when he acts in a way he believes will affect the putative prudential interests of others, he does not consider the (ethical) justification of his behavior; what the appraisive norms should be remain, from this vantage, entirely open to debate.

On the other hand, actions bearing on one's own life rather than another's cannot be said to be constrained by the same consideration, simply because one may actually not subscribe to the prudential interests sketched (as in suicide); and because to justify the constraint would require arguments bearing on what obligations and the like are thought to be derivable from the concept of human nature as such (as in natural-law and natural-right doctrines); and because if a man acts contrary to what might have been supposed to be his prudential interests (without assuming obligations derivable from human nature), we may ask whether he is mad or distraught or irrational, rather than whether he has acted immorally. There is, therefore, an important asymmetry exhibited by ethical questions regarding oneself and others: to affect the putative prudential interests of others is, minimally, to act in a way that at once calls for ethical appraisal; to construe one's actions with regard to one's own life as directly open to ethical appraisal is to presuppose that there are discoverable values or duties or norms or the like governing the mere use of one's own life. It may be so, but it is debatable in a way the other is not.

Recently, episodes of a sort related to war and revolution have noticeably accumulated, episodes that are perhaps not yet of the same magnitude as important wars and great revolutions. They pose an identical conceptual issue, however, and are useful for that reason to notice; for their limited potency permits us to examine the matter without comparable urgency or partisan pressure. Furthermore, it is a striking fact that observers of such events, observers by way at least of the news media, are quite willing to tolerate the loss of life and loss of property involved, provided only that certain kinds of claims (usually and variably fashionable) about a just war or a just revolution or the like are advanced in their favor, in a spirit of sufficient seriousness—and this not necessarily by people who are themselves strongly committed in a partisan way to the issues or who would be willing to commit similar acts for the same or similar causes. Typically, they would be appalled by such losses under easily formulable alternative circumstances, particularly those in which they would take themselves to be directly affected.

With this in mind, I canvassed the *New York Times* for August 1970, in order to find some fair specimens of the taking of life and destruction of property, or jeopardy of life and property, where a significant fraction of world or regional public opinion seemed either notably neutral or noncommittal in the face of substantial violence, or else rather inclined to admit or at least entertain the moral defensibility of the actions at stake. Leaving aside all the current wars in the world (and all the incidental violence attending them); whatever local violence does not bear on our issue (as for instance apparent murder for revenge or profit or malicious mischief); controversial cases where the details are in considerable dispute (as in the Kent State and Jackson State episodes, or in trials like that of the Black Panthers involving the apparent execution of one of their number or like the Charles Manson case concerning possible ritual murder)—all of which might well augment our list of possible specimens—and leaving aside all instances (including those bearing on pollution, health, subsistence) that might be construed as cases of double effect (where the loss or jeopardy of life and property is not deliberately aimed at but nevertheless known to be entailed by what is deliberately aimed at), a very striking range of specimen cases may yet be detailed:

ITEM: about eighteen persons have been kidnapped in assorted politically motivated incidents in Latin America, including a former president of Argentina, the foreign minister of Guatemala, a former foreign minister of Colombia, various ambassadors and consuls, and also Mr. Dan A. Mitrione, an officer of the U.S. Agency for International Development, who was taken as a hostage by the Uruguayan urban guerrilla group known as the Tupamaros and killed when the Uruguayan government refused to exchange one hundred and fifty prisoners for Mitrione—the U.S. government did not attempt to induce Uruguay to make the exchange;

ITEM: political terrorists have executed at least three prominent persons in Argentina in the last fourteen months, including José Varela Alonso, the Peronist head of the garment workers' union, the head of the metalworkers' union, and Lieutenant General Pedro Eugenio Aramburu, a former president of Argentina, who was kidnapped and apparently sentenced by a revolutionary tribunal;

ITEM: Israel formally detained a BOAC airplane and removed two Algerian nationals, Major Khalid Julul and Mr. Ali Belaziz, said to be Algerian security officers, to be held in custody in hopes of exchanging them for Israeli prisoners held in Egypt, Syria, and Jordan—following an Algerian precedent;

ITEM: Indian police arrested forty Samyukta socialist party demonstrators, including two members of Parliament, who were on the point of seizing Prime Minister Indira Gandhi's farm some eighteen miles from New Delhi, apparently for unauthorized redistribution to poor peasants;

ITEM: the FBI entered the investigation of the bombing incident at the Army Mathematics Research Center at the University of Wisconsin, in which more than six million dollars' worth of damage (and, apparently, an incidental death and some wounding) was caused by a bomb detonated in a stolen automobile parked outside the Center—for which a revolutionary group has claimed responsibility, a group threatening wider guerrilla warfare if its political demands are not met;

ITEM: thirty persons were injured, three by police bullets, in a seven-hour battle between police and hippies in the heart of Amsterdam (with apparently incidental looting of a jewelry and a perfume shop), following a protest against a municipal ban on overnight sleeping on the steps of the national war memorial in front of the royal palace—a favorite haunt of Dutch and foreign hippies;

ITEM: inmates at Manhattan Men's House of Detention deliberately rioted, took hostages, and broke windows and furniture in order to draw the public's attention to allegedly brutal treatment in prison and the violation of their rights;

ITEM: five persons hijacked a Polish Airlines plane and forced the pilot to land on one of Denmark's Baltic islands, in order to defect to the West; elsewhere, a Trans-Caribbean Airways plane was hijacked to Cuba;

ITEM: members of various Indian tribes affirmed their right to occupy Alcatraz Island, apparently Federal property, which they have held since November 15, 1969;

ITEM: the Reverend Daniel J. Berrigan began serving his prison sentence for having destroyed draft records, while forty persons conducted a "prayer vigil" in the heavy rain outside—there having been an estimated two hundred and seventy-one incidents of attempted destruction of draft records from January through August 1970;

ITEM: as part of a continuing contest over official Jordanian policy regarding the Arab-Israeli cease-fire, at least one Jordanian police officer and two guerrillas were wounded in a clash between the fedayeen and forces loyal to King Hussein near the Hussein Mosque; the incident appeared to reopen hostilities which, for months preceding an uneasy calm, had claimed about a thousand casualties;

ITEM: twenty sticks of dynamite blasted the Federal Office Building, the military induction headquarters in Minneapolis, causing an estimated damage of $500,000;

ITEM: a policeman was killed (and a number of others wounded) by a booby trap planted in a vacant house on the predominantly black north side of Omaha, Nebraska, where police had been lured by an emergency telephone call by a screaming woman;

ITEM: Superior Court Judge Harold J. Haley, two convicts (James D. McClain and William Arthur Christmas), and another man were killed in a shoot-out in San Rafael, California, in a foiled attempt to free several convicts—the so-called Soledad brothers, said to be the intended victims of a legal lynching—by using the judge, an assistant district attorney, and others as hostages;

ITEM: in Manchester, England, shoppers ran for cover from a gang of four hundred "skinheads" and "bovver" boys who invaded the business district—their favorite targets for harassment are homosexuals, Pakistanis, and other Asians;

ITEM: Roman Catholic bishops and priests of Maranhão state, Brazil, claimed that a young Brazilian priest, José da Magalhaes Monteiro, was tortured for two days by police after his arrest on charges of political subversion.

I have left out an enormous number of sustained street fights between police and blacks, police and Puerto Ricans, police and Chicanos, whites and blacks, as well as incidents of attempted bombing of police stations and of the killing of police officers and the like, which are typically confused but which, occurring in places like Hartford, the South Florida cities, Chicago, Houston, New York, are bound—on close review—to swell the range of cases here sampled. And if I had but added the first ten days of September, the list would have been increased in a most incredible way.

In any case, the phenomenon is clear. Thanks to the mass media, the world is informed, at once and in an increasingly detailed way, of the occurrence of relatively local episodes that tend to assume ethical importance in terms of global visions, both formalized and informal, of the objectives of, and practical measures available to, variously disadvantaged peoples. Under these circumstances, world opinion tends to be mobilized and polarized, in ethically partisan ways, on issues that themselves arise in a setting in which a relatively radical transformation of some sector of society is at stake. Black African nationalists, for instance, who bomb the Portuguese embassy in Washington, D.C., on grounds of attacking colonialism and advancing the cause of self-determination, can count on an unprecedented willingness on the part of educated and informed persons everywhere to consider seriously the possibility of ethically justifying their action. It is, obviously, easy to be a partisan in these matters, but it is rather more difficult to say whether and how ethical debate may proceed at all objectively, faced with the mere eligibility of such questions; and yet, if they were not eligible, ethical debate could hardly claim to be seriously relevant at all. All of the episodes culled from the *Times,* for instance, involve certain persons very substantially and very deliberately affecting others' putative prudential interests—in fact, assuming those interests, many of the episodes were disasters for the persons involved. Yet, they are not, and have not been, easily and uniformly condemned. The conceptual issues call for clarification.

For one thing, the incompatibility of the ideological convictions of contending factions—with one or another faction often being in a privileged or controlling position relative to the state or government—argues the practical impossibility of pursuing certain prominent objectives without the deliberate destruction of life and property. For a second, faced with this prospect, would-be rational agents are drawn to assess the justice or worth of their objectives in the face of offsetting the prima facie evil or loss of value entailed in the destruction or disadvantage or jeopardy contemplated. And for a third, with an eye to convincing others of, or confirming in themselves, the moral superiority of their position, such agents are bound to theorize about the conceptual grounds on which their own justificatory principles rest. What can be said about all such efforts? Are policies of deliberate violence and destruction significantly less defensible, ethically, than policies of nonviolence and nondestruction of life and property? The decisive considerations are, surprisingly, not too difficult to muster—and most instructive and serious.

It is idle, in the face of the evident conflict of conviction that our array of specimen cases exhibits, to hold that there are ethical values that all men are bound to support—in the sense either that men everywhere actually do support them or that they ought to. For any such values could not but be vacuous (as permitting, *ex hypothesi,* the contending parties to appeal to the same justifying values); or else the contending claims would be hopelessly partisan (in the sense that each party sincerely condemns the other by appeal to his own favored and competing principle). The only possible way out of this impasse lies with the tenability of some form of ethical cognitivism, that is, with the thesis that normative ethical values are, in some fair sense, open to discovery or discernment by perceptual, intuitive, revealed, or similar means—or, in particular, that some form of essentialism is tenable, that is, that a knowledge of human nature entails a knowledge of norms essential to human nature. This is emphatically not to say that, *given* normative ethical values, criteria, rules, principles, ethical disputes cannot be resolved in the same manner in which factual disputes are; but, of course, to admit this is to admit no more than needs to be admitted by the serious and opposed factions in our specimen cases.

The distinction between value judgments and factual judgments, as far as formal properties are concerned, lies entirely with whatever kinds of predicates may be ascribed to any given range of subjects. The distinction between factual judgments and value judgments is a distinction, therefore, involving a mixed classification, for factual judgments are properly distinguished solely in terms of the assignability of truth values: there is no reason to think that value judgments (at least a certain range of value judgments) are, on purely formal grounds, different from factual judgments.[1] The critical issue, consequently, is just the issue of whether the normative values that may be given—with respect to which, that is, ethical disputes may be resolved in the same way as factual disputes—may also be independently established as valid.

Alternatively put, we sometimes speak of factual judgments merely in terms of sentences so used that, on whatever basis we may choose, truth values may be assigned to sentences so used; and sometimes, in speaking of factual judgments, we speak of sentences whose use calls for the assignability of truth values on grounds specifically restricted to certain cognitive sources. Value judgments may, on the first condition, function as factual judgments if (as, for instance, in speaking of health, breach of law, infringement of moral conventions, and the like) formulable grounds may be provided for the confirmation of judgments rendered. To distinguish between value judgments and judgments that do not concern values is, from this point of view, to say nothing bearing on the assignment of truth values as such but to speak only about what bears on the theoretical grounds (quite possibly variable) on which given predicates (for instance, 'tubercular,' 'murdered,' 'ignored a call for help') are construed as valuational predicates or not. Their use may well be extensionally equivalent with that of non-valuational predicates but their sense, on some hypothesis, may be explicable only in terms of norms and normatively significant parameters (health and illness, for instance, lawfulness and lawlessness, morality and immorality). When the relevant norms are

1. Cf. Joseph Margolis, *Values and Conduct* (London, Oxford, and New York: Oxford University Press and The Clarendon Press, 1971), chap. 1.

themselves claimed to be open to cognitive discovery, value judgments may be said to be factual judgments in the second, more restricted, sense given.

There are any number of strategies that have been employed either to support cognitivism directly, as by supporting claims of an ethical faculty, or indirectly, as by supporting claims that entail some set of values thought not to be rationally replaceable.[2] Let me rehearse the principal alternatives here briefly—but say also at once that there is not a single familiar conceptual strategy by which the required claim can be satisfactorily sustained.

The frontal effort calls for epistemic faculties suited to discerning normative ethical values. Relevant claims are characteristically advanced in naturalistic and nonnaturalistic forms. The latter, holding that there is a distinctive faculty directly addressed to discerning normative values (possibly different faculties for discerning moral worth, aesthetic beauty, religious piety and the like), cannot support, in the face of the serious differences with which we began and of the obviously widespread ignorance of such a faculty among otherwise relevantly sensitive persons, a claim that is suitably separated from merely partisan rationalization: any effort to defend the seemingly privileged epistemic capacity of favored persons (in a nonpartisan way, as, analogously, telepathy might be defended) must in principle appeal to some antecedently and publicly accessible faculty for making the required discriminations—which, on the hypothesis, is precisely what is in dispute. Consequently, though the claims of ethical intuitionism or the like may be logically impeccable, there is no formulable procedure by which, under the circumstances, such claims can be publicly confirmed. The naturalistic alternative, correspondingly, cannot provide any compelling grounds for adjudicating among differences in conviction regarding the definition of what is right or good or obligatory or just, in terms

2. Ibid., chap. 6.

of the selection, among alternative partisan choices, of some set of preferred natural qualities or conditions—that is, qualities or conditions that, independently of value disputes, may be discerned by perceptual or similar means. Naturalism, unlike intuitionism or other nonnaturalistic doctrines, is not logically obliged to rest its case on the accessibility of a specialized faculty: it need demonstrate only that some natural quality is identical with some selected normative quality. But, under the circumstances, any particular naturalistic conviction simply raises an ethical dispute to an apparently metaethical level, without in the least advancing the issue in cognitive terms. Hence both naturalistic and nonnaturalistic forms of cognitivism merely provide complicated versions of the very quarrels with which we began.

It is often argued, also, that classification itself entails normative distinctions regarding what are normal or abnormal specimens of a given sort. If this thesis were true, it would not in itself sustain absolute values, for alternative systems of classification may always in principle be provided for any range of particulars identified under a given classificatory principle; but, in any case, the thesis is false, for things are classifiable solely in terms of resemblance to admitted specimens, where the initial specimens are not thought to be excellent or perfect or normal or mature or realized or the like in any particular regard. Crucially, the classification of human beings as such need not and does not, characteristically, depend on the assumption of any relevant normative values.[3] Hence, it cannot be supposed that the mere classification of men as men entails any relevant norms at all—nor, a fortiori, the distinctive ethical norms appropriate to human nature. Cognitivism is obliged, therefore, to take a more explicit form.

Again, it is often argued that the characterization of hu-

3. Cf. Stuart Hampshire, *Thought and Action* (London: Chatto & Windus, 1959), chap. 4.

man actions—the central items of ethical appraisal—cannot be altered or adjusted beyond certain formulable limits, which limits correspond to certain fixed interests or concerns or needs or the like of human beings as such. The limits of alternatively admissible descriptions of human action, on this thesis, either themselves entail ethically relevant appraisals (as in describing someone's action as a murder) or entail ethically pertinent distinctions that are neutral to particular appraisal in particular cases (as in describing someone's action as the killing of another, which requires but does not decide ethical appraisal). Both forms of the thesis are untenable, however, without the defense of an ulterior cognitivism (that would enable us to determine the normative interests or needs of men). Furthermore, it is logically possible to elide any given description of an action with its consequences in order to yield a new description of the apparent action in question (as in redescribing killing a man with the consequence of succeeding to the throne merely as succeeding to the throne) and also to defuse the direct ethical force of any given description (as in redescribing an action said to be a murder as the action of taking another's life—which, on the original thesis, merely raises an ethical question).[4]

Here, we may admit, following our minimal characterization of what is of 'ethical' concern, that where actions impinge on the prudential interests of others, ethical questions arise. But the description and redescription of actions that are preferred by certain individuals and certain societies may, at the same time that the merely formal precept respecting responsibility is admitted, accommodate the doctrinal or ideological convictions of the parties concerned respecting, precisely, what the *determinate* ethical import is of whatever may have occurred. The point may be put in another way. Ethical con-

4. Cf. Eric D'Arcy, *Human Acts* (Oxford: The Clarendon Press, 1963).

siderations may be said to be overriding considerations with respect to conduct. That is, whatever the interests of a rational agent may be, just as he considers problems of efficiency, compatibility among particular interests and objectives, the coherence of his pursuits, provision for possibly changing interests, so too he will consider the ranking of the values he pursues relative to his entire life: whatever takes precedence over all other values vis-à-vis his conduct as a man (and no man is exhausted by his roles, relationships, offices, and the like), may be fairly counted as his ethical values. But to grant this—without the comforting support of some cognitivism or essentialism—is tantamount to the admission that, although whatever an agent does that impinges on the putative prudential interests of others has ethical relevance, an action provisionally identified in this respect is not yet determinately characterized as far as its ethical import is concerned. It is entirely possible that competing ethical doctrines, ideologies, and the like may, without ignoring the minimal (but formal) sense of 'ethical,' redescribe whatever has occurred in ways that are significantly divergent ethically, at the same time that each competing account remains internally coherent. And they may do this not only in the sense that descriptive expressions with explicit ethical import '(murder,' 'mayhem,' for instance) may be replaced by others that are ethically provisional but call for additional ethically freighted judgments ('kill,' for instance), but also in the sense that such ethically provisional expressions may be replaced by others that do not construe what has occurred as an action or as an action calling for such additional judgments ('killed' may be replaced by '. . . caused the death of,' where '. . .' is not replaced by an expression designating an agent; and it may be elided with the expression designating some consequence so that it may be replaced, say, by 'succeeded to the throne'). Under these conditions, the purely formal consideration of being an ethically responsible agent is accommodated by doctrinally diverse and competing ethical systems. For one thing, though it is ethically relevant always to consult the putative prudential interests of men, it is not logically necessary that *any* ethically viable system commit itself to realizing those prudential interests as its own overriding values (for instance, the asumption that a war is ethically just entails going counter to the prudential interests of the enemy and jeopardizing the prudential interests of the warring party itself). And, for another thing, *every* network of act-descriptions employed to provide characterizations relevant to ethical review—that is, in the context in which men qua men pursue their overriding values—cannot but be doctrinally, ideologically, qualified in the respects just given (as entailing a determinate ethical appraisal ['murder'], as entailing the need for a further determinate appraisal ['kill'] or as entailing the ethical neutrality of what occurred or of what was done ['merely turned the ignition on' or '. . . caused the death of,' where '. . .' is suitably filled in]).

The admission, therefore, of a minimal (and entirely formal) sense of ethically responsible behavior is entirely compatible with any substantive (ideologically or normatively informed) network of act-descriptions otherwise internally coherent. Without the benefit of some form of moral cognitivism, it is impossible to justify substantive constraints on admissible act-descriptions or elisions of act-descriptions—which, without cognitivist support, must be seen as entirely partisan in nature. To put the matter heuristically, the prudential interests of others is the material but not necessarily the final cause of ethical conduct; one's conviction regarding overriding values fixes the (variable) final cause (unless cognitivism or essentialism holds); conceptual distinctions governing the description of action and corresponding with one's overriding values mark the formal cause of the ethical import of one's conduct; and actions and intentions serve as the efficient cause of whatever has ethical import.

Again, it is often maintained that a merely linguistic analysis of such exressions as 'I promise' yields ethical consequences, since consistent adherence to the alleged linguistic rules governing the use of such expressions—and adherence to the linguistic institutions embodying such rules—entails ethically substantive commitments. But this is to confuse linguistic and ethical questions by failing to take note of the distinction between performing ethically significant actions by means of speech and the analysis of ethical institutions as distinct from the analysis of linguistic institutions. It may well be impossible, for instance, to construe the performatory act of promising—uttering under appropriate circumstances the expression 'I promise' or some cognate expression—as a purely linguistic act. But this means that the very concept of a speech act (or of certain speech acts) may be incapable of restriction to purely linguistic conventions (as opposed to ethical conventions)—not that substantive ethical issues can be resolved by purely linguistic means.[5] For example, whether one can or cannot enter into a promise unless he is able to renege on his promise or unless he has good reason to believe (or no reasons for not believing) that he would be able to renege on his promise is a substantive matter affecting the institution of promising; but the matter cannot be construed, by any stretch of the imagination, as a purely linguistic consideration.[6] Similarly, there are no purely linguistic means, as by way of a study of the rule-governed use of 'good,' by which to decide whether man qua man has a function, in

5. This is the fundamental mistake, for instance, in John Searle's analysis of speech acts and, in particular, of the act of promising; cf. *Speech Acts* (Cambridge: Cambridge University Press, 1969), chap. 3.
6. I have discussed this issue at length in an as yet unpublished paper, "Promising and Linguistic Acts."

terms of which normative questions may be validly decided.[7]

Finally, and perhaps most important, there is no indisputable set of ethically critical cases that are not open (unless they are trivialized) to plausible ethical disagreement on the strength of alternative ethical principles; in fact, what the admissible central cases and paradigm judgments of ethical concern are is itself a matter that is not independent of the very principles one adopts. But this means that the adequacy of first principles cannot be straightforwardly tested by reference to antecedently determined cases and judgments, and fitting first principles to runs of cases does not conform to the model of science—a model that rests, in however complicated a manner, on the relative independence of *explanandum* and *explanans*. In the ethical domain, we cannot confirm, but only exhibit, the scope of a principle.[8] If cases are described in ethically neutral ways, they will be open to plural and nonconverging ethically relevant identification and interpretation controlled by alternative systems; and if cases are described in ethically freighted ways, they will, inevitably, favor just those theories in terms of which the favored identification and interpretation are actually provided.

Such, then, are the principal strategies by which cognitivism and cryptocognitivism have been advanced. They are all demonstrably question-begging, and their failure in this respect confirms the sense in which the claims of the irreconcilable partisan factions of our specimen cases cannot normally be undermined or disqualified by an appeal to settled public procedures for fixing the appropriate normative values for particular disputes.

It is also of crucial importance, in assessing the possibility of objective ethical appraisal, to take notice of the fact that

7. For instance, as in the view of Zeno Vendler, "The Grammar of Goodness," in *Linguistics in Philosophy* (Ithaca, N.Y.: Cornell University Press, 1967).
8. Cf. Margolis, op. cit., p. 8.

none of the engagements of our specimen cases are, in any obvious sense, irrational. In fact, it is impossible to show that
the taking of life—one's own or another's, deliberately or by
way of a double effect—or the corresponding destruction of
property is inherently irrational. Here, we need merely distinguish between moral and prudential considerations, that
is, between those values that are said to be overriding values,
said to take precedence over all other possible values as far as
deliberate conduct is concerned, and values that merely answer to the putative interests of all human beings, values
based on some generalized reflection regarding the usual policies of men. Thus, for instance, preserving one's life is a putative interest of men: we are thought to be rational in acting
to preserve our lives, in the minimal sense that so acting does
not require any special justification in order to qualify as rational. But a man may, in specifiable circumstances, suicide
or sacrifice his life by way of a double effect and yet, although
it can hardly be deemed prudent, to act so is not necessarily
to act contrary to reason. For a moral or overriding cause
may well be proposed as justifying, in the belief of the agent,
the act of sacrificing his life; and the complete loss of any desire to preserve one's life, as for reasons of failing health or
loss of fortune, may at least explain the sense in which suicide may be the act of a quite rational man. To go beyond
such admissions, as by conflating prudence and morality, is to
presuppose one or another of the versions of cognitivism already dismissed. Departure from the putative prudential concerns of men obviously calls for defense in order to qualify as
rational, but such defense is not unavailable. Thus it is conceivable that men may rationally advocate the wholesale destruction or jeopardy of life and property in the name of
some supposed moral objective: their claim may be disputed
by partisans of another persuasion, but their claim is not obviously self-contradictory, incoherent, or morally ineligible.

To have sorted out the conceptual issues here considered, however, is in effect to have demonstrated the impossibility of formulating any objective grounds on which validly to condemn as such the destruction of, or threat to, life and property characteristically entailed by our specimen cases—in any manner, that is, that escapes mere partisan advocacy. It may well be that, in particular instances, agents do behave inconsistently or in ways that may be condemned in accord with the normative values to which they themselves are in some relevant sense already committed; but it seems flatly impossible, by any conceptually defensible means, utterly to disqualify, as being morally incoherent or morally objectionable, policies and commitments that deliberately advocate the selective destruction of life and property. Once we give up the pretense of ethical cognitivism and cognate doctrines, we are reduced to partisan advocacy. But this is not to say that arbitrariness, inconsistency, expediency, insincerity, special pleading, or ad hoc qualification cannot be detected; nor is it to deny that entire societies are in effect committed to particular normative values relative to the framework of which value judgments may be objectively validated.

A further consideration is in order. It may reasonably be argued (as has been remarked) that the deliberate destruction of life and property must go contrary to the prudential interests of some human agents—and hence, on certain views, must be morally indefensible. It is indeed very probable that the violation of some agents' interests will be entailed under the circumstances. But though it is true, this itself is indecisive, for it is a substantive—and therefore disputable—thesis that no policy ought (in an ethically relevant sense) to be pursued unless every human agent could, convincingly, acknowledge that it was a policy actually in his interest or at least not contrary to his interest. For one thing, it is extraordinarily unlikely—as our specimen cases suggest—that any significant policies *could* satisfy the ethical condition proposed. For another, drawing on a previous argument, the thesis confuses ethical and prudential considerations: particular prudential interests are not, as such, either ethical concerns or necessary conditions for ethical concerns; and any prudential interest may in principle be ethically overridden. For a third, one can always universalize any policy favoring preferred interests merely by identifying relevant agents and interests in terms of suitable historical qualifications. This is, in fact, precisely what every faction advocating violence—as, for instance, in our specimen cases—implicitly does and, rationally, may do. Furthermore, if, as some hold, it is permissible to take another's life only when acting as a legitimately authorized agent of the state (as a soldier, for instance), then it is clear that the thesis is itself both partisan and conservative; for, short of some suitable cognitivism, it is impossible to separate the question of ethically justifying the practice of the state and the question of ethically justifying the practice of revolutionaries who would bring the state down.[9]

But then, repugnant as it may be, there are absolutely no grounds on which policies of selective violence and destruction of life and property can be shown to be conceptually dubious or defective or inferior to policies that embody what are said to be the most generous or altruistic or nonviolent or enlightened values that the civilizations of the world have yet advanced. And this means once again that we are, in a most profound sense, moral partisans, pitted against or joined to one another solely in terms of our convictions—and that given the mounting evidence favoring a reliance on violent and destructive means, we had better understand the import of this condition of the radical equality of alternative ethical visions.

9. Cf. G. E. M. Anscombe, "War and Murder," in Walter Stein, ed., *Nuclear Weapons: A Catholic Response* (New York: Sheed and Ward, 1961).

3

Reform and Revolution

PETER CAWS

The first step alone is decisive: discourse or violence, affective chaos or reason, which should I choose? This initial question once resolved—and it is because I am writing—what follows from it can be thought clearly: no existence is now possible for me except in conformity to reason; my first decision circumscribes me completely; it implies that my life will be lived according to a system of norms and that these norms will be brought to light by a form of knowledge.

— Lucien Sebag
Marxisme et structuralisme
(trans. P.C.)

AUTHOR'S NOTE

This essay is part of a longer work dealing with the relations between philosophy, politics, and education. It addresses itself ultimately to the question of what the philosopher, *in his capacity as such,* might reasonably try to do to affect the course of political events. Philosophy has for a long time held itself apart from such events, not because its practitioners found themselves in "a mean city, the politics of which they contemned and neglected"[1] (the only excuse Plato offers for not being politically involved), but because they accepted a view of philosophy as *essentially* detached from the practical affairs of the world—a view of which Plato, and later Marx, were extremely critical. For Plato and Marx philosophy had a

1. Plato *Republic* 496.

responsibility to put its knowledge and its critical perception at the disposal of the state or of civil society, even at the price of scholarly calm. "The world's becoming philosophical," said Marx (by which we are to understand its becoming a *practical* object of philosophical interest), "is at the same time philosophy's becoming worldly; its realization is at the same time its loss."[2]

The dilemma that arises, according to Marx, cannot be resolved *within* philosophy. "The *practice* of philosophy is theoretical." But after his own excursion into economics he is reported to have said, at the end of his life, that his enterprise as a whole had been at bottom a philosophical one—it was just that the point of application of philosophy could not be determined without the understanding of the world the economic studies were intended to provide, and that these studies had in fact come to occupy all his remaining energy outside the political activity of the middle years. The political activity had not succeeded in being philosophical, as might have been expected from the citations given.

It is not clear that the dilemma has to be accepted on Marx's terms; it may be that there is a way of remaining philosophical and yet at the same time making a contribution to politics. What will be lost will not be philosophy, but the luxury of philosophical remoteness and isolation. This is Plato's version of the matter, and it is further developed in what follows. But before adopting that solution it is necessary to be persuaded that there is some point in trying to remain philosophical—that, confronted with the choice between violence and discourse, there is some point in choosing discourse. Marx might just as well have abandoned the philosophical enterprise altogether, as some people think he did

2. Karl Marx, "Philosophy After its Completion," *Notes to the Doctoral Dissertation,* reprinted in Lloyd D. Easton and Kurt H. Guddat, trans. and ed., *Writings of the Young Marx on Philosophy and Society* (New York, 1967).

and as many of his followers have done, in favor of more or less direct political action. I have tried to show that it is reasonable to choose discourse rather than violence, reform rather than revolution, on two grounds: first, that the alternative of direct political action is not, in the present context, a particularly promising strategy; second, that there are unexplored avenues of philosophical activity, of a heuristic rather than an analytic kind, that should perhaps be exhausted before recourse is had to more desperate measures.

This attempt is open to a possible misunderstanding, which it is one of the purposes of this note to dispel. I have argued, on historical and not philosophical grounds, that political revolutions are at best double-edged weapons and that there is little evidence that they have been efficacious in producing the changes that their originators envisaged. But I do not intend by this argument to imply an adverse judgment of those who, examining their circumstances and their consciences, conclude that they are obliged to follow a violent or a revolutionary path. I think it likely that philosophers will make, on the whole, poor revolutionaries, and I think they have failed to investigate the resources of their own profession, or perhaps rather failed to estimate accurately what the reaction of people in power might be—given that such people are, on the whole, not much less or much more intelligent and rational than the philosophers themselves—if those resources were put at their disposal. But this is a strategic and not a moral dispute. If a philosopher believed his duty to be the abandonment of philosophy for a life of political action, because after examination of the alternatives all seemed to him futile, that decision would deserve the deepest respect. My only contention is that, if such a move involved the replacement of discourse by violence, it really *would* be an abandonment of philosophy, not temporarily but definitively. And I do not believe that this is necessary.

*　　*　　*

Discontent with the state of things in society, when it becomes acute enough to stimulate action, will produce different effects according to whether or not it attaches to particulars. To the question of what causes the discontent there are two kinds of response. One consists of making a list of the things that are wrong, one at a time (Vietnam, poverty, racial discrimination, hard drugs, and so on), but the other refuses to do this, saying in effect that the nature of the wrong is such as to make such lists futile, that nothing can be corrected short of a new beginning altogether, that the whole *system* is wrong. The first kind of response will lead, when it comes to the question of strategy, to proposals for reform; the second will lead to a call for revolution. The relation between the two ideas, then, can be provisionally understood in terms of generality and specificity: reform proceeds piecemeal; revolution overturns the basis of the system, so that no part remains unaffected by it.

The content of reform can usually be specified more or less exactly because a given reform is a partial change in a system whose other elements are thought of as remaining constant. Thus one might seek to reform foreign policy or education or electoral practices, on the assumption that such elements of the system can change radically without necessitating radical changes in the other elements. There will of course be causal influences of the elements on one another, and various mutual adaptations will have to take place. These adaptations will require a certain amount of systems-theoretical sophistication if they are to go smoothly, but the understanding of complex systems has advanced sufficiently to provide that. There is nothing to rule out the possibility that reforms might proceed in all the elements of the system simultaneously; the effect would be total, but since each component would have the partial character of a reform the whole process would not be thought of as revolutionary.

This last remark, however, suggests a rather special meaning for "revolution," not necessarily in agreement with its general use. For in the ordinary way, at any rate after the event, we would certainly be prepared to say of a process that had changed every aspect of the system, leaving nothing the same, that it had amounted to a revolution. It is just in this sense that we speak of the Industrial Revolution or the Copernican Revolution, and these may be taken as paradigms for one of the two usual meanings of the term. I will call them *epochal* revolutions. The other familiar use refers to a process which precisely does *not* have the global character that, in the first instance, I relied on to distinguish revolution from reform, but which takes place primarily in one component of the system, the political, and consists of a more or less rapid and more or less violent seizure of total political power—legislative, executive, and judicial—by a revolutionary group. The paradigms for this use are the familiar ones— the French Revolution, the October Revolution, and so on. I will call them *political* revolutions. Of the two types of revolutionary change recognized by Aristotle—"the one affecting the constitution, when men seek to change from an existing form into some other, for example, from democracy into oligarchy, and from oligarchy into democracy, or from either of them into constitutional government or aristocracy, and conversely; the other not affecting the constitution, when, without disturbing the form of government, whether oligarchy, or monarchy, or any other, they try to get the administration into their own hands"[3]—only the former would count as a political revolution in this sense.

Now the Marxist theory of revolution, as is well known,

3. Aristotle *Politics* 1301b.

considers that the main focus of attack must be the set of economic relations in bourgeois society that constitutes the base on which bourgeois politics, law, religion, and the like have been erected as a superstructure. Here enters another possible distinction between revolution and reform: reform touches only the superstructure, revolution changes the base, whether one considers that to be economic or otherwise. But would not a series of reforms that affected every element of the superstructure turn out to have changed the base? And if politics belongs to the superstructure, is there any guarantee that a political revolution will affect the base? A political revolution can clearly be only part of the story, and it is an open question whether such a revolution can ever be successfully linked to an epochal one. Marx's revolution is in fact epochal: it envisages a complete change in men's social and historical condition, in their relations to each other and to the world. In particular the class structure of society is to disappear, and the system of economic relations is to be changed in such a way as to overcome the alienation between man as a producer and the means and fruits of his production. This will naturally involve changes in the political power structure, and at various times during Marx's life he thought he perceived conditions, in different countries, that would make the violent seizure of power appropriate and possible. But none of the political revolutions with which he had anything to do were in the slightest degree successful, while on the other hand the epochal revolution that he heralded is well under way—although not only or even mainly in the places where successful political revolutions have invoked his name.

What led to the association of the two kinds of revolution in Marxist doctrine was, among other things, Engels's adoption of the Hegelian law of the passage from quantitative to qualitative change, a piece of romantic philosophizing on a mistaken scientific model. The accumulation of small quan-

titative changes in society, thought Engels, produces internal
tensions which mount towards a critical level without producing any great apparent change; when the critical level is
reached, however, a sudden and violent change occurs which
overturns the society and gives birth to a new and qualita-
tively different social order. The sequence of cumulative
changes looks like an epochal revolution; the sudden transformation looks like a political one; *ergo* the epochal revolution is achieved by political action. Typical of the examples
from nature on which Engels based this view (which I have
represented freely but, I think, accurately) was the change of
water into steam at the boiling point.[4] But in fact the change
of water into steam is not particularly sudden or violent. It
takes seven times as long to turn a pint of water into steam as
it takes to boil it, starting at room temperature; and provided
the steam has space to expand into, the process goes perfectly
smoothly. What makes it look so dramatic in teakettles, for
example, is that the change takes place at the bottom where
all the available space is already occupied by water, so that
the steam has to bubble to the top. As an analogy for *re-
pressed* change this is not bad, but it is not a mass phenomenon—a very small amount of water will make a very large
bubble of steam—and there is nothing inherent in the
change from water to steam that would sustain the revolutionary analogy.

The law of quality and quantity does not necessarily have
to be abandoned, but it is capable of a very different application. At the end of an epochal revolution a man might realize, on looking about him, that everything had *gradually* altered until the whole was *completely* different: compare the
beginning and the end, and the change is qualitative, but examine the details and nothing can be found except quantita-

4. Frederick Engels, *Anti-Duhring*, trans. Emile Bottigelli (Paris: Editions
Sociales, 1950), pp. 157-58.

tive change. So a series of reforms might, by sound dialectical standards, *constitute* a revolution; and this suggests that the opposition revolution/reform is an artificial one. Unfortunately it is enshrined in current usage as an opposition between the rapid, total and (probably) violent on the one hand, and the deliberate, partial, and nonviolent on the other. If revolutionary strategies are *opposed* to reformist ones, then reforms that might be carried out while awaiting the revolutionary opportunity (or working to create it) will appear counterrevolutionary; but failing to carry them out means either the rapid forcing of the revolution—whence the probable violence—or an apparently unnecessary delay in the correction of undesirable conditions. The opposition to reform may of course be due, as I shall suggest later, to the covert fear that if allowed it will, as it were, spike the guns of the revolution; but this indicates an undue attachment to a component of revolutionary activity that may in fact not be necessary to the achievement of genuinely revolutionary ends —a preference for political-revolutionary form over epochal-revolutionary content.

Epochal revolutions tend to be rather long-drawn-out affairs, and there is a theoretical limit on the speed with which they can be achieved. Jefferson was fond of pointing out that the statistical tables of his day gave the adults of the human race a half-life of nineteen years.[5] He did not use that term, but the idea is exactly the same as in modern physics: the period after which half of the material initially present has changed into another form; that is, in Jefferson's case, died. He cited this fact as the basis for an argument that there should be a constitutional convention every nineteen years, because on the one hand an inherited constitution is an infringement on the liberty of the new generation, and on the other the new generation might reasonably expect, after the

5. Thomas Jefferson, letter to James Madison, September 6, 1789.

half-life, to be in the majority. The relevance of this to epochal revolution is obvious if stress is placed on the disappear-
ance of the old generation rather than on the emergence of
the new one.

Now, of course, thanks to medicine, etc., the half-life is
much longer, which makes epochal revolutions even slower.
While some people are humble and open enough to change
their own minds during the course of their lives, the fact has
to be faced that most are not, so that the only way to be sure
that an epochal revolution is safely established—even assuming that the new ideas are presented to everybody at once,
which of course never happens—is to wait until the people
who grew up with the old beliefs are dead or outnumbered.
This is one reason why the explicit invocation of an epochal
revolution by a political one is so dangerous—the temptation
to hurry the process along by eliminating the unregenerate
may grow too strong to resist.

A political revolution, or at least the operative part of it,
takes place of necessity in a very much shorter period of time,
certainly much less than the half-life, because in order to
maintain the society at an even minimally operating level
power has to be wielded more or less continuously; such a
revolution cannot therefore (in the absence of a massacre or
a long suppression of civil liberties or both) take on the character of an epochal revolution, with the changes of habits and
attitudes that entails. One difficulty is that the dominant figures in the revolution must have grown up in the old epoch,
and will except in very rare cases carry with them the unconscious baggage of that epoch. This makes dissension under
the new regime almost inevitable, and an internal struggle
often ensues; it is remarkable, in fact, how few of the princi-
pals in political revolutions with epochal overtones survive.
The half-life of this group in the French Revolution must
have been about eighteen months.

In advocating revolutions it is important, therefore, to know what one has in mind. The advocate of an epochal revolution cannot, as a rule, expect to live to see the full results of his work; he can only make his contribution in the hope that the movement as a whole will follow the right direction. The figures who appear in retrospect to have been important in such revolutions often did not seem so at the time, or at any rate not in the same way. The pattern is of clear vision, continual effort, personal sacrifice, and disappointed ambitions. Effort and sacrifice are involved in political revolutions too, but they are more consciously directed towards an immediate end, and they are much more quickly disappointed or rewarded. The point I want to stress is that anybody having in mind the necessity for an epochal revolution, who advocates a political revolution as a means towards it, will almost certainly be disillusioned and will probably at some stage in it be brushed rudely aside if not liquidated.

As I have indicated, I believe that an epochal revolution is in progress—one perceived as necessary by Marx, among others, and argued for by him with passion and eloquence in his early writings. But the categories in terms of which he came to analyze it later—class and capital—have turned out to be largely irrelevant to the course it has taken. The character of this revolution has been convincingly described by Jean-François Revel in his recent book *Ni Marx ni Jésus;*[6] he believes that the main locus of it at the present time is America, and he is undoubtedly right in this. That is one reason why it is so important for Americans who are participating in it not to endanger it by mistaking it for a political revolution. For a successful political revolution is not remotely possible in America at the present time—not, at least, one that would be in any way friendly to the epochal revolution in

6. Jean-François Revel, *Ni Marx ni Jésus* (Paris, 1970); published in the U.S. as *Without Marx or Jesus* (Garden City, N.Y., 1971).

question. And to suggest, as some people have done, that a revolutionary situation could be brought about in America over a period of years, raises again the question of the revolutionary's attitude to reform. In the absence of any reform, assuming a continued deterioration on all fronts—unending war, deepening poverty, increasing alienation, worsening pollution, and so on—an explosive state of affairs might indeed develop, which would issue in violent revolutionary action. People who work to end the war, mitigate poverty, decrease alienation, reduce pollution, etc., might therefore be said to be unfriendly to *this* revolution. But to argue that they should therefore cease their efforts at reform would require not only a confidence in the outcome of the eventual revolution that (as I shall now try to show) cannot be justified by any appeal to history, but also an apparently cynical indifference to the immediate plight of those affected by the conditions in question.

Political revolutions may have various causes and various reasons, but their immediate end is always political power, even when this is intended to serve more distant ends such as peace and justice. (Such ends cannot make a political revolution into an epochal one.) The major political revolutions of the last few centuries have taken roughly the same direction, as part of a general movement away from tyranny and towards democracy. As the later stages of this process—which has been going on globally and has not depended for its progress on revolutions—begin to unfold, it is as well to remember that a contrary movement is possible: "In oligarchies the masses make revolution under the idea that they are unjustly treated, because . . . they are equals, and have not an equal share, and in democracies the notables revolt, because they are not equals, and yet have only an equal share."[7] The military *coups d'état* that have become so frequent of late have

7. Aristotle *Politics* 1303^b.

generally been counterrevolutionary—against the threat or in the fear of revolutions of the first kind, rather than examples of revolutions of the second kind. The Fascist régimes in Italy and Germany that precipitated World War II also took over far too soon to make them suitable examples of Aristotle's second category; they were (so far) *sui generis* bits of practical insanity, but they serve as reminders that *belief* in equality has as yet only a precarious hold even on populations that have been among the leaders of civilization.

A plausible case can be made for the essential similarity of all the standard examples of political revolution. The first important one in modern history was the Puritan Revolution of 1640-49. This broke genuinely new ground and constituted an "existence proof" of enormous importance. It served to establish a precedent and a principle: that the rights of kings could be successfully challenged, and that the supreme authority lay in the legislature. Once demonstrated in practice, it was in one sense unnecessary for these propositions to be worked out again by revolutionary action. They did have to be reiterated, since the notion of Divine Right died hard, and were given definitive form in Locke's *Two Treatises of Government*. This work, as Peter Laslett has convincingly argued,[8] was written well before the Glorious Revolution of 1688, and the fact that that revolution took the course it did suggests that the propositions had by then been widely accepted. To conjecture what might have happened if James II had been Protestant is beside the point, which is that when Parliament, even after the Restoration, saw the need of moving against the King, it felt free to take action.

The other two great revolutions of the Western world, the French of 1789-99 and the Russian of 1905-17, were in an important sense mere repetitions of the Puritan Revolution.

8. Peter Laslett, *Introduction* (chap. III) to John Locke, *Two Treatises of Government* (Cambridge, Eng., 1960).

The parallels among the three are striking. The points of overt conflict, although complicated by local differences (religious in England, economic in France, ideological in Russia) were strikingly similar: the despotic behavior of a monarch on the one hand and the assertion of parliamentary rights on the other. In each case a more or less representative body, called together out of reluctant necessity by a ruler convinced of his right to supreme power, took the law into its own hands: the Long Parliament declared that it could not be dissolved without its own consent, the States-General turned itself into the National Assembly, the Duma refused to recognize its dissolution by the tsar. In each case the symbol of monarchical tyranny was eventually executed.

But in guillotining Louis XVI and shooting Nicholas II, whatever the immediate and local causes of these acts, the French and Russians were symbolically re-enacting the beheading of Charles I. For Charles I stood exactly for what political revolutions have wished to destroy: a stubborn conviction of superiority and privilege, an establishment determined to cling to its social, political, and economic advantages. Every dictator against whom revolutionary energy has been directed has been, to some degree, a reincarnation of Charles I. By comparison George III is of no real importance. The American Revolution, it is true, was also unnecessary; in addition, however, it was not really a revolution, but rather a war of colonial liberation.

By saying that these later revolutions were unnecessary, I do not mean of course that in the context of their times they were either avoidable or unjustifiable, only that their social (as distinct from their ideological) objectives would probably, sooner or later, have been attained by other means. In every case, no doubt, the immediate situation appeared incapable of any other resolution: injustice had become intolerable, economic conditions were deteriorating, social stability was shaken, patience was exhausted. But in France the king had already accepted the principle of constitutional rule by October 1789; in America the colonists had powerful friends in the English Parliament itself, who before many more changes of administration would no doubt have won the concession of representation if not of self-government; in Russia the end of the war would almost certainly have brought constitutional reform. Such conjectures aside, however, my point is that the *ideas* of the limitation of dynastic power and the self-determination of representative assemblies were in circulation after 1649/1688 as they had not been before. In England at any rate it was thereafter possible to proceed explicitly by successive reforms.

One or two more notes from this historical excursion and we can return to contemporary problems. (1) It is clearly important, in deploying revolutionary force, to know who the adversary is; it is best of all if he declares himself, as Charles I did at Nottingham in 1642. In France a lot of revolutionary energy was set in motion without any very clear idea of what it was directed against, and it quickly turned on itself, with extremely grisly consequences. In Russia the power of the tsar was so weakened by 1917 that almost anything would have removed him; after February the conflict was internal to the revolution, and October and the civil war of 1918-20 followed for reasons which had little to do with the original grievances against the Romanovs. (2) None of the major European revolutions—and to them might be added the incredibly complex and protracted Chinese revolution, which lasted in one phase or another from 1912 to 1949—led in the end to anything like what their original authors expected or intended. The Stuart and Bourbon restorations, and repressive and bureaucratic communism, would have appalled most of the men who set in motion the chains of events that produced them. In none of the cases after 1688 can it be said with any certainty that things were on the whole better afterwards than they would otherwise have been, even in the country primarily concerned (the possible exceptions to this generalization are China and Cuba). And it is quite certain that the pattern of violence established in modern political revolutions has, by the fear it has instilled in the governments of other countries, led to a slowing down and even reversal of benign epochal changes elsewhere. Imagine the political history of the United States in the last half century, supposing the Kerensky régime in Russia to have stabilized, liberalized, and perpetuated itself!

History does not under any circumstances permit the drawing of definite morals. I am far from saying that political revolutions are never necessary, only that we know almost nothing about the laws according to which they proceed after the initial outbreak, and that such historical evidence as we have about their effectiveness in realizing what people want is extremely depressing. The point of the exercise has been to show that the question is academic: a truly revolutionary outbreak in America is, as I have said, strictly inconceivable at the present time, the distribution of economic, political, and military power being what it is. King and Parliament were almost matched in 1640; the colonies were being administered at a distance by men of already mixed sympathies in 1776; the French government was bankrupt in 1789; Russia was torn by war in 1917, and ruled in the tsar's absence by the tsarina, still under the posthumous influence of Rasputin. There is little evidence of such vulnerability today: the government is firmly in position and the people, even those who disagree with its policies, are in virtually unanimous support of its title to power.

When therefore Justice Douglas compares the present Establishment to George III and says that if it continues to "adhere to his tactics . . . the redress, honored in tradition, is also revolution,"[9] the historical analogy is misleading. In 1776 it was not merely a question of disapproving of George III's acts or believing that he abused his legitimate powers; the Founding Fathers came to the conclusion that under the circumstances he had no legitimate powers. That is the great difference: today, people who think that the administration's policies are hideous, and its arrogation of power to itself thoroughly unconstitutional, still for the most part concede that it is at any rate the legitimately elected administration, whose executive appointments have been legitimately confirmed. This throws into sharp relief the perplexity of the revolutionary in present-day America: whereas former political revolutions have been against systems whose injustice was apparent on their face, his would be against a system which, in formal terms at any rate, seems genuinely to have been designed to serve justice; what system will work better, as long as men continue to behave as they do? And even if the new men brought to power by the revolution represented a change for the better, what would guarantee that human weakness would not soon reassert itself, as has happened in every revolution so far recorded? No falling back on economic or class dogma can successfully evade this problem.

The motive force of revolution, said Marx, is a numerically dominant class suffering from an unqualified wrong.[10] His hope that the class he meant by this description, the proletariat of the late Industrial Revolution, would rise up and become the revolutionary engine needed for the *Aufhebung* of his own dialectical dilemma was never realized; Lenin, a man less concerned with philosophical than with political problems, abandoned it altogether and embraced a party élitist view. Lenin's success, as I have hinted, was the fruit of a

9. William O. Douglas, *Points of Rebellion* (New York, 1970), p. 95.
10. Karl Marx, *Toward the Critique of Hegel's Philosophy of Law*, reprinted in Easton and Guddat, op. cit., p. 263.

negative breakdown rather than of a positive outbreak: he saw an opportunity, and he took it. In the absence of such an opportunity, no amount of party organization would have been able to seize power by revolutionary means. Every successful political revolution has been opportunist in this way; there is no case on record of a revolutionary seizure of power at a time when the majority of the people were, for good or bad reasons, more or less contented with their lot. In France in 1968 there was a disturbance so severe that it seemed briefly to present a truly revolutionary opportunity, but the French Communist Party, the only organized group that might have taken advantage of it, declined to do so.[11] And in 1970 in Chile a Marxist administration came into power for the first time in a democratic election. So that *this* line of political revolutionary development, for the time being at any rate, seems to be at an end. President Allende, it is true, speaks of the Chilean Marxist victory as a "revolution of revolution,"[12] a new manner of arriving at revolutionary ends. But it is hard to see how this differs from ordinary parliamentary democracy, a stepwise process of reforms.

The fact is that most people instinctively reject revolutionary activity, unless it is clear to them in their immediate lives and persons that conditions have reached a point of desperation. Very few have the sporting attitude of Jefferson, who thought that an occasional rebellion was good for the political health of the state: "What country can preserve its liberties, if its rulers are not warned from time to time, that their people preserve the spirit of resistance? Let them take arms. The remedy is to set them right as to facts, pardon and pacify them. What signify a few lives lost in a century or two? The tree of liberty must be refreshed from time to time, with the

11. See my article "What Happened in Paris," *Partisan Review* (Autumn 1968), pp. 519-25.
12. See C. L. Sulzberger, *New York Times,* March 31, 1971, p. 45.

blood of patriots and tyrants."[13] And even Jefferson, in the Declaration of Independence, recognized the reluctance of the people to resist: "Prudence, indeed, will dictate that governments long established should not be changed for light and transient causes; and accordingly all experience hath shown that mankind are more disposed to suffer while evils are sufferable, than to right themselves by abolishing the forms to which they are accustomed."[14]

The crux of the matter is that, while the Vietnamese are suffering and some of the blacks are suffering and the poor are suffering and the relatives of the 45,000-odd dead soldiers are suffering, the solid majority of America's 200 million inhabitants is not suffering. One of the novel and extraordinary features of the so-called revolutionary movement, and one of the most admirable and hopeful things about it, is that the energy of many of those who participate in it is aroused by the sufferings of *others,* and by the objective failures of the government, rather than by conditions affecting them directly. The call for revolution becomes a question of morals as much as of politics. Unfortunately, "such revolutions happen not upon every little mismanagement in public affairs. Great mistakes in the ruling part, many wrong and inconvenient laws, and all the slips of human frailty will be borne by the people without mutiny or murmur. . . . For till the mischief be grown general, and the ill designs of the rulers become visible, or their attempts sensible to the greater part, the people, who are more disposed to suffer than right themselves by resistance, are not apt to stir. The examples of particular injustice or oppression of here and there an unfortunate man moves them not."[15] And even if the oppression

13. Thomas Jefferson, letter to Colonel Smith, November 13, 1787.
14. The Declaration of Independence.
15. John Locke, *Second Treatise of Government,* chap. XIX, paras. 225 and 230.

affects a number of people, and they become aware of it, still, knowing as they do that the rest of the population is not immediately affected, they themselves may decline to be drawn into revolutionary action. (It must be remembered that very often the oppressed do not realize they are so until brought to consciousness of the fact by political workers—"agitators," in the strict etymological sense of the term—believing otherwise that their misery is the natural condition of man; and that many of them remain convinced of the hopelessness of the situation even when they *have* become aware of it.) "Though they have a right to defend themselves, and to recover by force what by unlawful force is taken from them, yet the right to do so will not easily engage them in a contest wherein they are sure to perish; it being as impossible for one or a few oppressed men to disturb the government where the body of the people do not think themselves concerned in it, as for a raving madman or heavy malcontent to overturn a well-settled state, the people being as little apt to follow the one as the other."[16]

To sum up: political revolutions are hard to start, and they hardly ever work. Epochal revolutions are slow, and they may in fact consist of a series of reforms. To be a revolutionary in the political sense at a time when the conditions for political revolution are not present or likely to come about or able to be brought about is irresponsible, even supposing political revolution to be a sound strategy when conditions make it possible, which on the evidence is dubious. But it is possible to be an authentic revolutionary in the epochal sense by pursuing feasible reforms in limited areas, having in mind while doing so what the eventual state of the whole would ideally be after all the reforms had been accomplished. There is clearly a sense in which to talk about revolution *is* just a hy-

16. Ibid., chap. XVIII, para. 208.

perbolic way of talking about reform, which derives its plausibility from the fact that within the domain affected by the reform its consequences may seem revolutionary: a plan for university reform that called for the abolition of the office of president might appear genuinely revolutionary as seen from the president's office. It is in this sense that it is appropriate to speak, for example, of the sexual revolution, or to characterize black power or women's liberation as revolutionary movements.

But the term "revolution" sometimes has additional connotations and overtones in the light of which reforms cannot *possibly* be revolutionary or satisfy the true follower of the revolution. An analogy for this use is to be found in religious language. There too the idea of mere reform is considered inadequate; the believer will insist, rather, on *conversion*. Conversion is the evangelical counterpart of revolution, and has some of the same drawbacks. It takes place rapidly, indeed instantaneously, and with a good deal of interior melodrama; changed behavior is supposed to follow, but is less important than the changed state and the changed attitudes of the convert. A man who improved himself *practically,* who stopped committing certain acts he perceived to be wrong and started committing other acts he perceived to be right, if he did this by dint of his own efforts, would in spite of the genuineness of his reform be considered by the evangelist to have achieved literally nothing: "All our righteousnesses are as filthy rags." A convert, on the other hand, even though he continues to fall into the old temptations ("The good that I would, that I do not; the evil that I would not, that I do—O wretched man that I am!" says St. Paul,[17] writing to the church in Rome many years after the vision on the road to Damascus), is considered through grace to

17. Romans 7:19-24.

have turned the essential corner, to *be* different even if he doesn't *look* different.

So, one is sometimes tempted to think, with the revolution: if the triumphant régime is just as oppressive (towards different victims, to be sure) as the one it overthrew, still its ideological virtues more than make up for that; whereas a government which over a long period really managed, in spite of setbacks and reverses, to bring a society nearer to the ideals of equality and justice might seem, if this were done without a political revolution, to have somehow cheated history. The committed revolutionary is the fundamentalist of politics; his attitude towards the old régime has something in common with the preacher's attitude to sin, and the moral intensity of his message, like that of the gospel, may be quite as persuasive as its content, if not more so. The revolution may come to seem more important as a struggle between good and evil, in which the wicked are to be punished, than as a means of liberating the oppressed.

These reflections, however, provoke another: exploiting Plato's analogy between the individual and the state, there may be a use for the notion of revolution as *interior,* to refer precisely to a kind of secular/political conversion which consists in the refusal in one's own person of the inequities of the repressive régime, without involving its actual overthrow as a matter of immediate strategy. It was in this sense that the Surrealists, for example, were revolutionaries, even though their brief attachment to a political revolutionary movement ended bitterly. Revolution becomes, under this interpretation, a question of attitude rather than of activity; the individual or the group is in a state of permanent revolution, i.e. of openness to radical change, denying the fixed categories of the received social, economic, and political order. According to Kojève, this is just the condition of Hegel's Slave when he has transformed the world by work

and is about to achieve the final dialectical overcoming of
the Master.[18] It is characteristic of the Master, a warlike man
whose only route to self-realization lies in a fight to the death
for pure prestige, to depend on a fixed order, particularly in
what concerns the Slave's relation to him; he is the true conservative, embodying the values of the old régime. What he
does not understand is that the Slave has already become
more human than himself—that the Master's humanity has
always been parasitic on the Slave's, while the latter has won
an autonomous humanity against a hostile world and can
afford to dispense with the rigidity of an unchanging system.

The interesting thing about this is that although Kojève
represents the Slave as ready, now, to take up again the fight
for recognition that he previously abandoned by capitulating
to the Master (thus originally entering into his condition of
slavery), the revolution that he accomplishes is not against
the Master but against the world. He becomes for the first
time in history the man who is adequate to the world, who
by conquering its hostility has brought himself into harmony
with it. The process by which this comes about can only be
an epochal revolution, and one might say that the final epochal revolution, the one now going on, is the realization of
the permanent revolution, i.e. of a human condition liber-
ated from the Manichaean categories which have marked
political history and which alone make political revolution
plausible. No political revolution can even help this process,
since some opposition—between king and parliament or between bourgeois and proletarian or between radical and conservative—is not only necessary for the occurrence of such a
revolution but also necessarily survives it, whereas *such* oppo-
sitions, under the conditions of the permanent revolution,
might be expected to disappear or to be reduced to a formal

18. Alexandre Kojève, *Introduction to the Reading of Hegel,* trans. Allan
Bloom (New York, 1969), pp. 21-23.

level (e.g. a two-party system in which the policies of the two parties are very close to one another). In connection with this last point, it is quite conceivable that institutions suitable to the permanent revolution might come into being before a population prepared to take advantage of them. If this were to happen the challenge would be double: to raise the population to the level of its opportunities by a program of education, and in the meantime to resist the temptation to destroy the institutions because they failed to prevent errors and abuses on the part of leaders as yet uneducated.

Something like this, I believe, is true in America today. But there is yet another reason why arguments that defend current institutions are unattractive to a certain class of revolutionaries. Not only are political revolutions sudden and morally dramatic, but they are also often *violent,* and the notions of revolution and of violence tend to become confused in the minds of some advocates of revolution as well as in the minds of those whose fear of revolution is really fear of violence. Violence is inherently satisfactory to certain temperaments and under certain circumstances, e.g. a conviction of long-standing injustice. "In all of us, even in good men, there is a lawless wild-beast nature, which peers out in sleep";[19] if objective conditions have become a nightmare, who is to insist that it be kept in check? The current oligarchy exercises violence regularly, at home and abroad, "and shall we say that the violence, if exercised by a rich man, is just, and if by a poor man, unjust? May not any man, rich or poor, with or without laws, with the will of the citizens or against the will of the citizens, do what is for their interest?"[20]

This is plausible enough, but it is extremely risky, and the advocate of violence needs to be aware of this. The argument against the hasty use of violence is similar to the argument

19. Plato *Republic* 572,.
20. Plato *Statesman* 296.

against precipitate political revolution. Both reduce, essentially, to this: that the *chances* of change in the desired direction are less by these means than by almost any others, and this for the very general and practical reason that whenever energy is expended in a limited space-time region, the greater the energy and the smaller the region and harder it is to keep the process under control. If violence has already entered the situation on the part of an oppressive régime, for example, it may be necessary to meet it with violence; in this case the response needs to be appropriate to the attack it is designed to neutralize. But the danger of initiating violence in an otherwise calm situation (no matter how oppressive) is that it is likely either to provoke a *disproportionate* reaction or, worse, to be taken advantage of (as in judo, where it is a cardinal rule not to throw weight in such a way that the momentum can be utilized by one's opponent). In either case things rapidly become unpredictable. Note that this is not an argument against *any* use of violence, only against its hasty or spontaneous use. It is questionable, however, whether its prepared, calculated and restrained use is ever possible outside a full-fledged military organization, for example a disciplined guerrilla force. And in that case the opponent also has to be estimated in military terms, and the disposition of the local population—its preparedness to tolerate acts of war in its midst, rather than a few thousand miles away—has to be carefully assessed. On neither count does any advocacy of guerrilla warfare in the United States make the slightest sense.

The argument has often been heard in recent years that violent action is the only way to draw the attention of a slow-moving and virtually blind social and political system to the glaring injustices it perpetuates. This argument is unconvincing; it overlooks the whole range of rational and moral susceptibilities, which, just because they have not been intelligently exploited, or have even been allowed to atrophy, cannot be written off. There are some nice historical counter-examples: the abolition of child labor, and of slavery, did not result from violent manifestations by slaves and children but from the moral concern of men firmly embedded in the Establishments of the time. (The violence of the Civil War was not revolutionary violence but sprang rather from economic and political contradictions internal to America.) The more people there are who have achieved the permanent revolution—and the number is growing—the less need there is for violent means of commanding attention. To do the proponents of the argument justice, it has hardly ever been followed by genuine *violence*, as distinct from local disturbances; apart from one or two bombings whose consequences, when they affected persons directly, appear to have horrified even their own perpetrators, and some explosions in the ghettos set off by heat and poverty, the only violence of any magnitude on the American scene in the last few years has come from the police and the National Guard. If the spontaneous anger of students can be met with rifle fire, can anybody doubt what response would be called forth by calculated violence of revolutionary magnitude? And this being so, can there really be any point in even entertaining the idea of a strategy that involves it?

If there were no prospect of effecting change in *any* other way, a fanatical revolutionary might justify a violent initiative even against such overwhelming odds, on the grounds that it is better to go to certain defeat for a principle than to let the principle lapse by default. But in an open society—which, in spite of Marcusean gloom on the subject, contemporary American society genuinely is—there are many other ways; and fundamental changes of policy and outlook are in fact occurring now at a more rapid rate in America than in any society at any time in the history of the world. From the Glorious Revolution to the first Reform Bill, 144 years elapsed; from the Emancipation Proclamation to *Brown v. Board of Education of Topeka,* 92 years. In the seventeen years since 1954 reforms surely associated with the epochal revolution already referred to have followed one another at decreasing intervals. It would be tedious to list them all, and they have not occurred uniformly or without resistance; but one has only to think of the status in 1954 of the universities, women, sexual mores, censorship, ecological awareness, political awareness on the part of the young, and so on, not to mention the blacks themselves, to perceive that a shift of very considerable magnitude is taking place.

It would be obtuse to pretend that violence and the threat of violence have had nothing to do with this shift, but it is important to put this influence in perspective. At close quarters angry blacks and angry students can be terrifying, of course, but by comparison even with local and familiar models—from recent memory in lynching and gang warfare, or from present observation in organized crime, traffic deaths, the guns and clubs of the police—the sum of black and student violence is relatively insignificant. It is not clear that such violent tactics as have been employed, and the sympathy that has been expressed for them, have yielded a net advantage, although it is clear that they have damaged the reputation of intellectuals as reasonable persons and have raised a spectre of interference in academic affairs by the legislatures and the courts, the full menace of which is only just becoming apparent. By far the larger share of the credit for the changes referred to above must go to the nonviolent tactics of Martin Luther King and to the voter-registration workers, the civil liberties lawyers, the journalists and writers and publishers, the socially conscious scientists, the peace marchers and the peace candidates, the legislative leaders, the lobbyists and letter-writers, the hundreds of thousands of local workers and supporters and sympathisers on all issues

from integration to pollution to Vietnam, who without re-
sorting to violence in any form have helped to shape public
opinion and exert political pressure. Vietnam still dominates
all, but this does not mean that these efforts have been
wasted. Indeed it has partly stimulated them, and their effects
will outlast it.

There have been and will no doubt continue to be setbacks and betrayals, but when the effective half-life of twenty-
five to thirty years has elapsed and the generation that has
grown up since 1954 is in the majority there can be little
doubt that many more changes will have been brought about,
including some in those parts of the system, such as the military establishment, that have so far been most recalcitrant.
The likelihood of this depends, it is true, on there being no
revolution from the right, and this in turn depends partly on
the political skill and restraint of those who wish to see the
epochal revolution accomplished. The way to ensure this is
to concentrate available energy and information behind reforms in those parts of the system most likely to yield to rational reconstruction in the short run, while at the same time
pursuing a strategy of education with respect to principles
and the less tractable parts of the system. For reasons already
suggested it is preferable to avoid a stance which makes the
reformer an enemy of the system. For one thing, given present circumstances it is much easier to change the system than
to replace it; for another, in so far as it is a system of self-
government, the reformer is unavoidably implicated in it.
Either his reforms will be acceptable to the people, or they
will not: if they are acceptable, the people have in principle
the power to implement them, and it will be a question not
of overthrowing the system but of making it function; if
they are not, he has no business to impose them.

What is at stake, as Hamilton correctly saw, is "whether
societies of men are really capable or not of establishing good

government from reflection and choice,"[21] and it is to the reflection and choice, that is, to the *reason,* of the people that the reformer must appeal. The alternative is to accept Plato's pessimistic conclusion that "man never legislates, but accidents of all sorts, which legislate for us in all sorts of ways. The violence of war and the hard necessity of poverty are constantly overturning governments and changing laws."[22] That Plato should have implicitly classed violence with poverty as accidental (for the "necessity" of poverty is what follows it, not what determines it) seems to me significant; what he has in mind is the possibility of a state in which man will have overcome both, a state that he despaired of seeing realized but which the present epochal revolution may for the first time put within our reach.

Even in his earlier, more hopeful days, Plato was convinced of the necessity for careful, stepwise intervention in the processes of government: "Let the change, if possible, be of one thing only, or, if not, of two; at any rate, let the changes be as few and slight as possible."[23] It may be that the upheavals he had witnessed in Athenian politics had left him with a distaste for violent fluctuations in government. In the light of what has already been said the change he went on to propose has, suitably interpreted, a surprisingly practical interest at the present time. "I think that there might be a reform of the State if only one change were made, which is not a slight or easy though still a possible one. . . . *Until philosophers are kings, or the kings and princes of this world have the spirit and power of philosophy, and political greatness and wisdom meet in one, and those commoner natures who pursue either to the exclusion of the other are compelled to stand aside, cities will never have rest from their*

21. Alexander Hamilton, *The Federalist,* no. 1.
22. Plato *Laws* 709.
23. Plato *Republic* 473.

evils,—no, nor the human race, as I believe,—and then only
will this our State have a possibility of life and behold the
light of day."[24]

The passage is celebrated, and in danger of being read as
a cliché. The "philosopher-king" has become the paradigm
of the conceit, of the Utopian irrelevance, of philosophy. But
by "philosophy" Plato did not mean an academic discipline,
as that expression has come to be used, at least not an academic discipline *among others;* and the philosopher-king is
not necessarily a philosopher who becomes a king—he may
equally well be a king who becomes a philosopher. The philosopher, as Plato goes on to define him, sounds very much
like the man in whom the permanent revolution has taken
hold, who refuses the fixed and closed and maintains an attitude of openness towards the world. "He who has a taste
for every sort of knowledge and who is curious to learn and
never satisfied, may be justly termed a philosopher? Am I not
right?"[25] As the *Republic* proceeds, it is true, the specification
of what a philosopher must be and know before he is qualified to assume political power grows into something much
more elaborate and rigorous than this, and in keeping with
the constructivist mode of the dialogue the formation of such
a man is envisaged as starting in youth and unfolding over a
long period of time. But it is not clear that some aspects at
least of the "spirit and power of philosophy" might not be
acquired in a shorter time or with a later start, and it is this
reflection that suggests a possible strategy for practical reform.

Possible solutions to most of the problems that confront
the world are already known. What is lacking is education,
i.e. the communication of these possible solutions, along with
the facts to which they address themselves, to people who are
in a position to implement them justly. Men are rational, not

24. Loc. cit.
25. Ibid., 475.

in the sense that they can by the aid of reason solve their immediate problems, but in the sense that, other things being equal, they tend to recognize rational solutions when they see them. Other things are usually not equal: all sorts of prejudices and dogmas intrude themselves. True education performs two functions; it makes it harder and harder for the prejudices and dogmas to survive, and it makes available the accumulation of selected rational strategies (selected in a Darwinian sense) that we owe to preceding generations and to men in other parts of the world. At the present time there is almost no true education in America, and any proposal for reform must in the long run involve the creation of an educational system that will provide it. But long-run solutions are too slow, if the reformed system is to begin with infants and produce an informed electorate which will in time elect a reformed government.

The short-run strategy is to concentrate on the education, not of the electors, *but of the elected*. The task for philosophy, in the narrow professional sense but also in the wider sense that Plato would certainly have recognized, according to which it would include a larger part of the intellectual community, is, in his language, to educate the kings: to address itself explicitly, not as an adversary but as an ally, not patronizingly but as sharing common concerns, to those who are already in positions of political power. If this sounds like a recommendation of partisan alignment, that is only because our conceptions of government have become degraded to the point where it seems natural to suppose that a political leader's first thoughts will be of his ambitions rather than of his responsibilities. But once the election is over, there is no point in lamenting that it might have gone differently; a particular human reality confronts us, an administration composed of individual human beings, with greater or lesser gifts, charged with decisions that affect the lives and fortunes of men all over the world. What can philosophy possibly have to say to such people? It will clearly do no good if it just tells them that they have got it all wrong, that they are morally bankrupt, dishonest, expedient, and the rest. It will do as little good if the philosopher attempts to tell the politician what he ought to be doing rather than what he is doing; such technical advice has not been asked for and will not be welcomed; moreover the philosopher is not as a rule competent to give it. There will be plenty of other people to give advice and exert pressure, but those are not roles for the philosopher in his professional capacity.

Also there will be no point at all in addressing some of the elected, "those commoner natures" who pursue political greatness to the *exclusion* of wisdom. This expression is typical of what many people take to be Plato's snobbery, as "compelled to stand aside" seems typical of his totalitarian impulses. But the judgement is symmetrical, and also condemns as "commoner natures" those who pursue wisdom to the exclusion of political greatness. They of course do not need to be compelled to stand aside; they stand aside, if not aloof, already. The question is, who is to compel the others? It is clearly not implied by what Plato says (whatever he may in fact have thought, given the condition of the democracy in Athens) that they have to be compelled dictatorially, and one might look at the democratic process as developed in America as a series of compulsions to stand aside, by losing elections, being removed from committee chairmanships, and the like. So there is plenty of precedent—it is just a matter of exerting pressure in the right direction, and this is the task of those among the elected who are acquiring the spirit and power of philosophy, which is to be translated simply as that breadth of curiosity and moral concern which will enable them to transcend the narrower interests on which political behavior has traditionally depended. Most political figures will claim at least to aspire to this, to be in pursuit of wisdom, to have a conception of an interest larger than the personal or regional or factional, even if the claim is only rhetorical.

This aspiration is usually safe enough, since nobody is arrogant enough to claim to know what political wisdom is. But perhaps this arrogance is something philosophy should be prepared to take upon itself. Socrates was thought arrogant, but his arrogance was one of challenge and not of assertion: it would be a start, at least, if some of those in power could be persuaded that the received wisdom—the genius of pluralism, the equilibrium of partial interests, and the like—is not necessarily wisdom at all, that we do not know what we think we know about what is best for the world. And once some of the kings have become philosophers in Plato's sense they may be encouraged to become philosophers in Marx's sense, men who can recognize not only reason but also alienation when they see it, who arrive not only at theoretical understanding but at "practical criticism," i.e. the overcoming in their own persons of the alienation of economic and political institutions and the modification of the institutions in the direction of lessening the alienation for others.

To achieve this they need not become political revolutionaries; although Marx was in the habit of talking about "critical-revolutionary practice"[26] it should by now be clear that the concept of revolution even in his works is much more complex than any merely political shift of power. The profession of philosophy might make its best contribution to public affairs by exposing and if necessary ridiculing—but not, at any cost, being indignant or self-righteous about—the pretensions and inconsistencies of leaders who think them-

26. Karl Marx, *Theses on Feuerbach* nos. 1 and 3, reprinted in Easton and Guddat, op. cit., p. 401.

selves politically wise, and identifying and working with those who by their words and actions show most clearly a potential concern for true political wisdom. There are many men in the second category, not just one or two; a given local philosophical community might begin with its local representatives. I have in mind not an individual message, a letter to the press, a resolution passed at a meeting, but a collective, prepared, *worked* presentation, of limited scope, put forward with the weight of the intellectual tradition of which philosophers are the guardians but adapted to contemporary exigencies, offered as *seriously* bearing on the issues being considered by the men to whom it is addressed and as embodying the virtues of scope and rigor, of scepticism and hesitation, that philosophy cherishes, and followed up by sustained personal contact, public announcements, local discussions, and so on. The fact that Plato did not succeed in improving matters at Syracuse, although often taken as a sign that philosophy belongs in another world, that, as Hegel put it, it always comes on the scene too late to be of any help,[27] is no excuse for not trying. It is not, I repeat, a question of offering advice, but of offering analysis, and analysis of a kind that has made genuine progress since the Greeks and a fortiori since Hegel. Also the number of available practitioners is greater than it was. There could be no more appropriate time at which to try once again to develop the "this-sided" character of philosophy to which Marx refers in the third thesis on Feuerbach.[28]

Imagine us received by the kings and princes of this world. What would we, in fact, say?[29]

27. G. W. F. Hegel, *The Philosophy of Right,* trans. T. M. Knox (Oxford, 1942), p. 12.
28. Marx, loc. cit., no. 2.
29. This essay was written during the tenure of a grant from Carnegie Corporation of New York, whose support I gratefully acknowledge.

Two
DEFIANCE OF THE STATE

Introduction

In what ways and to what degrees are citizens, alone or in groups, justified in defying their government? If legal restraints prevent the assertion of legitimate social or political interests, should the law be superseded? If the political process, democratic or other, denies to groups which have serious grievances but little power the chance to influence policy, how ought they to protest? If an individual's conscience requires him to violate an unjust law, does this take priority over his obligation, if he has one, to obey the law? How far should governmental toleration of dissent, civil disobedience, and defiance be extended, and to what extent is the resistance of the citizen morally acceptable?

These are among the questions taken up in the section that follows. In the *Crito*, Socrates argues that if one lives voluntarily under a system of laws, one has tacitly accepted an obligation to obey all the laws within that system, even those laws one considers to be wrong. It is generally agreed by philosophers writing today that such a position is seriously inadequate. Obviously, however, it does not follow that if a citizen is justified in defying some laws and governmental decisions, he is justified in defying all or even most laws and governmental decisions. What are needed are criteria and guidelines indicating when and how defiance of particular aspects of governmental authority may be justified.

Virginia Held considers what it may mean for citizens to go on strike against a political system or a unit of it, and suggests that justifiable political strikes may well involve actions considered illegal, just as labor strikes involved such alleged infringements of law as "conspiracy" and "restraint of trade" for many decades.

Hugo Bedau examines the concept of obligation and what he calls "the transitivity of morality"; he disputes the view that a young man has a moral obligation to serve in the armed forces if called upon through the draft to do so.

Whether or not to prosecute, and how severely to punish, persons engaged in civil disobedience are choices in which political and judicial authorities have considerable latitude. Sidney Gendin argues for a much wider toleration of illegal dissent, when based on grounds of conscience, than has been practiced in the United States in recent years.

A number of recent discussions of civil disobedience have suggested that a person violating a law for moral reasons ought to accept willingly the penalty attached to this violation. By not resisting the punishment, the disobedient, it is claimed, demonstrates his moral sincerity and his loyalty to the wider system of law, though he breaks a particular law within it. Sidney Gendin and Gordon Schochet dispute such a view, and Schochet discusses forms of resistance.

That defiance of the state may sometimes be justified, and is at present morally defensible in a significant number of cases, is a position shared by all the writers in Part II.

4

On Understanding Political Strikes

VIRGINIA HELD

In the current language of political argument, the term "strike" is frequently used in distinctly unordinary ways. Students in recent years have claimed to be "striking" against their universities, "striking" against a political system that has continued to engage in a war they consider evil and misguided, and even "striking" against a corrupt society. Some professors have declared their sympathy with what they have been willing to call student "strikes"; some have declared themselves on strike for political reasons and have refused to hold normal classes. For some years an organization called Women Strike for Peace has been urging housewives and other women to "strike" against U.S. foreign policy in Southeast Asia. In the spring of 1970, whole universities were sometimes described as being "on strike" against the American political system or the wider society to protest the U.S. invasion of Cambodia and the shooting of students at Kent State University and at Jackson State College. Frequently, those who have been "striking" have been concerned less with their own interests than with the interests of some other group, or acting more on grounds of conscience than of self-interest.

At times the term "strike" has seemed a mis-description,

too far removed from the economic context we have come to think of as normal. Sceptics have wondered how students could "strike" when they were not earning money from the university or laboring for it. As recently as 1968, a philosopher who thought himself a radical explained to students that the model of the university they should strive to bring about was not that of workers vs. management, but that of medieval apprentices learning with love the skill of the craftsman. But "strike" it continued to be in the language of the participants: administrators and professors, in the eyes of some students, had the role of management; the "striking" students said they were refusing to submit to the educational processing that was to turn them into products for the consumption of the military-industrial complex.

The picture of the university-as-corporation, with periodic rounds of bargaining and striking and acquiescence, is disappointing still to those who would hope for a more satisfactory model for both university and corporation. But the notion that a university's members, especially its students, may withhold their "work" in order to protest, directly or indirectly, the "conditions" in which it is performed, and that they may thus be described as being "on strike," seems by now almost acceptable. That sit-ins and obstructions of various kinds can be expected to occur along with refusals to work is now generally acknowledged; whether some of these activities may be considered to be components of "strikes" in these and other contexts is a possibility to be examined.

All sides have presumably become more sophisticated in their predictions of just what it may or may not be possible to accomplish by student and other comparable "strikes." But as the history of labor disturbances makes evident, a strike does not have to be successful to merit description as such, and, in the early days of industrial labor stoppages, workers refusing to work were undoubtedly as confused and uncertain about the nature, the justification, and the effectiveness of their actions as were students and other protesters in the 1960s. Prior to 1842, American courts generally held *all* labor organizations to be illegal per se, indictable as criminal conspiracies no matter what their aims or activities. It was almost a century after that before the rights of workers to organize and defend themselves against corporate tyranny were clearly established.[1]

What it can mean for a whole university to be "on strike" is more difficult to specify, except by analogy. But just as students refusing to "produce" trained and willing personnel for the industrial state may consider themselves "on strike," so the various sides at the faculty-student-administration negotiating table, recognizing a common discontent with the wider society, may act in common to withhold their work. It may seem self-defeating to close down the discussion of literature and philosophy and history to protest a political decision or a social condition. Yet in the spring of 1970, various universities and colleges, refusing to continue with production-as-usual, began to act as collective entities to influence the social and political "conditions" in which they do their work. To describe some of these institutions as having been "on strike" does not seem utterly far-fetched, although, again, the question of effectiveness is another matter altogether. As with a labor union's strike, a university strike may reduce funds, encourage harmful legislation, and discourage members rather than accomplish the strikers' purposes.

We seem not yet to have developed a clear idea of what can best be meant by "striking against the political system," or a unit of it, for political and social rather than for primarily economic reasons. But actions are occurring, and

1. For a brief history of labor and labor law in the U.S., see Merle Fainsod, Lincoln Gordon, and Joseph C. Palamountain, Jr., *Government and the American Economy*, 3rd ed. (New York: W. W. Norton, 1959), chap. 7.

others appear foreseeable, which seem to call for just such an idea. When the primary objects of protest are the decisions and conditions provided by the political arrangements within which people live, can "strikes" be directed against political institutions, and can they perhaps achieve good results? Could such strikes be among the actions called for by Arnold Kaufman, for instance, in saying that "the strategic concept I am proposing is that of using any device, short of open rebellion or revolution, to bring pressure to bear in support of liberal aims"?[2] Would they be in line with the dominant intent of mass protest in recent years: to redress grievances through political action? The study directed by Jerome Skolnick concludes that "almost uniformly, the participants in mass protest today see their grievances as rooted in the existing arrangements of power and authority in contemporary society, and they view their own activity as political action—on a direct or symbolic level—aimed at altering those arrangements."[3] Would political strikes be appropriate forms of such action? Would such strikes have to consist in the usual withholding of the striker's own work, or could there be other, and perhaps more effective, forms of political strikes? *What would citizens' strikes for better political conditions look like?*

The 1968 *International Encyclopedia of the Social Sciences,* classifying "Strikes" under the heading of "Labor Relations," defines strikes as "collective stoppages of work, intended to influence those who depend on the sale or use of the products of that work."[4] There are no articles at all under

2. Arnold Kaufman, *The Radical Liberal* (New York: Atherton Press, 1968), p. 73.

3. Jerome H. Skolnick, director, *The Politics of Protest* (New York: Simon and Schuster, 1969), p. 7.

4. David L. Sills, ed., *International Encyclopedia of the Social Sciences* (New York: Macmillan and Free Press, 1968), vol. 8, p. 500.

such headings as Defiance, Demonstrations, Dissent, Disruption, Disturbances, Interferences, Protest, Resistance, or Violence.

Historically, there have of course been political strikes, in the sense of workers refusing to work for political as well as for economic reasons, and in Europe such strikes are still fairly common. In 1842 the Chartists in England called on workers striking against a serious reduction in wages to stay on strike until Parliament extended the suffrage to all adult males.[5] While this general strike was unsuccessful, labor demonstrations and disturbances were important in enacting the Reform Bill of 1867 doubling the size of the electorate. Later, international socialist congresses demanded mass strike actions, and in Austria and Sweden mass walkouts did achieve important electoral reforms.

In the Revisionist debates in Germany after 1904, the general strike was seen by some as an instrument of revolution. Bernstein, although not opposed to the general strike as such, thought it should be used sparingly and only as a tactical weapon, because its chances of success were small; he suggested that it must involve workers in essential categories such as transport, light and power, communications, and food distribution. Bread-and-butter-minded trade union leaders, however, agreed with the quip of the even more sceptical socialist Ignaz Auer that "general strike is general nonsense." In France, Sorel celebrated the myth of the political general strike as opposed to the proletarian strike for mere economic purposes, but he did so with more fervor than realism. In 1926, in England, half of the six million organized workers took part in a general strike to support particularly hard-pressed coal miners seeking government help for their plight, but their concerns were largely economic. In France, a gen-

5. In line with the most entrenched position of privilege, this was called, even by Chartists, "universal suffrage."

eral strike in 1934 contributed to the emergence of the Popular Front and the ministry of Leon Blum. A general strike called by the socialists in Belgium in 1950 succeeded in preventing Leopold III from resuming the throne. The most dramatic political strike in recent times has probably been the French one of May 1968, when workers joined students to bring the nation to the brink of revolution.

In the United States, since the ascendency of the tactics and policies of Samuel Gompers in the 1890s,[6] labor strikes have been almost entirely confined to economic issues, and even these have been narrowly construed to include workers' wages and direct working conditions rather than questions of industrial organization and control. This narrow orientation —sometimes credited with success if not with vision—has held for so long that the very possibility of workers striking for broad political objectives seems somehow out of the question. Scattered instances of longshoremen refusing to unload goods from communist ships or typographical workers refusing to set copy they have considered obscene are hardly reminiscent of the European tradition of the workers' political strike—general or not—to achieve liberal or broadly Marxist reforms of the political arrangements under which they labor. While the future may see interesting changes, there is little evidence yet of rank-and-file opposition to the gradual inclusion of labor in the military-industrial complex.

It can be hoped that in coming years in the United States various professional groups will recognize their power and their social responsibilities and will use bargaining, and, if need be, work stoppages to further justifiable social and political objectives rather than merely their own interests. One can well imagine medical personnel demanding, on a sig-

6. See Philip S. Foner, *History of the Labor Movement in the United States* (New York: International Publishers, 1955), vol. II, and Daniel Bell, *Marxian Socialism in the United States* (Princeton: Princeton University Press, 1967), chap. IV.

nificant scale, reforms in health care from their institutions, and teachers regularly demanding of their employers better services for children. One can even imagine, with some effort, scientists negotiating with manufacturers to refrain from producing certain armaments, and technical personnel striking against corporations that refuse to decrease their pollution of the environment.[7] One can even imagine, with only slightly more effort, coordinated efforts among various such groups at a national level. In this paper, however, I shall be concerned with strikes that might include large numbers of less highly trained persons.

In the United States today, even were the tradition of the general labor strike for political objectives to be adapted at some level, it would probably not result in large-scale participation that would further the purposes of the Left: the "essential workers" would be likely to be on the other side. At best, perhaps, they could be asked to be neutral. Labor strikes with distinctly limited political objectives should not be ruled out; one can certainly hope for efforts by workers to democratize somewhat their own highly authoritarian corporate structures,[8] but the attitudes of labor at the present time are not such as to indicate much likelihood of achieving fundamental political reforms through such means. And students, however united they might become, could hardly shut down the society or starve the bourgeoisie by refusing to open their books, no matter how many professors joined them. Women walking off their unpaid or poorly paid "jobs" could cause vast inconvenience to those who benefit most from using them; but the independent resources of

7. For a discussion see Abraham Edel, "The Scientific Enterprise and Social Conscience," *Philosophic Exchange*, State University of New York, College at Brockport (Summer 1970), pp. 39-57. (Also forthcoming in *Trans-action*.)
8. See Michael Walzer, *Obligations: Essays on Disobedience, War, and Citizenship* (Cambridge: Harvard University Press, 1970), chap. 2, and Robert A. Dahl, "Citizens of the Corporation," *New York Times*, March 17, 1971, p. 45.

women are thin indeed, and they are the least likely group to risk the welfare of their children for political goals. Many blacks, the poor, the recipients of welfare, are similarly apt to be in nonessential jobs, or unemployed, and again can often exert relatively little pressure by refusing to work. In short, those who might be expected to be most inclined to favor large-scale strikes against the present political system or units of it are those who can wield the least power by "stoppages of work" in the normal sense of refraining from doing their jobs. The analogies must be re-thought from the foundations.

Where the object of discontent is not primarily economic, or even political to the extent that a political arrangement affects economic conditions, but is itself, and directly, political, *who* can appropriately strike, and *how*, to bring about more humane political conditions?[9]

Let us begin with some standard attitudes towards the political system, and see if descriptions of them bring us anywhere near the domain of strikes. Let us then see if an analogy between a strike in the economic sphere and a strike in the political sphere might suggest that, just as a withholding of one's work is an appropriate form of collective action directed at the managers of industry, so some other form of collective action—say, an interference with *their* work—might be an appropriate way to "strike" against the managers of the political system.

9. To many students and sympathizers, the revolution that is needed is less political than cultural, but they have perhaps lost sight of a necessary step. Thesis 29 of *The Appeal From The Sorbonne,* June 13-14, 1968, declared: "The bourgeois revolution was judicial; the proletarian revolution was economic. Ours will be social and cultural so that man can become himself." (Reprinted in Carl Oglesby, ed., *The New Left Reader* [New York: Grove Press, 1969], p. 273.) Charles Reich and his followers appear to count even more heavily on a changed culture (Charles Reich, *The Greening of America* [New York: Random House, 1970]). I am assuming in this paper, however, that those who wish to transform the society will not be able to leap over the political, although they may of course not wish to stop there.

We must first of all consider the justification for drawing an analogy between a labor strike and a citizens' strike. The political sphere is usually described as being governed by a framework of constitutional and legal provisions quite unlike those controlling the economic sphere; politicians are still, it is pointed out, subject to the approval of the voters, and the pursuit of political power is conducted quite differently from the pursuit of profits.

With regard to the democratic political system, the citizen who is morally disconcerted is accustomed, traditionally, to thinking of a number of alternatives: he can work for better candidates and try to get them elected; he can try to apply pressure, alone or through an interest group, upon his representatives and upon governmental administrators; he can mount marches and demonstrations; he can perform acts of civil disobedience or resistance; he can consider violence or, ultimately, revolution. But perhaps some economic analogies would be suggestive, and would sharpen or focus our view of these alternatives.

Perhaps there is some justification for drawing an analogy between the relation of worker to corporation and the relation of citizen to state.[10] And perhaps the counter-pressures citizens could exert on government can then be thought of in terms analogous to the counter-pressures workers are able to exert upon a corporation.

The government of the United States at present seems to be, in significant respects, rather like a super-corporation, in some ways not much more subject to electoral control than are business corporations. Seymour Melman has claimed that the loose collaboration of the military-industrial complex has now been replaced by "a formal central-management office to administer the military-industrial empire," and has ob-

10. See Morris Cohen, "Property and Sovereignty," in *Law and the Social Order* (New York: Harcourt, Brace & Co., 1933), and Michael Walzer, op. cit.

served that the "state-management" system through which the Defense Department affects that part of the economy related to defense is, "by the measure of the scope and scale of its decision-power . . . the most important single management in the United States."[11] Even those who view the significance of the developments referred to somewhat differently acknowledge that the defense-industrial managers are extraordinarily impervious to criticisms or even inquiries from the elected representatives of the voters.

There has been, in any case, a vast increase in the importance and number of governmental decisions that are relatively unaffected by the electoral process. This follows the earlier trend in industry, discernable by the 1930s, in which power shifted from the owners of stock to the managers of large corporations.[12] Now, in the sphere of super-government, politicians win or lose, and, in important respects, the managers of the military-industrial complex hardly notice. Professor Harrison Brown, with considerable experience of the bases for such claims, thinks it fair to say, for instance, that

> the Department of Defense has become de facto the primary executive body of the Federal Government. It comes close to being the primary legislative body as well. Numerous decisions, which have been made in large measure by men of good will, have narrowed the area within which Congress and the President can effectively maneuver to one which is very small when compared with that which is dominated by the Pentagon—the largest and most generously financed organization ever created by man.[13]

11. Seymour Melman, *Pentagon Capitalism: The Political Economy of War* (New York: McGraw-Hill, 1970), p. 2.
12. The well-known classic study of this development is A. A. Berle, Jr., and G. C. Means, *The Modern Corporation and Private Property* (New York: Macmillan, 1934).
13. Harrison Brown, *New York Times Book Review,* May 24, 1970, p. 1.

And there is, of course, in addition, a vast managerial bureaucracy for nonmilitary governmental activities, including regulatory agencies which serve the interests regulated more effectively than they do the public, and layers of "professionals" and "civil servants" who increase in various ways the distance between the citizen and the source of the decisions made for and about and upon him.

Perhaps, with respect to both industry and government, *the key relation now is between the managers and the managed*. If that is admitted, a number of traditional conceptions may need to be radically revised.

To tell a citizen who is profoundly dissatisfied with his "political conditions" to go out and work for better candidates may seem not utterly unlike telling a working man profoundly resentful of his working conditions to try to persuade the stockholders to select a new management. Formally, stockholders "control" the corporation, and it might be suggested that to get the corporation's management to change its policies, the worker could organize rallies, circulate petitions, leave literature at appropriate doorsteps, and have students with fresh haircuts present to stockholders (sometimes their fathers) face-to-face the arguments for higher wages. The fact that some stockholders hold many votes and others few, while in the political system we are said to be moving closer to what is called a one-man-one-vote electoral process, does not destroy the analogy, because in the realities of contemporary politics some persons have the means to control any possible candidate, or to multiply votes through buying television time, hiring advertising agencies, or employing the services of pollsters and influencers.[14] In any case,

14. By the time John W. Gardner writes that "campaign spending has gotten wildly out of hand. . . . Venality is a harsh word, but in the simplest terms, a good many of our public officials are being bought and paid for," one can no longer take at face value, if one ever did, the notion of one-man-one-vote electoral control (*New York Times*, November 23, 1970, p. 37).

as we have seen, winning an election in no way assures a significant change of management policy.

As to influencing government through normal interest-group channels, here again economic factors become salient. Citizens' groups can hardly hope to pay lobbyists, finance campaigns, and marshal influence in favor of their policies on a scale comparable to that of the Department of Defense and the industries that received $45 billion from its contracts in fiscal 1970, and countless other billions in advantages and favors. Just as in gaining control of a corporation, gaining favorable political decisions normally requires vast amounts of money or positions already held.

Pursuing the analogy with regard to the final alternative, it may seem that acts of violence or attempted revolution in the current situation are not entirely unlike smashing the windows of a factory or bombing the manager's office. Such acts may have some possible symbolic or psychological value, they may give credibility to effective threats, but they often accomplish little to improve the economic conditions of the worker. One of the more useful segments of history for radicals to study is the American labor movement, which has already provided examples of massive discontent, the destruction of property, violence, and the shooting of strikers.

Two evaluators have concluded that

> the effect of labor violence was almost always harmful to the union. There is little evidence that violence succeeded in gaining advantages for strikers. Not only does the rollcall of lost strikes confirm such a view, but the use of employer agents, disguised as union members or union officials for advocating violence within the union, testifies to the advantage such practices gave the employer. . . . A community might be sympathetic to the demands of strikers, but as soon as violent confrontations took place, the possibility was high that interest would shift from concern for the acceptance of union demands to the stopping of violence. . . . The evi-

dence against the effectiveness of violence as a means of gaining concessions by labor in the United States is too overwhelming to be a matter of dispute.[15]

Although this conclusion may be an overstatement, thoughtful radicals at the present time are often wary of agents of reform bearing arms; the latter may even be in the pay of the local police. Workers, however, have obviously not given up violence merely to acquiesce in the decisions of corporate management. They have developed the strike as their weapon, and those who control the conditions of work have learned to bargain with workers' groups. As such staid observers as Robert Dahl and Charles Lindblom note:

> The strike is such an essential technique of collective bargaining that it cannot be eliminated without eliminating collective bargaining itself. Collective bargaining is a form of reciprocal control which workers and their leaders have developed with the passive or active consent of the dominant decision makers in Western societies. They have developed it as an alternative to the combination of hierarchical control by the employer and spontaneous field control exerted through the price system, a combination they felt intolerable. The main techniques by which workers' organizations enforce bargaining as a substitute is the strike, a device through which workers' organizations can influence the behavior of employers. In short, the strike is a fundamental technique of control requisite to bargaining. It does not represent an abnormality or breakdown in collective bargaining any more than the practice of voting unpopular officials out of office is an abnormality or breakdown in the reciprocal arrangements customary in polyarchies.[16]

15. Philip Taft and Philip Ross, "American Labor Violence: Its Causes, Character, and Outcome," in Hugh Davis Graham and Ted Robert Gurr, eds., *Violence in America:* A Report to the National Commission on the Causes and Prevention of Violence (New York: Bantam Books, 1969), pp. 382-83.
16. Robert A. Dahl and Charles E. Lindblom, *Politics, Economics, and Welfare,* 2d ed. (New York: Harper & Row, 1963 [1953]), p. 485.

A problem, however, is that at the present time many unpopular officials are beyond the reach of the voters, and many governmental policies unacceptable on grounds of conscience simply cannot be altered by the electoral process. A question many who would wish to change present tendencies in the political system may now ask is: can the politically discontented develop a form of action as justifiable and effective as the labor strike? Bargaining has of course been at the heart of politics from the beginning of time, but political bargaining now seems comparable to such a stage of economic bargaining as that between, say, one group of stockholders and another, or one faction of management and another. That kind of bargaining was not what brought workers decent wages and hours, and it is clear that bargaining between management and workers would never have developed as it did if workers had not fashioned the technique of the strike. Can there not be a meaningful political analogue through which the politically managed can acquire an appropriate position from which to bargain with the political managers?

If the object of conscientious protest is a governmental policy or law, we are accustomed to thinking of the possibilities of civil disobedience, or resistance, rather than of striking. But perhaps the techniques of the economic strike could be transferred to the political sector of the society with good results, although the action might no longer simply consist in a refusal to work. Even industrial strikes can often be limited to a simple withdrawal of work only after the cohesion and corporate recognition of workers has been achieved. As Michael Walzer notes, "The first strikes may have to take more direct and coercive forms. Generally, they involve the physical occupation of the corporate plant and the expulsion of nonstrikers," as illustrated by the autoworkers' sit-down strikes as late as 1936-37.[17] The labor strike has undergone a long evolution.

17. Walzer, op. cit., p. 31.

The first characteristic of a strike that must be noted is that it is a *collective* action. An individual acting alone cannot conduct a strike. A strike must involve significant numbers of persons acting together. If a non-violent protest involving civil disobedience and directed specifically at a political target is a collective action, its collective nature may distinguish it from civil disobedience, or even resistance, as frequently understood. Civil disobedience is a violation of law on grounds of conscience; resistance is a refusal to accept the legal penalties of such violation. Both are associated with individual action and individual conscience. Of course many persons can together perform such actions, but they are acting as individuals, and the participation of others is in no way required for the acts in question to be acts of civil disobedience or resistance. Nonviolent collective protests, on the other hand, may well be such that their collective nature is essential to them. They may involve no intentional violation of *law* as such, as when large numbers of persons block streets or passages; and the question of whether a resulting penalty is accepted or rejected may be quite incidental to them. Their purpose may be to exert political pressure rather than to seek legal redress.

After the multiplicity of nondisruptive demonstrations in recent years, demonstrations have almost come to be ordinary parts of the political scene, so ordinary as frequently to be of little significance and less effect. Violent revolution continues to appear to most of its potential recruits as either unnecessary or impossible, and isolated acts of individual civil disobedience often seem futile, however justified. What may now be sought are intermediate forms of action: collective, frequently but not necessarily in violation of law, and capable of exerting real pressure on the political managers the way strikes are capable of exerting real pressure on the managers of corporations. Perhaps the term "citizens' strike" could appropriately be used for such collective political interferences with the normal activities of the political system, even though a withholding of the participant's own work would no longer be a dominant feature of them.

Certainly, the participants in such strikes might hope for a deeper reform of the society than could be achieved by such means, and for a time when justifiable moral judgments would have the edge over effective power in the making of social and political decisions. In the meantime, however, political strikes with specific objectives and some chance of success may well be worth consideration.

The political system, like the economy, is broken up into units or subsystems of varying dimension: there is this city agency, that federal department, this armed forces unit, that county office. The medium of exchange, and what everyone is trying to get more of when the edges glint, is power rather than mere profit,—but egoism is hardly less pervasive in the polity as presently constituted than in the economy. And just as corporate management determines the conditions under which the worker must either labor or go elsewhere, so, in important respects, political management determines the public conditions under which the citizen must live or go elsewhere, if he can.

A political system is that which authoritatively makes rules, decides policies, and allocates goods in a society. The authority with which this may be done may be *formal,* such as that possessed by officials with governmental titles, or *effective,* such as that possessed by a commercial interest group which turns out to have the political power to get a policy accepted. Formal authority approximates previously established effective authority and makes it possible to predict future decisions on the basis of who occupies what offices. Effective authority approximates future power, which can only be guessed at until after the fact.

In a cohesive system, many persons translate the sentence

"X has authority" into "what X commands ought to be done"; for political decisions to be authoritative in almost any sense, however, they must be accepted at least grudgingly by those affected by them. And just as the corporation cannot turn out products unless the workers put up with the working conditions, so a political system cannot turn out authoritative decisions unless its members put up with the conditions it provides.[18]

If groups of members of a political system or a subsystem of it refuse to accept the conditions they are offered, and if this refusal is organized and substantial, an appropriate description of the situation might seem to be: *the citizens are on strike.* As such occurrences become more and more frequent, as they appear to be doing, the political managers, to avoid them, may begin to bargain in earnest with those whose grievances cannot be met by a suggestion that they take their problems up with "the voting public." All too often, the voting public reveals itself to be a reflection of the selfish interests of the regnant majority rather than a collectivity concerned with the requirements for social justice still glaringly outstanding in the world's richest nation, or aware of the minimal responsibilities a political system must meet to assure its own future and the possibilities of international peace. With the development of political strikes, citizens of conscience may perhaps not remain at the mercy of electoral

18. A comparison between the shaping of power and the production of wealth is suggested by Harold D. Lasswell and Abraham Kaplan in *Power and Society:* "The *arena* of power is the situation comprised by those who demand power or who are within the domain of power. . . . An *encounter* is an interaction in the power process. . . . An encounter in the arena sets in motion a process of focusing the activities of all concerned to the end of affecting the outcome. The process is equivalent to the *production* of wealth, which is not concluded until the claim to the service is offered for exchange in the market. Power is not completely made available (shaped) until it is involved in fighting, arguing, boycotting, negotiating—all of which may be resorted to in a particular process of power determination." (New Haven: Yale University Press, 1950, pp. 78-81).

largesse or judicial innovation. To the extent that their actions may be coercive upon those in power, this coercion should be no less justifiable[19] than that already employed by the political system. But evaluations along these lines should lead to recommendations for restraint, not to immobility.

To be effective, such political strikes will probably have to be organized, collective refusals to accept specific political decisions, such refusals being registered through an impeding of the work of the political unit being "struck," and, sometimes, through disobedience of various of its legal requirements. Familiar forms which may be improved upon may be blocking of entrances to governmental buildings, deliberate interference with military or defense-industrial activities, nonpayment of kinds or percentages of taxes, refusal to move from an official's office, and so on. Certainly new forms may be imagined and developed, but with the growing awareness of the purposes of such strikes and the grounds for their justification, the particular form adopted may be less important than the organization of large numbers of persons to go on strike against a unit of the political system, or against the system as a whole, when they consider it appropriate and justifiable to bring about specific and genuine good consequences.

For such persons, the citizens' strike, even when it involves civil disobedience, will not be thought of as a rare and extreme response, appropriate only for the most outrageous or tyrannical of governments or laws, or the most blatant violations of fundamental rights. It will be directed toward decisions and policies which the political managers faced with it can change, and will come to be thought of, perhaps, by participants and observers alike as no more outlandish than

19. For a discussion of the grounds on which such judgments might be made, see Virginia Held, "Coercion and Coercive Offers," in J. Roland Pennock and John W. Chapman, eds., *Coercion: Nomos XIV* (New York: Atherton, 1971).

a labor union strike. To be out on bail or in jail as a result of such activities may come to seem rather like refusing to work—uncomfortable, costly, and sometimes painful—but hardly cause for much more righteous fury than a banker now expends on a striking hard-hat.

Of course, the worker's right to strike against a corporation is now acknowledged by law, while the citizen who commits an act of civil disobedience is by definition acting illegally. But prior to 1921, labor picketing of any kind was held by some courts to be unlawful, and for almost two decades after that judicial definitions of the kinds of picketing which were legal and the kinds which were not were confused and contradictory. Until the mid-1930s, an employer could fire an employee for union activity, and require workers to sign contracts binding them not to join a union, much less strike. Both arrangements are somewhat comparable to ones the political system thinks it has with those for whom it makes authoritative decisions.

Which sorts of political strike activities may be justifiably coercive and which sorts may not will have to be worked out in detail, just as the lines between acceptable and unacceptable union "coercion" have had to be worked out. The lines for labor have obviously shifted from pre-1914 conceptions allowing injunctions to be issued forbidding even attempts to persuade, and from the days afterwards when a single picket for "communication and persuasion" was allowed at each gate, but mass picketing was prohibited. The uses made by the courts of injunctions in the 1920s, when any union action which intentionally interfered with interstate commerce could be interpreted as an illegal "restraint of trade," belong clearly to the past. Similar shifts may be appropriate in our conceptions with regard to political strikes.

By the time legislation was enacted requiring employers to bargain collectively with workers, the strike was a familiar occurrence. Various forms of what is now thought to be civil disobedience might begin to be worked out such that some obstructions of the production of authoritative governmental decisions might similarly be permitted by law, and some could by agreement go unprosecuted, while enforced restrictions against violence remain. Hannah Arendt has suggested that the political system give recognition to groups of persons engaging in civil disobedience just as it now recognizes organized pressure groups whose lobbyists are permitted and expected to influence governmental decisions.[20] Alternatively, since decisions to prosecute or not prosecute are frequently political decisions, the threat of political strikes by citizens' groups could come to be seen as calling for negotiations rather than for a rigid enforcement of law.[21]

Most citizens have come to take it for granted that in attaining an acceptable level of wages, workers may be justified in going on strike against a corporation. It is not much more difficult to argue that, under present conditions, in the process of gaining morally acceptable political decisions, citizens may be justified in going on strike against a political system or a unit of it. Unless forms of political action that exceed the present bounds of electoral and interest-group politics are developed, and in time given legal scope, discontent among conscientious citizens with the political conditions within which they live may well reach flood proportions.

20. Hannah Arendt, "Civil Disobedience," *The New Yorker,* September 12, 1970.

21. Hugo Bedau has pointed out that "the law has long managed to obviate much civil disobedience by clauses providing exemption for conscientious objectors," and that similar exemptions from prosecution and penalty for violations of law on conscientious grounds could well be provided for other laws than those concerned with military service (Hugo Bedau, "On Civil Disobedience," *Journal of Philosophy* 58 [1961], p. 655). Long before such legal provisions were enacted, political decisions to refrain from enforcement might become frequent.

5

Military Service and Moral Obligation

HUGO ADAM BEDAU

I

Since 1948, thanks to Congressional legislation and presidential policy, compulsory military service has been the law in this country. Every male resident, upon reaching the age of eighteen, has been subject to the provisions of the draft law. Unless a registrant could produce evidence to warrant some other classification, deferment, or exemption, the law required him to be classified 1-A. Depending upon the manpower needs of the Defense Department, he was liable to be inducted into the armed services (usually, the Army) for two years. In the past generation millions of men have been drafted under the authority of the Selective Service Act. Hundreds of thousands of draftees have seen combat service in Korea and Indochina.

An integral feature of the draft throughout its history has been the idea that every American male has an *obligation* to render military service to the nation. The idea is found already in the first court case on selective service, which upheld President Lincoln's authority to draft men into the Union armies in 1863.[1] It reappeared during the First World War;

1. Kneedler v. Lane, 45 Pa. St. 238 (1863).

A revised version of an essay first published in *Inquiry*, vol. 14, no. 3 (1971), Universitetsforlaget, Oslo, Norway. Reprinted with revisions, by permission.

in 1916, one Massachusetts congressman unsuccessfully urged deletion of the term 'draft' from the title of the proposed legislation then under debate, in favor of the phrase 'personal obligation to service.'[2] Two years later, the Supreme Court vindicated the draft law by declaring, in part, that "the very concept of a just government and its duty to the citizen includes the reciprocal obligation of the citizen to render military service in case of need."[3] Within the past decade, the Supreme Court has again spoken of the "imperative obligations of citizenship," including military service "in time of war and national emergency."[4] The president of Yale University has referred to our "national obligation" and "national duty" to serve.[5] Several of the invited speakers at the University of Chicago's Conference on the Draft in 1966 alluded to our "obligations of military service."[6] In his message to Congress in 1967 recommending renewal of the Selective Service Act, President Johnson invoked on behalf of that legislation what he called "the obligations and benefits of military service."[7] Congress, too, in prefacing the Military Selective Service Act of 1967 (the law in force at the time of this writing), spoke of "the obligations and privileges of serving in the armed forces" and declared that these "should be generally shared." The unpopularity of the war in Vietnam

2. Quoted in Warren S. Tyron, "The Draft in World War I," *Current History* XIV (1968), p. 342.

3. *Selective Draft Law Cases*, 245 U.S. 366 (1918).

4. United States v. Mendoza-Martinez, 372 U.S. 144, 159-60 (1963).

5. Quoted in Harry A. Marmion, "A Critique of Selective Service with Emphasis on Student Deferment," in Sol Tax, ed., *The Draft* (Chicago: University of Chicago Press, 1967), p. 55.

6. Samuel H. Hays, "A Military View of Selective Service," in Tax, ed., op. cit., p. 14; S. L. A. Marshall, "The Search for an Ideal Solution in a Natural Game of Chance," in Tax, ed., op. cit., p. 62; and Donald J. Eberly, "Guidelines for National Service," in Tax, ed., op. cit., p. 110.

7. "The President's Message on Selective Service to the Congress," in Tax, ed., op. cit., p. 466.

has not wholly effaced this century-old style of talk. Earlier this year, President Nixon's Commission on an All-Volunteer Armed Force referred to "the traditional belief that each citizen has a moral responsibility to serve his country."[8] And of course General Hershey, for thirty years the director of Selective Services, has assured us that "military service," in our "American heritage," is both "an obligation and privilege."[9] The idea that we have a military obligation, therefore, is not merely invented and propagated by recruiting sergeants, draft boards, and the American Legion. It is an essential feature of how we understand our Selective Service System—of how we talk about it, appraise its claims upon us, gauge our response to it.

That the lawyers, soldiers, politicians, behaviorial scientists, and scholars who have written so much on the draft in the last few years have ignored this language is all the more surprising. One would have thought that this putative obligation raised questions at least as fundamental as other moral questions about the draft (such as whether its statutory provisions and administration are fair and efficient) and like all such assumptions it would receive its proper review.[10] Instead, all these writers have looked right past this much-touted military obligation. The interested reader may well wonder whether these authorities are cautious cynics (not caring whether there is any such obligation, but having no

8. *Report of the Commission on an All-Volunteer Armed Force* (Washington, D.C.: Government Printing Office, 1970), p. 14.
9. Lewis B. Hershey, "The Operation of the Selective Service System," *Current History* LIV (1968), p. 3.
10. The only exception I have noticed is Michael Walzer, "Political Alienation and Military Service," in J. Roland Pennock and John W. Chapman, eds., *Political and Legal Obligation: Nomos XII* (New York: Atherton Press, 1970), pp. 401-20, also published in his *Obligations* (Cambridge: Harvard University Press, 1970). The draft, of course, has been much criticized from a moral point of view as in, for example, American Friends Service Committee, Peace Education Division, *The Draft?* (New York: Hill and Wang, 1968).

intention of challenging the conventional wisdom either way) or hypocrites (taking for granted in their public discussions that there is such obligation, but in private not believing it), or whether they are simply blind to this matter.

I propose to look at this issue squarely: do we in fact have an obligation to render military service (a military obligation, as I shall usually call it, for brevity's sake)? If so, what is the source of this obligation? What makes this obligation universal among American men (and only men!) today? What fault accrues to us if by evasion or repudiation we fail to discharge this obligation? The matter is a grave one for anyone concerned with moral conduct, because to have a moral obligation to do something is always to have a special kind of good reason for doing it. Today, few things can have greater moral urgency for young men in this country than to be assured whether they have that kind of good reason for accepting the military draft. To anticipate my conclusion, I shall argue that there is not any plausible theory in terms of which we can understand our military obligation as a moral obligation, and I am prepared to draw the inference that in all likelihood there is no such moral obligation at all.

II

At the threshold of my argument, it is necessary to supply some elementary clarifications so that the issue and my position on it are not grossly misunderstood. In the first place, when I say that the topic of this inquiry is whether men have a military obligation, I mean to challenge their obligation to obey the Selective Service Act. Since I concede that the Selective Service Act is valid law, I do not intend to dispute or cast into doubt whether that body of law imposes *legal* obligations on all who are subject to it. (The possible unconstitutionality of that law, however, I do not foreclose; see below, section III.) My question, therefore, is not whether men have a military obligation in the sense of a legal obligation to render military service if ordered to do so. Rather, I am concerned with whether that legal obligation is in any sense a *moral* obligation, and how it is to be shown that it is a moral obligation. I am aware that many Americans subject to the draft think that a man's military obligation is a moral obligation, and that many others not subject to the draft also think so. Far from denying these beliefs, I insist upon them because they point up the genuineness and relevance of the questions we are to discuss. What I do not concede is (a) that this legal obligation is *ipso facto* a moral obligation, (b) that this legal obligation is decisive evidence that there is a concurrent, antecedent, or subsequent moral obligation, and (c) that the source of this legal obligation also causes the obligation to be moral. All three points, (a)–(c), should be clear, for they do not arise only in the present context. Few legal obligations are *ipso facto* moral obligations; e.g. the legal obligation to pay a monthly interest charge of one and one-half percent of the unpaid balance on one's charge account is not anything a person is morally obligated to do just because it is enforceable against him as a legal obligation. Nor does the existence of a legal obligation, e.g. for a tenant to give thirty days notice prior to terminating a lease, show that there is some antecedent moral obligation to which this legal duty gives shape or substance. In general, then, persons can have a legal obligation without having any correlative moral obligation of the same sort or to the same end. In the present context, it is even possible that a man's legal obligation to render military service to his country is contradicted by a moral obligation not to fight his nation's declared enemies, a possibility of considerable interest in light of the Vietnam war, but not something there is space to pursue here.

Secondly, the question I am raising is related to but is not identical with the question whether men *ought* to render military service. Whether someone is *obligated* to do something, and whether he *ought* to do it, are in general two very different kinds of questions—as many philosophers have been trying to show for some years.[11] In general, sentences of the form 'You are obligated to do *x*' and 'You ought to do *x*' do not have the same meaning. Nor do the kinds of reasons which show that one of these utterances is true always show that the other is true. In general, we establish obligations for ourselves and others in virtue of making promises, voluntarily accepting benefits from others, incurring debts to them, placing ourselves in roles with defined duties, and so forth. But what persons ought to do will be determined by a much wider range of considerations, including selfish and prudential considerations. Thus, perhaps a person ought to take his umbrella with him (because it looks like rain), but only if something very different is true (he promised his wife) will he have an obligation to take his umbrella. We are often blinded to this distinction because, normally, if a man has an obligation to do *x*, then (barring certain contravening considerations of a moral sort) he ought to do *x*. Whether a man's moral obligations are always and only what we "morally ought" to do[12] is also dubious. Morally, a person ought to help someone in need if he can do so without grave risk or cost to himself; only under unusual circumstances (the person is his companion in a joint venture, e.g. spelunking) will it be thought that he has a moral obligation to help him here and now. The reason for insisting here on a distinction between obligatoriness and oughtness is to allow for the pos-

11. See, for example, P. H. Nowell-Smith, *Ethics* (London: Penguin Books, 1954), pp. 190-212.
12. Cf. Kurt Baier, "Obligation: Political and Moral," in Pennock and Chapman, eds., op. cit., pp. 132 ff.

sibility that even though there may be no moral obligation whatever to serve one's nation militarily, still it might be true that a man ought to (and, conversely, even if there were a moral obligation to serve it might still be true that a man ought not to). I shall not attempt to argue to this conclusion (or its converse). Though much of what I say against the morality of military obligation will count as well against military service being what a man ought (or morally ought) to render to his country, the two issues are separate, and to distinguish them is not to indulge in an evasive quibble.

Finally, when I challenge the nature and basis of a man's military *obligation,* I do not mean to put in doubt whether some American men today are *obliged* to render such service. There is no doubt that they are, viz., most of those who are ordered to report for induction. It is true that anyone who is so ordered has alternatives. He can "go underground" into the "dropout culture," or emigrate, or suffer imprisonment. But none of these alternatives (save the last) is legally permitted, much less officially encouraged, and for most inductees all are practically out of the question. It is these facts, deriving from the imposition of sanctions for draft law violators, which oblige them to serve. This is what makes their service compulsory; it does not make it morally obligatory, however. Nor can we explain or justify what is called a man's military obligation by invoking the fact that he is obliged to such service. Although obligations may have an aroma of something onerous, of requirements contrary to the desires of the person bearing the obligation, and not of benefit to him nor desired for their own sake in the normal course of events, we are in trouble if we try to identify *being obliged* with *being obligated.*[13] Were we to do so, in this case, we could not understand the words of all those quoted earlier (the

13. See, for example, H. L. A. Hart, *The Concept of Law* (Oxford: The Clarendon Press, 1961), pp. 80-81.

courts, the Congress, the president, the director of Selective Service) who speak for the larger society. We could not understand why, for example, the public high schools so readily cooperate with the military recruiting officers but reject would-be draft counselors, why volunteering for military service is so widely esteemed whereas seeking an exemption as a conscientious objector has been stigmatized as evasive and little short of disloyal. The putative morality of one's military obligation would be hidden, perhaps completely destroyed, if it were collapsed into being obliged.

In sum, then, I concede that there is at present a *legal obligation* on American men to serve in the armed forces, and that many of them are *obliged* to render military service; I leave open whether anyone *ought* to serve in the armed forces—and I question whether anyone is *morally obligated* to such service.

III

The most convenient way to proceed would be as follows. First, we should identify what in general are the defining conditions of a moral obligation; then we should determine whether our alleged military obligation meets all of these conditions; finally, we should draw the inference that it does, or that it does not, with the consequences in either case. Regretfully, moral philosophers, as recent discussions show,[14] are far from agreement on what a moral obligation is. The explanation of this disagreement is complex; it lies partly in

14. See, for example, H. L. A. Hart, "Legal and Moral Obligation," in A. I. Melden, ed., *Essays in Moral Philosophy* (Seattle: University of Washington Press, 1958), pp. 82-107; Richard Brandt, "The Concepts of Obligation and Duty," *Mind* LXXIII (1964), pp. 374-93; Kurt Baier, "Moral Obligation," *American Philosophical Quarterly* III (1966), pp. 210-26; John Ladd, "Legal and Moral Obligation," in Pennock and Chapman, eds., op. cit., pp. 3-35.

the heterogeneous uses to which 'obligate' and its cognates are subject, in the vagaries in the idea of the moral itself,[15] and in the evident heterogeneity of the things which morally obligate a person. These together allow different interpretation and emphasis, so that a clear and coherent theory of moral obligation has yet to emerge. Some features about moral obligation do seem to be generally accepted: the personality of obligations (only persons or their organizations are obligated), their universalizability (whatever serves to obligate one person would serve equally well to obligate anyone else, were he in the same situation), the inequivalence of feeling obligated and being obligated, of being obligated and being obliged, of a thing's being what one is obligated to do and its being what one ought to do, the notion that to have a moral obligation to do something is to have a special reason for doing it. Beyond this, however, it is difficult to go, and these agreements are not of much help here. Short either of inventing an entire theory of moral obligation for use in the present context, or of accepting one of the existing theories, warts and all, we will have to abandon the plausible way to proceed which I outlined above in favor of a less straightforward strategy.

Let us begin, then, in a different way. It seems quite clear that a man can come under a moral obligation to serve by volunteering for military service. In the absence of defeating conditions (e.g. his failure to understand the consequences of being sworn in) such a man would have a moral obligation to serve his country; how could this be disputed? For centuries men have understood that for a man to give his consent (to agree, to promise) to do something is to undertake a moral obligation to do it, to be morally bound to render a certain performance as a consequence of his promise. A man's

15. See G. Wallace and A. D. M. Walker, eds., *The Definition of Morality* (New York: Barnes and Noble, 1970).

word is his moral bond, and in his giving his word we have the paradigm of how a moral obligation is created.

The trouble with this line of thought in the present context is twofold. The most obvious difficulty is its inapplicability in the overwhelming number of cases, since we know that most men do not volunteer for military service. No doubt the boldest attempt which history records to disguise this fact was contributed by President Wilson in 1917, when he said on behalf of the pending draft bill in Congress that it provided "in no sense a conscription of the unwilling; it is, rather, selection from a nation which has volunteered in mass."[16] The simple truth, of course, is that if it were a necessary and sufficient condition of a man's having a military obligation that he be a volunteer, then not all servicemen and only a small proportion of draft registrants would have any such obligation at all. This unwelcome conclusion cannot be surprising, since no one really believes that the morality of the military obligation young men are supposed to have is something which their volunteering for service creates. At most, the act of volunteering is thought to ratify a man's recognition of his being morally obligated to serve, and to bring the volunteer under the legal obligation to serve. Or, it might be argued, the act of volunteering adds a further and special moral obligation (derived from an explicit promise) to serve, over and above the standing moral obligation of service which all men have. Whereas the ordinary citizen has only the standing obligation to serve if needed, and the draftee has his obligation to serve because he has been ordered to do so, the volunteer has both the standing obligation and a special obligation because he offered to serve. These possibilities, however, do show that insofar as volunteers, draftees, and ordinary citizens all have a

16. Quoted in Tyron, op. cit., p. 342.

common moral obligation to serve, then that obligation cannot arise from any volunteering. It must arise in a totally
different way. The problem is, what is that way; what is the
way in which a person without doing anything special (such
as volunteering), incurs a moral obligation to serve his country? I am not, it should be noted, implying that the model of
consent is irrelevant to understanding the morality of this
obligation. I am only showing that acts of volunteering (and
the same could be said for the act of oath-taking performed
by all servicemen, volunteers and draftees alike) for military
service will not be the relevant, or obligation-making, feature.

If we proceed on the assumption (a) that the moral obligation we want to account for is shared equally by draftee and
volunteer, it will be plausible to assume also (b) that this obligation is simply a special case of the citizen's general legal
or societal obligations, all of which are moral obligations for
the same reasons. Philosophers have provided many theories
to account for the morality of legal and political obligations,
including these:[17] (i) the government is the earthly representative of a divine power, and whatever the earthly power
commands (not expressly contrary to the divine will) imposes
a moral duty on those subject to it (Thomism); (ii) the government has the rightful authority to command military
service, because whatever the government commands imposes
a moral duty upon those subject to it (positivism); (iii) the
government is the creation of the members of the body politic,
who have voluntarily covenanted to create it in authority

---

17. A. J. Ayer, *Philosophy and Politics* (Liverpool: Liverpool University Press,
1969), identifies no less than a dozen attempts by philosophers to answer the
question, 'What is the ground of political obligation?' (pp. 9-10). All of these
theories, he implies, are intended to show that political obligation is in general
a moral obligation, but none of them, as he rightly remarks, is "very impres-
sive."

over themselves, and whatever issues from such a government the members are morally obligated to obey (contractualism); (iv) the government is the device through which the society secures the greatest good of the greatest number, and this makes strict obedience to the law a moral obligation (utilitarianism); (v) the nation has a life and purpose logically independent of, and morally superior to, the lives and purposes of its individual citizens, and this moral superiority legitimizes the authority of the state over the individual and imposes an obligation of obedience by the latter to the former (organicism); (vi) through social organizations, including the nation-state, unique benefits are secured to all citizens, but only by the willing acceptance of various burdens by all, chief among which is dutiful obedience to the law; so that it is unfair to accept these benefits without accepting one's share of the burdens—including military service—which alone make the benefits possible.[18]

I shall not attempt to assess the merit of these theories, one by one, as they relate to the problem at hand; what that might gain in thoroughness it would surely lose in tedium. Besides, all of these theories share in common one vulnerable feature which can be isolated for direct scrutiny. I shall call it *the transitivity of morality*. The point of all these theories is to show the citizen in general and in advance why he has a moral obligation to obey particular laws independent of any further moral test for those particular laws. Each theory proceeds on the assumption that if the purpose, end, system, or structure—the *constitution*, in short—of the so-

18. Theory (vi) is the Hume-Kant-Rawls theory summarily stated by John Rawls, "Legal Obligation and the Duty of Fair Play," in Sidney Hook, ed., *Law and Philosophy* (New York: New York University Press, 1964), p. 17. For a criticism different from but consistent with mine, see Richard A. Wasserstrom, "The Obligation to Obey the Law," *U.C.L.A. Law Review* X (1963), pp. 790-807, reprinted in Robert Summers, ed., *Essays in Legal Philosophy* (Oxford: Blackwells, 1968), pp. 293-302.

ciety meets certain tests of moral worthiness, then every valid or legitimate act of the government in that society must be no less morally worthy.[19] The transitivity of morality guarantees that it would be inconsistent both to grant the morality (by whatever test is deemed appropriate) of the political structure and still doubt or deny the morality, including the moral obligatoriness, of a particular policy, statute, or court decision which some appropriate agency in that structure issues.

We may illustrate the difficulty of accepting any theory which relies on this assumption by considering two questions: Is the constitutional structure under which our society operates, including the avowed and tacit ends to be secured by that constitution, morally acceptable? Are the particular laws and policies which create our legal obligation for military service valid? On the theory we are considering, only if the answer to both questions is in the affirmative will the legal obligation in question also be a moral obligation. What we are considering, in other words, is simply an application of the thesis that a person has a moral obligation to obey whatever law is validly enacted by whatever political authority is constitutionally authorized to do so, provided only that constitutional structure itself has moral authority.

In the present case, it is impossible to give a fully convincing answer to either question; all I can do is sketch the outline of an answer. As to the first question, the moral acceptability of our constitutional system is chiefly to be determined by whether it is founded on principles of justice and equality, and whether it gives operating effectiveness to those

19. An instructive instance of the pervasiveness of this assumption can be seen in the theory of why political obligations are moral obligations advanced by J. R. Pennock, "The Obligation to Obey the Law and the Ends of the State," in Hook, ed., op. cit., pp. 77-85, and the critique therein of Rawls' rival theory. Pennock and Rawls share this assumption, and by comparison with this tacit agreement their differences shrink into relative insignificance.

principles.[20] If only for the sake of argument here, let us concede that our constitutional structure is not an unjust one, and that it does operate effectively. As for the second question, an affirmative answer depends to some extent on accepting a distinction between what is legitimate (or valid) law, and what is constitutionally permissible. The former is to be determined chiefly by reference to whether the legislation in question arises in the constitutionally authorized way. The latter, however, is to be settled by reference to whether the legislation is in violation of any constitutional prohibition as determined by the courts. More than one statute has clearly passed the former of these tests, and yet failed the latter, as the history of state and federal legislation before the bar of appellate courts will testify. I am unwilling, as I have already made clear, to challenge the validity or legitimacy of the draft legislation as such. I have, however, doubts about its constitutional permissibility, as do many others. I do not concede, for example, that a perpetual peacetime military draft is consistent with the constitution, nor that the constitution permits the use of draftees in overseas combat with foreign nationals in the absence of a declaration of war.[21] Even if the Supreme Court were to continue to evade

20. By far the best attempt to show what is involved in this question (though not an attempt to answer it, even implicitly, for the United States) is to be found in the essays by John Rawls: "Justice as Fairness," *Philosophical Review* LXVII (1958), pp. 164-94; "Constitutional Liberty and the Concept of Justice," in C. J. Friedrich and J. W. Chapman, eds., *Justice: Nomos VI* (New York: Atherton Press, 1963), pp. 98-125; and "The Justification of Civil Disobedience," in H. A. Bedau, ed., *Civil Disobedience* (New York: Pegasus, 1969), pp. 240-55.

21. That Congress has the power to conscript men into military service during wartime was settled by the Supreme Court in *The Selective Draft Law Cases* (1918). Subsequently, however, only lower court holdings and Supreme Court dicta have endorsed the power of Congress to draft in peacetime and of the president to send draftees overseas into combat in an undeclared war. An unusually explicit avowal from the bench of these powers as constitutional may be found in the opinion of Judge Charles Wyzanski, Jr., in United States v.

these "political questions" (as I expect it will), that evasion need not be construed as a favorable judgment on these constitutional questions. Nevertheless, we may be required to give an affirmative answer to the second question before us.

But surely the more interesting question in the argument we are assessing is not the truth of the two premises we have been discussing but the validity of the inference, which depends on the transitivity of morality. Such transitivity is dubious at best. I believe that we do not and should not accept the argument that a given law creates not only a legal but a moral obligation because it is a valid law and it issues from a government authorized by a constitution that is morally sound. The chief objection to accepting such a form of argument is the best reason for rejecting any form of argument as invalid: it would allow one to infer false conclusions from true premises. Consider some examples of the moral obligations we would find it necessary to recognize if we were to accept the transitivity of morality: the manufacture of intoxicating liquors during the reign of the Volstead Act would have violated not only a legal but also a moral obligation; today, it would be not only legally but morally impermissible to travel to North Vietnam and China, given current State Department directives; all persons having taxable income would be under a moral as well as a legal obligation to pay that portion of their taxes which finances the Vietnam war, CBW research, endless stockpiling of nuclear weapons, etc. There is no end to these examples, but is not any one of them too much to accept? In order to avoid such counter-intuitive consequences, we must abandon the as-

Sisson, *Selective Service Law Reporter* I (1969), pp. 3354 ff. For further discussion, see Carl Brent Swisher, "The Supreme Court and Conscription," *Current History* LIV (1968), pp. 351-55, 365-66; *Selective Service Law Reporter* (1968), p. 1005; and American Civil Liberties Union, "Memorandum of Points and Authorities in Support of Motion to Dismiss the Indictment," United States v. Zimmerman (S.D.N.Y., 1969) mimeographed).

sumption I have called the transitivity of morality and be prepared to face directly and piecemeal, in each case where we have a legal obligation, whether we also have a moral obligation.

Some may object that any society which would permit such preposterous things as cited in my examples cannot be founded on a morally sound constitution. One recalls Thoreau's explicit condemnation of the constitution of his day for its tolerance of slavery. This line of objection claims that my examples quite fail to establish their point. For I am purporting to prove by examples that morality is not transitive, and to do that I must rely on the morality of the constitution, which my own examples impeach! There is some truth in this objection, and it prompts two comments. Perhaps the transitivity of morality is theoretically a tenable assumption; even so, it remains practically useless because at no stage in history has any constitution been sufficiently just to entitle inferences of the sort we are discussing. If, however, transitivity of morality is accepted, despite the existence of morally obnoxious laws, we are entitled to reverse the argument, with the result that we destroy the moral authority of the constitution itself. For example, anyone in 1859 who judged that he had no moral obligation to assist in the return of fugitive slaves, but who accepted the transitivity of morality, would have had to judge the constitution grossly immoral (as Thoreau said he did). The lesson is that one must be cautious in insisting upon the transitivity of morality lest the immoralities sanctioned by law turn out to destroy the truth of the major premiss (that the constitution is just).

IV

Another line of interpretation ancillary to the foregoing line of argument is the possibility that a military obligation is made moral by being a *status* obligation, an obligation on those who hold the status of citizen in a republic. This idea emerged from the development of conscript armies in the Napoleonic era. The military historian, B. H. Liddell-Hart, no admirer of conscription, once described it as "the misbegotten child of [French] revolutionary enthusiasm."[22] An armed citizenry (so this view would hold) is the natural result of an egalitarian and democratic basis of political authority and at the same time the best protection against counterrevolutionary efforts by reactionary elements in society or in neighboring nations. So, along with our right to vote and other rights of citizenship there are certain responsibilities, duties, or obligations, including the defense of the society in which we are full and equal members, Citizens. That this line of thought is still pertinent can be seen from the recent remark of an American military officer: "To divorce military service from the duties of citizenship would be the height of folly, inviting ultimate disaster."[23] The Supreme Court has already been quoted in its endorsement of this idea of citizen soldiers, in language hardly less categorical.

The idea that status provides (indeed, is to be defined in terms of the exercise of) certain responsibilities, privileges, rights, duties, is generally accepted. Elective and appointive offices in all organizations, roles earned by dint of qualifications and merit, jobs assigned or otherwise obtained, titles inherited and awarded—all these amply illustrate the notion that with certain status go certain duties. Do we then have in the role or status of citizen a special case of this general idea, and if so, can it be used to show why a citizen's military

22. Quoted from B. H. Liddell-Hart, *Why Don't We Learn From History?* (London: Allen and Unwin, 1944) by Senator Mark O. Hatfield, in *The Congressional Record* (July 7, 1970), p. S10634.
23. Hays, op. cit., p. 20.

obligation is also a moral obligation? So long as we extend general moral approval to the ends and constitutional structure of political society, the morality of the ensuing rights and duties of citizen membership in that society is guaranteed— at least, if we accept the transitivity of morality. But the only way to guarantee that there is a universal moral obligation upon (male) citizens to render military service is by stipulating that this is one of the duties of their citizenship. Historically, something like this may be seen in the claim that citizens have a moral duty to volunteer when their country needs them (the theory on which England raised its first armies in World War I). Logically, however, the status of citizenship can bear the weight being put on it by this argument only if the question is begged, or else if there is tacit reliance on other notions such as those criticized elsewhere in this essay.

V

The argument of the two preceding sections has relied on the assumption that a man's military obligation is simply a special case of a more general legal or political obligation. Natural though it may be, this assumption is neither historically sound nor logically necessary. Traditionally, moral obligations have often been divided into three categories: obligations to God, to others, and to oneself. A man's military obligation to serve his country presumably would be a special case of the second sort of obligation, and all other legal or political obligations would also fall into this category. The distinctive thing about military service is that it creates a cadre of persons subject to military orders and (in that sense) ready to fight so that the community in which they live can preserve its integrity, including its own legal, political, and social institutions. Now, suppose one thinks of the protection and defense of other persons, in particular of one's family and neighbors, as something which one is morally obligated to provide. Thus, a recent critic of pacifism has asserted that "the draft is morally justifiable if the defense of persons is considered a basic obligation of the citizen."[24] As such, it would be natural to think of this defense as being derived from his other obligations to other persons. In this way one might come to see the morality of a man's military obligation as a consequence of all his other legal or political obligations.

This, or something like it, seems to me to be a line of thought behind much talk of a military obligation as a moral obligation. In order to establish this obligation upon particular persons by means of this kind of argument, one must be relying on certain empirical assumptions. Chief among these is the belief that the presence of men in military service can and will in fact protect the rest of the community from aggression, in ways or with effectiveness superior to any alternative, e.g. by deterring aggressors, defeating attempted invasion, forcing a stronger aggressor to negotiate a less than unconditional surrender. Should this factual situation not obtain, then there seems no reason on this argument why anyone should see himself as morally obligated to provide what amounts to ineffective or futile military service.

In the present social and political climate, what can we say about this argument as establishing a moral obligation upon young American men to serve in the armed services today? Frankly, it strikes me as the moral detritus from a half-imagined and hardly to be reestablished period in hu-

24. Jan Narveson, "Pacifism: A Philosophical Analysis," *Ethics* LXXV (1965), pp. 259-71, reprinted in Richard Wasserstrom, ed., *War and Morality* (Belmont, Calif.: Wadsworth Publishing Co., 1970), p. 77. Narveson's statement would be more plausible if for 'if' he had written 'only if,' and if for 'persons' he had written 'fellow-citizens.'

man history when familial, tribal, communal, and civic loyalties dictated the chief features of civilized life, and from which recognizable political relationships eventually grew. This antique mode of thought about the fundamental nature of a person's military obligation has little if any relevance to the morality of a young American's rendering military service to the United States in the current decade of the present century. No one can seriously think of treating this nation as a community to which communal-like obligations are borne by each of us (or at least by each male during a certain period of his young manhood). Nor is it reasonable to see our economic, social, political, legal institutions—insofar as they are worthy of preservation and pride—both as seriously threatened by any nation or people outside (or inside) our borders and as defendable only by conscripted citizen service in the armed forces.

It must be kept in mind that the obligation whose morality we are attempting to establish is an obligation to others (insofar as it is to anyone) as defined by the limits of the nation-state. Obligations to one's neighbors as human beings, obligations to defend the weak and helpless, obligations to run risks for those in danger, obligations to come to the aid of the innocent, obligations to preserve the community—all these obligations are wholly indifferent to the nation-state system. But national territory, national citizenship, and the national state are of the essence in characterizing the military obligation we are discussing. It is not, after all, the town of Concord, the county of Middlesex, the Commonwealth of Massachusetts—nor the Anglo-American community, the English-speaking people of the world, nor even the United Nations—that propose to draft my sons if their volunteered service cannot be secured. No doubt it would be easier to establish the morality of our military obligation if the morality of the nation-state system could be established. In any case, it is military obligation within the framework of that system which is in question.

If I may hazard the idea, I suggest that if there were a universal moral obligation upon persons to defend their community, their duties would be confined to the protection of neighborhoods and towns, to keep them liveable and healthy, safe and available for the use of all, both today and in the future. The community's defenses, in other words, would be raised against polluters and despoilers, not only against criminals, and least of all against foreign enemies. Moral considerations adequate to justify a domestic police force cannot suffice to justify as well a conscript standing army in present international conditions. A nation's army is not a police force, after all, and least of all is it an international police force. It is not, therefore, a moral obligation to render community service which I dispute. I object only to the attempt to see in such a moral obligation the source or rationale of the morality of a military obligation to serve the present nation-state.

It must be clear by now that my attack on the morality of military obligation as derivative from the moral obligation to defend persons depends essentially on the insufficiency of this consideration in the economic, political, and social conditions which exist in this country and in the world today. Under altered domestic or international circumstances, approaches which I reject here might in fact prove sufficient to establish the morality of a military obligation. Thus, I would not argue from the absence of a military obligation which is also a moral obligation among young Americans today to the conclusion that their Israeli counterparts, faced possibly with a genuine struggle for ethnic survival, also have no moral obligation to serve in their nation's armed forces; or that Cubans have no moral obligation to provide the armed forces needed to defend their socialist society against a counterrevolutionary invasion by imperialistic neighbors to the north. The moral obligation of military service in such cases as these is not settled by my criticism of possible ways whereby that obligation might be established in American society. What I have been relying upon throughout this discussion is that having a moral obligation depends not only upon certain general principles and practices and conceptual truths, but also upon circumstances and situations which alter through history as economic, social, and other contingent relationships vary.

VI

Could it be argued that although the obligation to serve in the armed forces is imposed on young men, it is none the less moral? Is it possible to impose a moral obligation upon someone, to thrust upon him without his consent or desire the moral duty to perform or forbear certain undertakings? Are these circumstances under which I could *make* you morally obligated to do something, without your doing anything to undertake or acknowledge the obligation? Can you become liable to the imposition of an obligation without any offering (as the lawyers say) on your part? Surely, it seems, children have their status as children of their parents through no act of their own. Yet this status traditionally carries with it certain obligations beginning with the duty to "honor one's father and mother." Surely, this is an obligation which is a moral obligation, and it is imposed on all children without their consent.

There is, no doubt, something slightly archaic and quaint in the above reasoning. In earlier generations, to be sure, it would have been generally granted that children have obligations to their parents which are imposed on them and are yet moral. Locke, for example, certainly believed this (as his

Second Treatise shows) and he did not speak for himself alone. But it is doubtful that many would grant this conclusion in the same way today. Normally, it would be agreed, children are much obliged to their parents for the benefits and blessings of tender loving care. Also, children are obliged by their infancy to obey their parent's wishes. Perhaps for some philosophers this would be sufficient to establish that children have imposed on them moral obligations toward their own parents.[25] Yet most philosophers today, I venture, would grant both the premiss and the conclusion but deny the inference.

Even if the inference were granted, and it provided us with a clear case of the imposition of a moral obligation, it is not clear that it would provide us with a plausible model of the imposition of a moral obligation which could be used to explain how it is that the government (or Congress, by passing the Selective Service Act) imposes a moral obligation of military service on all eligible men. For it is not parents who impose moral obligations upon their children, but the circumstances in which children normally find themselves with respect to their parents: parents do not *make* children morally obligated to them merely by the act of procreation, but by the (usually, subsequent) things they do and forego for their children. If so, then we have not been brought to understand how it is that the government makes those subject to the draft morally obligated to obey it. Instead, we are again forced back upon one or another of the theories we have already examined, because it is those arguments which incorporate the circumstances in which the community finds itself and the previous acts of its members through which moral obligations arise.

25. Cf. Alan R. White, "On Being Obliged to Act," in G. N. A. Vessey, ed., *The Human Agent* (London: Macmillan, 1968), pp. 66 ff.

VII

I have reviewed and found wanting three different arguments *for* the view that our military obligation is a moral obligation. Now I want to consider much more briefly three different arguments *against* that conclusion, arguments which I also reject.

The first of these arguments would destroy any possibility of a military obligation ever being a moral obligation. Again, we must assume that a military obligation is simply a special case of a legal or political obligation—an obligation unlike ordinary family or contractual obligations, in not being owed to another person or specific organization, but owed to some abstract entity, such as the State or Society, and so akin to the obligation to pay one's taxes, obey traffic regulations, and assist the police when ordered to do so. Now, some philosophers have urged that there simply are *no* such obligations at all; they have advanced arguments to show that it is absurd to suppose anyone ever has *any* legal or political obligation.[26] Other philosophers have gone even further; they have urged us to abandon the concept of obligation, whether legal, political, or otherwise, insofar as these obligations are to be thought of as *moral* obligations.[27] These are large-scale and bold challenges, but there is not space here to give them the scrutiny they deserve. These extreme objections may be true, though I believe and have assumed that they are not. If I am wrong, and these objections are well-founded, of course, any such investigation along the lines I have taken would be obviated at the onset, and the falsity

26. See T. N. Macpherson, *Political Obligation* (New York: Humanities Press, 1969), p. 84, and Ladd, op. cit., p. 4.
27. G. E. M. Anscombe, "Modern Moral Philosophy," *Philosophy* XXXIII (1958), pp. 5-26, reprinted in W. D. Hudson, ed., *The Is-Ought Question* (London: Macmillan, 1969), pp. 179 ff.

of a military obligation being a moral obligation would be guaranteed.

A second line of argument urges that the very fact of compelling performance of military service, as is done by arraying the forces of the law against known evaders and draft resisters, shows conclusively that there is nothing moral in obeying the body of law thus sanctioned. That is, from the fact that the obligation to serve is made into a legal obligation backed by coercive force, it is inferred that whatever may have been moral in the obligation in the first place is now destroyed. To this objection I have two replies. (a) The idea of community or patriotic obligations being exacted from us, because the ordinary citizen cannot ordinarily be expected to render what he properly owes unless he is compelled to do so (or is subject to legal sanctions for failing to do so), is old and very familiar. For Americans, paying taxes, jury duty, and school attendance are all illustrations. All of these obligations are provided for by law, and a citizen may find himself coerced into performing any one of them against his will. But all three obligations have usually been thought to be moral obligations of good citizenship, and this conception of them has not been thought weakened or destroyed by their legal enforceability. The law, it would ordinarily be said, merely gives form, efficiency, and force to the moral obligation. So the fact that a man's military obligation is exacted from him by the coercive instrumentalities of the Selective Service System, the Federal Bureau of Investigation, the federal criminal courts, and the Bureau of Prisons will not of itself suffice to show that a military obligation is not a moral obligation. At the very least, it will have this consequence only if many other obligations enforceable as law which are thought to be moral cease to be so regarded. (b) While it is clear that no one general relation holds between law and morals, it is reasonably clear that the use of

force to exact performance or compliance does not of itself
—except on the most saintly ethic—destroy the putative morality of the conduct. Many philosophers would join John
Stuart Mill in insisting that one of the distinctive characteristics of a moral obligation is that "we should be gratified
to see . . . [it] enforced by anybody who had the power."[28]
Now it is true that the fact that someone complies with a
certain order or directive because it is backed by a threat to
use coercive force to secure compliance tends to show that
there is little or nothing moral in the compliance. But it
does not tend to show that there is no moral obligation to
comply with the directive or that it is morally wrong to use
force to back it up. Perhaps it is a failure to distinguish the
way coercion supplies a (nonmoral) motive from the way
reasons may (morally) justify the use of force that leads us to
disagree with the position Mill defends.

A third and very different line of criticism might be extracted from the apparent theory on which conscientious objection exemptions are established.[29] The exemption for conscientious objection is founded upon the language and intent of Congress as embodied in the Selective Service Act
beginning with the legislation passed in 1940.[30] Although the
basis of the exemption is not constitutional but statutory,
and what Congress can grant Congress can deny, the statutory exemption seems to acknowledge the existence of a
moral claim upon persons superior to any man-made law.

28. J. S. Mill, *Utilitarianism* (1861), chap. 5. Cf. Hart, "Legal and Moral Obligation," in Melden, ed., op. cit., pp. 102 ff.; Ladd, op. cit., pp. 14-15; and
Brandt, op. cit., p. 391.
29. Quite apart from defects in the underlying theory of political obligation,
the actual structure of exemptions is open to moral criticism, too. See John
de J. Pemberton, Jr., "Equality in the Exemption of Conscientious Objectors,"
in Tax, ed., op. cit., pp. 66-69; Carl Cohen, "Conscientious Objection," *Ethics*
LXXVIII (1968), pp. 269-79; and James Finn, ed., *Conflict of Loyalties* (New
York: Pegasus, 1969).
30. 54 Stat. 885, Sec. 5(g) (1940).

The underlying theory of the statutory exemption seems to be that there is a different source of moral regulation, indeed, an obligation more ultimate than any provided by statute (or constitutional) law, i.e. God-given commandments forbidding men to raise their arms in anger against their brothers, and by implication forbidding a man to do so at the behest of a secular government on behalf of policies the man may not understand (or may understand only to repudiate) and against persons he has never seen and who have done him no harm. The "ultimacy" of military obligation,[31] therefore, is tacitly denied by the very instrument which gives legal authority to that obligation. On the strength of this analysis, one might argue that the statutory exemption for conscientious objectors shows that there is nothing moral in the legal obligation to serve in the armed forces, because these statutes acknowledge a superior moral claim as the basis of a moral exemption to such service.

On at least two different grounds this is an inconclusive argument. (a) This objection simply assumes that moral obligations cannot conflict with each other, as though what a moral obligation overrides cannot be another moral obligation. Much moral philosophy in this century, however, has relied upon the notion that there are "prima facie" moral obligations, that they can and do conflict, and that a man's ultimate moral obligation in each situation (or, to put it another way, what he morally ought to do) is determined by a rational resolution of this conflict.[32] It would be argued by these philosophers that a man has prima facie moral obligations to obey the laws of his country, to obey the orders of those in authority over him, to avoid harming other men, and to do whatever he conscientiously believes he ought to

31. The term is from Michael Walzer, *Obligations*, pp. 89, 97, 105.
32. The doctrine originated with W. D. Ross, *The Right and the Good* (Oxford: The Clarendon Press, 1930), pp. 19-47.

do. But these prima facie obligations can conflict; a given act which satisfies some of these obligations can violate others, and there might be no act open to the agent (at least in certain situations) which will satisfy them all. If this is the way in which one understands the intersection of the legal obligation to serve and conscientious objection to such service, then it is quite consistent to maintain that there is at least a prima facie moral obligation to serve in the armed forces. (b) The exemption for conscientious objectors has always carried with it the statutory requirement of alternative civilian service "in the national interest."[33] So it could be argued that a man's military obligation is really a special case of a more general moral obligation to render service to the nation, and that *this* obligation is one to which there is *no* legal or moral exemption in principle. As the law stands, this, too, is a perfectly consistent interpretation of the conscientious objector exemption, which does not undercut the putative morality of a man's military obligation. I should add that I do not advocate the interpretations relied upon in (a) and (b); I am only pointing out that they are plausible and that they show the original argument to be far from conclusive.

VIII

I hope I have shown why I believe that there is no route whereby persons incur or create or undertake moral obligations which, if used as a pattern or model for the morality of the obligation to serve in the armed forces, will show that young men in our country are morally obligated to serve in the armed forces at this time. The consequence is that we must either develop some new theory which will produce this result, or reassess the many factual judgments I have (admittedly) all too briefly identified and rendered, or confess

33. See, for example, Military Selective Service Act (1967), Sec. 6(j).

that we have no adequate reason for supposing that a man's military obligation is at present also a moral obligation.

As we contemplate the last alternative, we should note that some recent commentators on the Selective Service System now describe it as a system of "impressment,"[34] deliberately using the term of opprobrium from previous centuries to reveal the true status of the system we have embraced during the past generation. Our draft boards have become little more than genteel press gangs, and our draftee army simply battalions of men dragooned into rendering a service which they are told on all sides they owe their country.

Impressment is strictly the forced contribution of private service in the public interest; it has its occasions and justifications. Imminent threat of community or public disaster (flooding waters, forest fire, volcanic eruption, famine, epidemic) can leave the authorities with no feasible alternative, in the face of the collapse of community life and essential social services, but to press all able-bodied persons in the vicinity into public service immediately. Whether one should invoke the doctrine of necessity to justify or only to excuse the use of force to secure compliance with orders in such situations will depend on one's theory of how a justification differs from an excuse. In either case, necessity makes it not wrong for the authorities to act as they do. Yet even the extreme circumstances and the extreme measures made morally appropriate in this way are appropriate only because of certain background assumptions which, conceivably, may be missing. For example, it cannot be right to impress persons into labor on behalf of preserving institutions which in normal times have exploited or otherwise unjustly treated them.

The problem with the draft for the past generation is whether one can reasonably invoke any such necessities on

---

34. Bruce Chapman, "Politics and Conscription: A Proposal to Replace the Draft," in Tax, ed., op. cit., p. 208; and Walzer, op. cit., pp. 177 f.

its behalf. American life and institutions do not seem, since 1948, to have been in jeopardy and saved from destruction thanks only to millions of draftees, in the way some village might have been lost if its mayor and council had not used the police to force all able-bodied persons to fill and haul sandbags to bolster sagging dikes against a rampaging river. Our much-touted "foreign policy commitments" have not created (nor been undertaken in response to) social needs tantamount to the necessities which alone could justify the conclusion that American men have a moral obligation to meet those needs with their personal military service.[35]

If I am right, then, a man's military obligation today looks, from a moral point of view, not significantly different from his obligation to get his dog a license. His obligation is a creature of the law, so that once a certain law is passed he has this (legal) obligation, but in the absence of the law he has no such obligation at all. One result of this is that the obligation men have today to serve in the armed forces may not be at all like the obligation their fathers or grandfathers had to render comparable service. *There simply is no standing and universal moral obligation upon persons to render military service which can be invoked to give a moral reason why a young man ought to obey a draft board.*

While I am unable to offer any fruit of research into American history to bolster the point, it is irresistible to speculate that the popularity of the idea of a military obligation in this country is chiefly a function of the actual imposition of a draft law over the past century: first, at the height of the Civil War (1863); next, immediately after American entry into the war in Europe (1917); again, a few days before the fall of France to the Nazi invaders 1940); finally, in our

35. See, for example, Gabriel Kolko, *The Roots of American Foreign Policy* (Boston: Beacon Press, 1969), and William Appleman Williams, *Roots of the Modern American Empire* (New York: Random House, 1969).

time, with the onset of the Cold War (1948), its subsequent quadrennial Congressional renewal always accompanied by predictable alarums and excursions. Is it not more likely that the presence of the draft in our midst explains the talk about our obligation to serve, rather than being explained by that alleged obligation? Is it not that the permanent military establishment in this nation encourages moralistic belief in our obligation to military service, rather than that our sense of obligation causes us to create our permanent military establishment?

What we are left with, then, is this. The Selective Service Act places on those subject to it a legal obligation to render military service if called upon to do so. Even if this law were to be abolished, there would remain the political capacity in Congress and the president to reestablish such a legal obligation at almost any time irrespective of the factual warrant for doing so (though this would not have been true in any other epoch of American history). The circumstances in community life, or in national survival, which alone could justify impressment are simply missing from the scene today and probably have not existed at any time in this century.

My arguments, as I have already implied, should not be construed as an attempt to show that we have a moral obligation to resist or repeal the draft. These possibilities go beyond my interests here, even if my arguments help pave the way for facing them. What I have tried to show is that repudiation, violation, or evasion of the legal obligation to serve in the armed forces today, if it incurs any moral taint at all, does not incur that taint brought upon a person who repudiates, violates, or evades his moral obligations.[36]

36. A revised version of a paper originally presented at the Ripon College Conference on Rights and Political Action, October 10, 1970. I am grateful to Constance Putnam for comments on an early draft, and to Virginia Held for comments on a later version published in *Inquiry* (1971).

6

Governmental Toleration of Civil Disobedience

SIDNEY GENDIN

Most discussions of civil disobedience proceed on the presumption that civil disobedience is a problem for the agent. For this reason the principal question is usually "When, if ever, are acts of civil disobedience justified?" I want to suggest the major issue is a matter not of deciding when civil disobedience is justified but rather of seeing what forms of behavior a government may tolerate.

Besides the question "When, if ever, are acts of civil disobedience justified?" another question philosophers have asked is "Just what is an act of civil disobedience?" It may be tempting to think that if we get clear about the meaning of 'civil disobedience' then we will be well on the way to providing a justification for acts of civil disobedience. I think, and will try to show, that this is not a profitable way of regarding the conceptual question. I will begin the discussion of the category of civil disobedience by examining one particular (alleged) necessary condition of an act's being classified as an instance of civil disobedience—the willingness to accept punishment for one's action.

Many writers have attempted to distinguish civil disobedience from defiance of the law by claiming that a *defining* feature of the former is that those who engage in it must be willing to accept whatever punishment is prescribed by law for their actions. This feature is not only said to be a logical characteristic of civil disobedience but is supposed to be one of the main justifications for it. Presumably it is *the* mark of conscientious dissension.[1] I shall argue that the distinction between civil disobedience and defiance of the law cannot be drawn in terms of one's willingness to accept a penalty. Further, by itself, such willingness contributes nothing towards either the legal or moral justification of one's act. After attending to this pseudo-criterion of civil disobedience I shall then explain what I think the purpose of the category of civil disobedience is and, finally, I shall turn to some more promising criteria of this category.

Among the distinguished writers who have emphasized that those who are conscientiously motivated in their objections to a law must be willing to abide by whatever punishment is decreed by law are Erwin Griswold and Sidney Hook. John Rawls, too, has included willingness to accept punishment as a condition of civil disobedience, although he has not gone so far in exaggerating its significance.[2] That persons of such differing philosophic persuasions are here united is itself formidable evidence of the correctness of their view. Nevertheless it seems to me that such willingness comes to very little. One thing these writers overlook is that among the things a man may find objectionable about a law is the penalty prescribed for its violation. Suppose a law prohibited the possession of marijuana and that the punishment for

1. See, for example, Darnell Rucker, "The Moral Grounds of Civil Disobedience," *Ethics*, vol. 76 (January, 1966), pp. 142-45.
2. Sidney Hook, "Social Protest and Civil Disobedience," in Paul Kurz, ed., *Moral Problems in Contemporary Society* (Englewood Cliffs, N.J.: Prentice-Hall, 1969), pp. 161-72; Erwin Griswold, "Dissent—1968 Style," The George A. Dreyfous Lecture given at Tulane University (April 1968); John Rawls, "The Justification of Civil Disobedience," in Hugo Bedau, ed., *Civil Disobedience: Theory and Practice* (New York: Pegasus, 1969), pp. 240-55.

possession was imprisonment for not less than fifteen years. Here a person who had no intention of using it or selling it might deliberately and openly violate the law in order to direct the public's attention to what he regarded as an unusually cruel punishment. Whether such a person should be punished is one thing; it is quite another thing to expect him to be willing to endure the very penalty he is protesting. Another thing that is overlooked or ignored is that the protest against certain laws is not directed just against their alleged immorality. Often enough, those protesting are persuaded that the laws they are challenging are unconstitutional or invalid in some other way. In maintaining that these protesters should be willing to accept their punishment one is begging the question against them. They are not claiming to have a moral right to disobey a bad law; rather they claim they are not violating the law. The question is not whether they are right. Nor is it a matter of claiming that we must presume a law is valid until it is ruled otherwise. The point is that since the dissenters do not regard themselves as breaking the law it is unreasonable to expect them to be willing to accept punishment. The willingness to accept punishment may be important in some other way but it isn't necessarily the mark of conscientious motivation.

Nor is willingness to accept punishment ever a sufficient condition for an act's being classified as one of civil disobedience, as the following example makes clear. It is not uncommon in the business world for corporations to pay their fines willingly and even cheerfully, because these fines are usually trivial in comparison to the profits reaped from the practices that result in them. The fact that the fines are so low results in the feeling that they are not to be taken seriously, that they are nuisance taxes. For this reason businessmen do not regard themselves as criminals. They regard the fines as legitimate options which the government grants them.

But this does not prove they really are within their rights. That businessmen do not regard themselves as criminals is about as relevant to deciding whether they are criminals as deciding whether prostitution is criminal by asking prostitutes if they regard themselves as criminals. It is worth mentioning that if the penalties handed out to prostitutes were as trivial in relation to their profits as the penalties given to businessmen are to theirs, then prostitutes would pay them cheerfully. Would that reduce their offences to civil disobedience? Finally, it happens occasionally that people commit serious crimes like murder and then, as a consequence of their remorse, turn themselves over to the police, willing to abide by whatever the penalty is. Surely such willingness does not show that they were only civilly disobedient, and of course it does nothing to contribute to the justification of their original crimes.

'Defiance of the law' is a phrase standing for a broad class of actions that includes civil disobedience as a special case. Therefore it is futile to seek a possible foundation for justifying acts of civil disobedience in a false bifurcation between them and acts in defiance of the law. Why then is it true that many persons engaged in civil disobedience are willing to accept punishment for their acts? My guess is that they are willing not because *they* think such willingness is morally obligatory but because they wish to impress upon *others,* who may be dubious, that their resistance is not undertaken for a self-serving purpose. But this reason for accepting punishment should not be underrated. In conjunction with certain other conditions it helps illuminate the purpose of the category of civil disobedience.

It is time now to consider why we are concerned at all about clarifying the criteria of civil disobedience. Many false issues have been raised on this matter. Some persons have said that it is morally right to disobey laws which either are not constitutional or have not been duly enacted. Others have said that it is morally right to disobey bad laws. Against these views others have replied that although a law may be a bad one or may not have been duly enacted the only correct way to dispose of it in a democratic society is by legal means. If it is a bad law, it should be repealed; if unconstitutional, it should be brought before the courts, which shall then declare it unconstitutional. In any event it should not be openly flouted because that creates disrespect for the law in general. When the issues are drawn in such oversimplified terms it is no wonder that we get oversimplified attitudes about civil disobedience. I have heard it claimed by one philosopher that acts of civil disobedience are *always* justified; it is just a matter of setting forth the criteria that determine which are the acts of civil disobedience.[3] On this view it is assumed that we can readily settle which laws are good, bad, constitutional, and unconstitutional. All that is left to decide are the appropriate methods of dissent. On the other extreme it is argued that acts of civil disobedience are *never* justified because their short-term gains are always bought at the cost of long-term damage to the rule of law.[4] Both sides assume that the problem of civil disobedience is *the agent's problem*. How should he behave?

This way of regarding the matter seems to me to be a

3. At the spring 1969 meeting of the Long Island Philosophy Society, Karsten Struhl, one of the two principal speakers in a civil disobedience symposium, made this point his major thesis, in an unpublished paper entitled "Civil Disobedience as Self-Justifying."

4. Archibald Cox seems to hold this view. See "Direct Action, Civil Disobedience, and the Constitution," in *Civil Rights, the Constitution, and the Courts* (Cambridge: Harvard University Press, 1967), pp. 2-29. And, in my opinion, the most outstanding example of an oversimplified approach to all issues in civil disobedience can be found in Abe Fortas' *Concerning Dissent and Civil Disobedience* (New York: New American Library, 1968).

mistake. It is of course true that when a person confronts what he takes to be a bad law he has the problem of deciding whether to obey it. But there are many ways in which he may defy the law; and not all of them give rise to questions of civil disobedience. The crucial question concerning civil disobedience is not merely whether to obey the law. The question "When, if ever, are acts of civil disobedience justified?" is distinct from the question "When, if ever, is it right to disobey the law?" The latter question is, I think, easily answered. There are many circumstances in which it may be right to disobey a law. Laws are always and necessarily expressed in a certain limited number of terms. A law is addressed to the standard circumstances under which the acts it covers occur. With a little ingenuity one can think up some extraordinary circumstances that the law was not designed to meet. Thus, for example, a man should ignore the posted highway speed limit if he has a dying passenger who must be rushed to a hospital, provided that traffic is practically nonexistent, his car is in safe condition, etc. Such cases are recognized by *everyone* as moral exceptions to the law. In contrast to this, civil disobedience raises a challenge to the very existence of a law. The one who engages in it does not think of his act as a proper exception to the law; instead, he is protesting that the law is not legitimate and/or moral even in its most central applications. But since it was precisely with an eye to those central applications that the law was passed in the first place, *it follows that there is bound to be serious disagreement over the justification for the protest.* So if anyone answers the question "When, if ever, is civil disobedience justified?" by saying, "It is justified when the law even in its most central applications is not moral," his answer is of no use at all. The situation is this: any actual law is such that one can spell out circumstances that ought to constitute an exception to it, and, since the law does not in fact provide for these circumstances, it ought to be broken when they occur and *when it is clear*[5] that more good will come of breaking the law than of obeying it. On the other hand, *no law* is such that on all sides it will be agreed that it should never have been made in the first place. Hence there exists no law which is uncontroversially immoral.

It may be objected that, merely because not all parties to a dispute admit that a law is immoral, it does not follow that the law isn't clearly immoral. But I think it does follow if the word 'clearly' is taken seriously. Now it is not my intention to claim that civil disobedience cannot possibly be justified. The point I have tried to make is that in practice, although not in theory, it is bound to be harder to justify acts of civil disobedience than to say when it might be right to break a law. This is because saying when a law should be broken does not require hypothesizing a bad law; it requires only hypothesizing certain circumstances unanticipated by the law. On the other hand, it is certainly true that many intelligent people will be found who favor the laws or government policies which the dissenters are protesting against. It is a disheartening fact that most of those who have set forth criteria for the justification of civil disobedience have, in the main, been addressing themselves to an audience already inclined to agree with them. (The situation is not dissimilar among those who have attacked civil disobedience.) But if the purpose of setting forth these criteria is to persuade, it is simply too much to expect criteria which will satisfy all sides that the acts of civil disobedience were undertaken for just

5. The catch here is the phrase 'when it is clear.' If the law one is contemplating breaking is known to be a generally useful one, it is not enough that one be inclined to think the law should be broken rather than obeyed. For more on this, see G. E. Moore, *Principia Ethica* (Cambridge: Cambridge University Press, 1903), pp. 162-64.

causes. However, something less than this can reasonably be hoped for. It is this: to recognize an act as civil disobedience is not to grant that it is right or that it is performed in pursuit of a good end, but simply to recognize that it has been performed in a permissible or tolerable manner. The problem is not to decide what ends may legitimately be pursued, but to decide what methods of pursuing ends, whether or not they are good, governments may tolerate. It is, then, a problem for courts and law enforcement agencies more than for those involved in acts of civil disobedience. For those who believe that their consciences require them to break the law there is very little else to do but follow the dictates of their consciences. Of course conscience is not an infallible guide to what is right. Still, society has an obligation to distinguish ordinary criminals from those who break the law because they feel it is the moral thing to do. Hence the problem for society is to find criteria which will allow it to treat the civilly disobedient in some way different from the way it treats ordinary criminals. I am saying that the purpose of developing criteria for civil disobedience is to discover whether and when governments can afford to distinguish between kinds of defiance. I believe that governments can afford to do this and that the commonly given lists of criteria (nonviolence, etc.) provide a way of recognizing a permissible form of protest. When I use the word 'permissible' I do not mean 'legally permissible' but 'morally permissible.' I am not saying that the government should formally recognize a legal right to civil disobedience. Rather I have in mind the sorts of things Ronald Dworkin has recently discussed, namely the special considerations the courts can give an offender. We need not revise our laws radically. As Dworkin points out, even under the laws as now constituted, prosecutors have a great deal of latitude concerning which offenders are brought to trial. Further, judges have a great deal of latitude in how they may

treat defendants once they are adjudged guilty.[6] Surely this
is how the notion of civil disobedience is of greatest useful-
ness—in providing a rational defense for judicial leeway, in
setting up prima facie cases for leniency of treatment.

There is one point on which I take issue with Dworkin.
Dworkin argues, quite ably, that our legal system thrives on
condoning a certain amount of conscientiously motivated
noncompliance with the law— that is to say, not only can we
tolerate it, we actually benefit from it. Although I was persuaded myself, by Dworkin's arguments, I know that they
cannot be at the heart of our respect for conscientiously
motivated acts. Thus I doubt that Dworkin himself would be
less sympathetic to whatever he takes to be conscientiously
motivated behavior merely because it turned out to have
consequences different from what the agent had anticipated.
The debate over what the ultimate consequences of civil disobedience will be, while very important, does not bear on
what our present attitudes toward it should be. The issue is
not whether civil disobedience has good aims and/or good
consequences. In discussing civil disobedience it is important
to separate out the concrete issues from the forms of protest.
Attitudes about civil disobedience ought to be attitudes about
the latter. One cannot call a protest justifiable because of its
form but one can say that it is permissible or that the dissenters deserve special consideration because of its form. It
is unfortunate that students all across the nation have been
alienating potential supporters lately, not on the basis of
their causes, but, more than any other reason, because it is
not possible for university administrators to sanction their
progressively less passive methods. Furthermore, they have
failed to see that, from a logical point of view, amnesty cannot be a general aim on a par with their other demands but

6. Dworkin, "On Not Prosecuting Civil Disobedience," The New York Review
of Books, vol 10 (June 6, 1968), pp. 14-21.

is a second-order demand which must be considered in the light of how they have advanced their other demands.

It has often been said that although there may be a legitimate difference of opinion between an individual and the government as to whether the individual's act is legal, ultimately the power to settle that question must reside with the government. This claim is true, but it is then falsely concluded that, while one may sympathize with the individual's point of view, once the government has declared his act illegal it can do nothing else but deal with him as it would deal with any other offender. Against this, however, it may be pointed out that at least some laws may be amended in order to make allowances for the special nature of civil disobedience. There is no compelling reason why the law could not and should not take cognizance of the fact that one man resists the draft because he is convinced that it would be morally wrong for him to serve in the armed forces while another man is a plain draft-dodger. True, there may be practical difficulties involved. One may think that if the grounds for conscientious objection were broadened there would hardly be any reason for anyone to be a draft-dodger. There is little doubt that broadening the grounds for conscientious objection would provide a means for some young men to dodge the draft. But it is an unwarranted and pernicious assumption that this would cause the draft to break down. It is simply not true that all young men are opposed to the war. Nor is it true that every young man who is opposed to the war thinks he should give priority to his opinion despite his government's call to duty. And just as we generally regard it as better to let one guilty person go free than to punish one innocent person, so, too, it is better to let one man dodge the draft than to force into service one man who has deep convictions that it is wrong for him to serve. But I do not want to insist particularly on this example. My point is that it is feasible to attempt revisions of certain laws, that we should not adopt an *a priori cynicism* concerning what would happen if we made special allowances for conscientious dissension.

Finally, I want to say something about the criteria which governments may use to justify special treatment for those who engage in civil disobedience. I do not claim that these criteria are necessary and sufficient conditions for special treatment nor that they are the sole marks of conscientious motivation. Rather, they are often sorts of things a government may take cognizance of in some informal way.

1. The most commonly referred to criterion is that of nonviolence. It must be obvious that an act's merely being nonviolent does not show that it is undertaken in a justifiable cause. And surely those who have stressed this condition cannot mean that violence is never justified. Certainly there are times when it is justified. The agent must decide for himself if and when violence is justified. He may decide (rightly) that violence is justified but he can hardly expect the government to be able to tolerate his decision. Nearly all persons I have asked have admitted that the attempted assassination of Hitler was right and would have had good results if it had succeeded, yet they recognize that from Hitler's point of view there was no way to treat the would-be assassins leniently. He could hardly have been expected to say, "I'll let you go because you followed the dictates of your conscience." We are inquiring into what kinds of cases cry out for special consideration, and surely violent activity is not one kind.

2. The act must not be seditious. However terrible a government may be, however deserving of being overthrown, it cannot tolerate sedition. Sedition may be justifiable but each government must presume its own legitimacy and cannot be expected to tolerate its own overthrow.

3. The act must be done publicly, usually with advance

notice. Without this condition it degenerates into simple evasion of the law and is not a challenge to it. Sometimes a man feels he is right to evade the law. He may feel that his taxes are being used for a purpose he disapproves of; but there is little a government can do if it detects that he has cheated on his income taxes. In such a case the government must presume that his intentions were not honorable. Far better is the method of Thoreau—a public refusal to pay taxes. I am not saying that once a person announces that he cannot in good conscience pay his taxes, the government should allow it. I am pointing out that his announcement gives it a ground for considering him and his case in a different light, so that the way is open for handling him differently from ordinary tax-dodgers.

4. The act must be directed not merely at a law one believes bad, but at one for which there is good reason to think legal means for redress are not available. This point is often misunderstood by students. I have heard students say that they were forced to take nonlegal means of getting what they wanted because they had exhausted all legal means without getting satisfaction. They concluded that legal means were not available to achieve their demands. This interpretation of 'available' makes a mockery of due process. One who is determined to have his way is simply giving lip service to democratic procedure. It is ridiculous to say, "I shall be democratic about the matter; I shall give you a chance to satisfy my demand legally but if you fail to see things my way, I shall have no choice but to use other methods; since, after your refusal, legal channels would no longer be available." This, of course, is not the proper sense of 'available.' The sense in which a legal means for redress is not available is the sense in which it is not available *ab initio*. Democracy is not a panacea for all social ills. There is no guarantee that it will give you what you want. All one is entitled to is a fair

hearing for one's demands, not that the demands will be granted. Any government must assume that if a legal solution is not being denied to someone then he must restrict his efforts to seeking that sort of remedy. Only if one is being systematically deprived of his opportunity to bring about changes can government take a tolerant attitude toward the individual's going outside the law.[7]

5. The morality or the constitutionality of the law must be seriously questioned by a significant number of competent persons. Toleration of civil disobedience cannot be allowed to deteriorate into toleration for each person's deciding for himself which laws he will obey and which ones he will not. Now one may be inclined to raise a theoretical doubt concerning which persons are competent and what constitutes a significant number of them. In practice, however, it is not all that difficult. When I say the constitutionality of the law must be questioned by a significant number of persons I mean 'questioned' and not 'denied.' It is a fact, for example, that almost all constitutional lawyers, no matter what they ultimately conclude, admit that the legality of the Vietnam war is a matter for serious debate. Naturally, there is no rule telling us when we have a significant number of competent persons agreeing that some issue is debatable. Such things are judgmental matters, and whether that is fortunate or unfortunate depends on the character of those who must decide these matters.

6. The act must be committed in the name of a fundamental right. There is something ludicrous, it seems to me, about lumping the demands of a Martin Luther King to-

7. For Abe Fortas the problem of civil disobedience is really quite trivial. He claims one is never justified in going outside the law and that government cannot give special consideration to one who does go outside the law. He says that civil disobedience is justified so long as the act is legal, orderly, not disruptive, and performed in a good cause. A very daring view! See Fortas, op. cit., especially pp. 57-71 and 121-26.

gether with the demands of students who want to be part of promotion and tenure committees. Perhaps students should participate on such committees but it can scarcely be maintained that the right is of such overriding importance as to justify the disruptions that have been resorted to. And even if they are justified, they are not clearly justified and there is no way government can make allowances for them. Men and women have a finite amount of energy and time at their disposal. The exigencies of life require selectivity in the causes they pursue. Thus the Supreme Court frequently refuses to hear cases, not on the ground that it presumes the cases have already been settled rightfully in the lower courts, but because demands on its time necessitate hearing only those cases whose ramifications go beyond the particular case in question.

Ideally, changes in the law should stem from the light of reason; but we know that in actuality changes often are made only because certain conscientious men and women have refused to comply with existing laws. The problem of civil disobedience is defining the forms of this beneficial noncompliance. And even if such noncompliance were not clearly beneficial, a politically advanced community must find the means to tolerate it when it is motivated by high ideals and expressed in sensible form. Such toleration does not imply that noncompliance with the law is right.

The six conditions discussed above are only sketches which need considerable elaboration to become working guides for legal purposes. Furthermore they are aimed at our particular society. Under some forms of government civil disobedience is not tolerated to any degree. Under such forms of government the only moral alternative may be outright revolution and killing. I take it that in our society that kind of defiance is never necessary although, to be sure, there are some who would try to justify it on grounds short of necessity. Even if it were true, i.e. that in the final analysis one came to see that killing had been justified, it would also still be true that there would have been no way that government could have allowed for it. And it is what government can allow for that civil disobedience is all about.

7

The Morality of Resisting the Penalty

GORDON J. SCHOCHET

It is widely agreed by scholars and laymen that there is a necessary relationship between engaging in civil disobedience and being required to pay the penalty for one's illegal acts. The prevailing conception of civil disobedience, almost as a matter of definition, includes the insistence that those who engage in this form of justified (or justifiable) law-breaking cannot escape what amounts to the criminal responsibility for their conduct. Despite the importance of this presumption, there have been surprisingly few attempts to analyze it. The entire issue raises a number of questions that are not sufficiently or often enough distinguished. Consequently, it is generally not clear what is intended by the assertion that paying the penalty is a part of civil disobedience. Why this is a special characteristic that ought to be singled out is equally difficult to determine.

In order to deal directly with this question, I shall assume that civil disobedience itself is defensible and that an acceptable account and justification have already been provided.[1] It does not matter what justification of civil disobe-

1. I have attempted to do so in my "From Dissent to Disobedience: A Justification of Rational Protest," *Politics and Society* I (February 1971, 235-56. However, my present argument is not specifically dependent upon that article.

dience is appealed to. My aim is to demonstrate that the punishment criterion is at best a contingent rather than an essential part of civil disobedience. While I believe my thesis does not turn simply on how civil disobedience is defined or characterized,[2] there are three qualifications to this claim, but I doubt that anyone who accepts civil disobedience in principle would have any theoretical or practical difficulty agreeing to them: (1) the civil disobedience must be seen as *morally* defensible behavior and not just a political or prudentially valid act; (2) the civil disobedience must in some sense be rationally and consciously undertaken and not the result of anger, sudden impulse, or mere circumstances; (3) the reason for the civil disobedience must be capable of being properly and accurately expressed in terms of some conception of "justice," "the public interest," or legality[3] as opposed

2. It follows, of course, that anyone who does not agree that there are conditions in which the resort to law-breaking is a justifiable method of protest will not accept the present analysis.

3. Appeals to "justice" and "the public interest" are relatively clear and almost universally accepted bases for civil disobedience, but legality is not. By this final category, I wish to call attention to the claim by civil disobedients that the laws or policies they are violating are actually prohibited by the constitution or positive laws of their state. Accordingly, they view their own behavior as completely lawful, since whatever it violates is itself unlawful. The view has been rejected by Carl Cohen; he recognizes that laws are disobeyed for constitutional reasons (which may be the only way to get a judicial determination of the law's constitutionality), but argues that calling such constitutional challenges "civil disobedience" would create the paradoxical and contradictory situation in which a right to disobey law was legally sanctioned. See Cohen's *Civil Disobedience: Conscience, Tactics, and the Law* (New York, 1971), pp. 94-101; his contribution to the symposium "Civil Disobedience and the Law," *Rutgers Law Review* XXI (Fall 1966), 1-17, esp. 7-9; and his earlier article, "Essence and Ethics of Civil Disobedience," *The Nation* CXCVIII March 16, 1964), 257-62. This position seems overly restrictive and posits too rigid and mechanical a distinction between moral and political considerations on the one hand and legal ones on the other. There are, I think, as ample reasons for distinguishing between politics and morality as for distinguishing between either or both and law, and it would be more reasonable to separate each of the three as different sources of civil disobedience.

to self-interest or the unavoidable and politically acceptable differences of opinion that characterize a society in which there are diverse and conflicting value standards. In short, I am presuming that civil disobedience is a morally and politically justifiable form of rational protest that accords with the premises of democratic philosophy.

There is something odd and puzzling about the contention that one ought to suffer the penalty for having committed a justifiable act. Penalties are imposed for wrongdoing; their purposes, broadly speaking, are to provide vengeance or retribution or to deter. Persons whose conduct was permissible ought not to be punished for that behavior, and it certainly makes little sense to deter people from exercising an apparent right. If punishment is a justifiable institution and if there are instances when disobeying the law is justifiable, then that disobedience should not be punished unless it is further shown that the grounds on which the punishment is justified are superior to those that sustain certain instances of law-breaking. Few commentators have actually confronted the issue this directly. Therefore, this latter requirement is not generally recognized, although it seems to be implicit in almost everything that has been written on the subject. The usual practice is simply to explain why a commitment to rational conduct requires that the penalty be paid and to ignore these other problems.

Some writers believe that by accepting the punishment the civil disobedient is merely discharging an obligation he incurred when he broke the law. Upon closer examination, this claim becomes a strange doctrine. The contention appears to be that the law confronts the individual with a simple choice: obey or suffer the consequences, but in the end it is all the same. The issue is far more complex than this would suggest. Assuming that the law is valid, enforceable, and has some determinate merit or justification, there is a presumption in its favor; it is decidedly preferable for people to obey than for them to disobey and pay the penalty. The penalty, so to speak, is a further inducement for obeying that extends beyond the inherent merit of the specific law and of law-abidingness in general. On the whole, we do not want laws disobeyed, and when it becomes necessary to punish as a means of securing obedience, the social fabric that underlies the law has already begun to weaken. Moreover, a willingness to pay the penalty does not *permit* one to break the law; we would not, for instance, say that a person was justified in commiting a robbery so long as he (willingly) went to jail for his crime.[4] Breaking laws is not like sinning; while there are *some* similarities that the retributive theory of punishment highlights, suffering the penalty does not "make up" for an illegal act in the way that "atonement" does for a sin. But even if we were to agree that paying the penalty is similar to atonement, this interpretation of punishment would have to apply to all law-breaking and not just to civil disobedience.

An interesting problem is brought to light by the comparison of being punished with atoning for sins: we do not normally speak of persons who break the law as *required* to endure the punishment unless we are thinking in essentially retributivist or theological terms. On the other hand, we regularly and quite clearly say that the state is justified in punishing genuine offenders. It may be a logical and moral consequence of this entitlement of the state's that the offender is required or even obliged to submit. If he were not, and if his guilt were properly and sufficiently established (which, of

4. See Marshall Cohen, "Civil Disobedience in a Constitutional Democracy," *Massachusetts Review* X (Spring 1969), 214. Further criticism can be found in John Ladd, "Legal and Moral Obligation," in *Political and Legal Obligation: Nomos XIII*, J. Roland Pennock and John W. Chapman, eds. (New York, 1970), p. 20, n. 17. The view I am objecting to has recently been set forth with exceptional clarity and fullness by John H. de Boisblanc, "The Dilemma of the Disobedient: A Solution," *Indiana Law Journal* XLII (Summer 1967), 521-34.

course, is a prior condition of morally justified punishment), we would have the paradoxical situation in which the state's entitlement would not have to be acquiesced in (and conceivably could even be resisted) by the party over whom that entitlement was to be exercised. Thus, there is a sense in which it is correct to say that criminals are required to pay the penalty. However, it is not clear what this sense is, and the entire formulation still seems odd. Perhaps this problem is simply a reflection of the inability of "liberal" political philosophy to account for the relationships of individuals to their communities, especially when those relations are rooted in conflict rather than cooperation. This dilemma is extremely close to the historical sources of individualist liberalism; it was precisely the question of whether or not one was required to accept legitimate punishment that constituted a major stopping point in Thomas Hobbes's theory of political obligation. Nonetheless, we may still speak of the requirement upon offenders to submit to punishment even though we cannot *fully* specify what we mean. This requirement would undoubtedly apply with equal force to all who violate the law and are not otherwise excused. However, the assertion with which we are presently concerned seems to entail a special and considerably stronger claim about those who engage in civil disobedience. Otherwise there would be no point in making liability to punishment a distinct characteristic of civil disobedience. And it has not yet been possible to clarify this claim.

The precise nature and content of the disobedient's requirement also needs clarification. Is he required to *seek* punishment (or at least prosecution) for his behavior or merely to accept what the system legitimately imposes upon him? It would not be sensible to insist that civil disobedients plead guilty and refrain from appealing their convictions. Such a restriction would deny dissidents judicial appraisals, which would be an especially invidious deprivation where disobedience was based upon constitutional challenges to laws or policies. As Joseph Ellin has observed, "The idea of taking the penalty probably should be understood to mean not willingness to accept jail but rather the renunciation of all non-legal means (concealment, flight) of avoiding jail. What is intended is the willingness to rely on the law alone as your protection."[5] If this interpretation is accepted—and I think it is an adequate and reasonable rendering of the notion—we are still entitled to ask why this condition should prevail, and as we shall see from the perspective of that question, reliance upon the law does not impose an absolute burden upon the dissident but is in force only so long as he has sufficient confidence in the legal system.

In fact, to understand the punishment claim, it will be necessary to examine the various reasons that are typically given in its behalf. While there are a number of distinguishable reasons, they are all based upon the reformist aims of civil disobedience and the commitment of the disobedient to the political system whose law(s) he is protesting. With one important exception, to be discussed separately, these reasons are generally reducible to the assertion that willingness to pay the penalty is a sign of that commitment and one of the essential means by which the civil disobedient can be distinguished from the revolutionary. In other words, the claim is that by recognizing that the system is entitled to punish him for breaking its laws, the civil disobedient is showing that he accepts the authority of the state and regards it as legitimate even though he feels justified in reacting against this identified breach of justice, the public interest, or constitutionality. The presumptions on which this position builds are that legitimate political authority has the capacity to punish offenders against its laws and that the institution of punish-

5. Joseph Ellin, "Fidelity to Law," *Soundings* LI (Winter 1968), 422, n*.

ment is itself sufficiently justified. Detailed analysis of these positions would require an analysis of punishment per se. Such an analysis would, I believe, suggest that a morally acceptable conception of punishment might be inapplicable to law-breaking that is genuinely undertaken in pursuit of justice or one of the other principles that may underlie rational protest.

For the sake of clarity and illustration, however, I shall assume that it is possible to set forth a theory of punishment that is compatible with the theory of civil disobedience. There is undoubtedly some merit to this assumption, for the power to punish is one of the greatest clubs the state has over an individual. What is more, a person's conscientious and honest recognition that the state is legitimately entitled to punish him for certain specified actions is a valid sign of his loyalty to the political order (and on normative and not merely coercive grounds). This recognition is also an explicit assertion that the conduct in question was genuinely improper and therefore punishable. Similarly, a denial of the state's entitlement to punish appears to be a rejection of its authority. But there is something wrong with both of these propositions. The negative claim is entirely too sweeping; it precludes the possibility of an individual's rejecting the right of the state to punish in a single, identifiable instance. Just as the civil disobedient is not disavowing his obligation *in toto*, neither is the person who resists the penalty denying the right of the state to punish in general when he refuses to accept a specific penalty.[6] Moreover, submission to punishment

6. Throughout this essay, I refer to persons who are otherwise civilly disobedient but who refuse to pay the penalty as "resisters" and to their conduct as "resistance." This terminology is directly borrowed from and inspired by draft "resisters," many of whom engage in or advocate civil disobedience (burning of draft cards, refusal to register for the draft, and refusal to answer induction notices) but who often deny that there is a corresponding requirement to accept the penalty for breaking the law.

is not the only way in which one can show his loyalty to the state, and it is certainly not the most important. If acceptance of penalties were so overriding, most people—because they are rarely in a position to accept or reject penalties—would be incapable of fulfilling their obligations in this manner, and we would be in the odd position of attributing greater political loyalty to criminals who acknowledged their guilt and the entitlement of the state to punish them than to ordinary, law-abiding citizens!

It may be, in fact, that such criminals are more *conscious* of their obligation than are most citizens. By the same token, criminals who *know* they are violating the law and are so successful at it that they are never apprehended and prosecuted are also fully aware of the responsibilities of citizenship. Consciousness undoubtedly has a great deal to do with the concepts of moral and political obligation; performing an obligation intentionally *is* distinguishable from and morally superior to doing so unwittingly, inadvertently, or through force of habit. But I cannot understand what advantage would be gained by making acceptance of lawful penalties a singularly important manifestation of the duty to obey the state. One can at least affirm his political loyalty in other ways than by going to jail willingly. He may obey the law in *general,* pay taxes, and take part in the civic life of the community. There is no reason in *principle* why these options would not be open to resisters. In *fact,* it is often difficult for a resister to register his loyalty in these ways, for he becomes branded as an outlaw and is pursued by the state; in order to save himself he frequently must resort to further and more dramatically illegal acts or leave the country and become a fugitive from the law. Yet this is not an initial sign of diminished loyalty on his part so much as it is a response to actions by the state. But to the extent that the state's actions reveal or are taken as evidence of further deterioration of its good faith, the resister's commitment and obligation may be correspondingly decreased.

None of this is designed to relieve the resister of any political responsibility. If anything, the foregoing should add to the weight of responsibility he already bears, for I have certainly not shown that resisters are free to avoid penalties. What I have suggested, however, is that arguments for a requirement to pay the penalty that are derived from an individual's loyalty to the political order are neither absolute nor unexceptionable. To say that there are exceptions to a principle is to place the burden of justification upon whoever claims to be exempt. Stating and defending one's position is inescapable in any rational enterprise, a category that includes ethics and ethical discourse as well as political action for which a rational or moral basis is alleged. The person who wishes to resist and at the same time wants to be identified as something less than a revolutionary must show that circumstances warrant his use of this tactic, but that he remains basically loyal to the state and, given the opportunity, is willing to discharge his obligations in some manner other than by accepting the penalty for his "criminal" acts. Just how he is to do this convincingly is another matter, but his entire demeanor and the history of his movement to lawbreaking and resistance will certainly be relevant criteria in attempting to assess his sincerity. In the last analysis, however, we are forced back upon good faith and the presumption that one who claims to be acting as moral agent is *in fact* doing so unless there are cogent and compelling reasons for believing the contrary. Perhaps, at this point, a man has nothing more to rely upon than his word; he certainly has the right to have that word taken at its face value. (I am presuming, of course, that the individual's previous behavior, his reputation for honesty, and similar factors will be examined. These are precisely the criteria that we consider in weighing someone's plea that he be regarded as a moral agent.)

As this discussion has made apparent, the purported requirement that civil disobedients pay the penalties (to say nothing of the justification of punishment itself) is closely related to political obligation, that is, the grounds on which it is assumed one is morally required to obey the political order. While it is not clear how being required to pay the penalty and political obligation are related, it is undoubtedly true that the principles justifying one support the other as well. The duty to obey any specific state is derived in part from the legitimacy of that state and its satisfaction of a number of normative and formal criteria, which are mutually supporting factors. The moral capacity of the state to punish —which is a necessary presupposition of the requirement that civil disobedients submit to punishment—is similarly dependent upon the state's being of a certain kind. The components of a minimal political morality would include the existence of periodic and meaningful (and genuinely competitive) elections, the provision of a system of rights and freedoms, the just distribution of political and other social goods, acceptance of formal equality, guaranteed protection of minority rights, and the provision of governmental accountability. A state that failed to live up to these criteria would be punishing people for disobeying unjust laws. The imposition of such penalties would undoubtedly be an important institutional support for an essentially unjustifiable regime, a regime, in other words, to which we would not normally presume any political obligation was owed. Such a political order would still have the capacity to coerce its subjects; in strictly legal terms, it would be entitled to do so. There might even be persons who, for whatever reasons— brainwashing, fear, or because they occupied a certain privileged status—would feel a genuine loyalty to the system and an obligation to it. This would not defeat the claim that the government was not *worthy* of the support of its subjects, for the problem of political obligation invariably includes an attempt to find *objective* criteria that morally justify the claim of any state to the allegiance of its people, regardless of how they might actually be disposed toward it. Furthermore, a state to which no obligation was owed would not be *morally* justified in punishing violators of its laws, for there can be no moral support for attempting to coerce people to act in immoral ways. Nonetheless, the traditional, *formal* justifications of punishment (retribution, deterrence, and reform) would probably apply as fully in such a state as they would in any other instance.

A possible exception to the conclusion reached in the preceding paragraph would be the claim that political obligation is always more pressing than the demands of substantive morality, when these conflict. This proposition cannot be accepted as general rule, for it is contrary to the belief that there is a significant relationship between politics and morality.[7] If political obligation is a species of moral obligation or somehow partakes of it, it is difficult to understand how there could be *any* obligation to a morally unjustifiable state, unless there were a substantive moral rule that proscribed all resistance. Such rules, it is worth noting, are characteristic either of authoritarian political philosophies (or philosophies that have no apparent way of staving off political absolutism) or of religious and mystical doctrines that predicate a "higher" order in which the evils and immoralities of this world assume a relative unimportance and therefore become less objectionable. It seems paradoxical, however, and quite immoral, to assert that there is a substantive moral rule that has

7. However, I acknowledge that moral considerations do not necessarily defeat all opposing claims. See, for instance, Huntington Terrell, "Are Moral Considerations Always Overriding?" *Australasian Journal of Philosophy* XLVII (May 1969), 51-70.

the effect of requiring one to cooperate in the perpetuation of immorality.

Christian casuists of the sixteenth and seventeenth centuries certainly recognized this dilemma but often refused to embrace what should have been an inescapable right to revolution. Instead, they advised their followers to obey God when the laws of the sovereign commanded them to sin but to endure the punishments of the temporal ruler for their defiance. Surely these men saw the absurdity of sanctioning a penalty that was imposed for the refusal to act immorally! Need I add, just to put all accounts in order, that in these terms I think Socrates was wrong to accept the sentence of the Athenian court and that he set a foolish, bad, and incorrect precedent?

The argument about the civil disobedient's taking the penalty presumes that the state punishing him is one to which he should (morally) be loyal and toward which he should display some signs of commitment. Without this presumption, there would be no point in saying that acceptance of the penalty is an indication of the disobedient's basic acceptance of the system. Showing loyalty and recognizing and acting upon one's political obligations are undoubtedly morally required and therefore praiseworthy acts; if they were not, they could not be used as positive normative supports for paying the penalty. This, in turn, presupposes that the political order punishing a disobedient is *worthy of* and *morally entitled* to his loyalty, which means that it is morally acceptable. Other things being equal, the presumption of moral acceptability should be made about any political order that, at least superficially and initially, does not appear to be immoral. But what if the presumption turns out to have been unfounded? How obliged is a civil disobedient to accept the penalty meted out by a state that is not objectively entitled to his allegiance? Political obligation is not an all-or-nothing relationship; one is not either totally bound to the state or altogether free of its claims on his loyalty. In part, political duty is a result of the state's having satisfied the criteria that would entitle it to be called "moral." Its failure to meet these standards decreases its moral hold over its members, and the resulting situation can be characterized as one of "diminished obligation." In the absence of a "perfectly and fully just and moral" state to which one would be perpetually and absolutely obliged,[8] men live under politics that more or less achieve justice and to which they are, accordingly, more or less obliged. A state to which something less than full commitment and obedience is owed is also less than fully justified in punishing violations of its laws. So long as the disobedience is part of a rational protest and is undertaken in concert with an appeal to those respects in which the state's claim to obedience is diminished, it seems especially difficult to justify punishing it.

One objection that should be dealt with is the claim that obligation is owed to the political system as a whole and not to specific laws. Therefore, disobedience of particular laws could not be an entitlement that followed from diminished obligation. An obvious difficulty with this position is its implication that obligation cannot be differentially acted upon. If obedience and disobedience to specific laws are not the instrumentalities through which obligation is expressed, one

8. This, in itself, is a paradoxical notion, for the possibility of disobedience would not be readily conceivable in such a state, and the problem of political obligation would therefore be irrelevant. Questions about the duty to obey are raised and dealt with only in the face of potential disobedience, which is a calling into question of the state's putative morality. To defend such a state would be to open that very question of its justness, which might well lead to change. See Alasdair MacIntyre, "A Mistake about Causality in Social Science," *Philosophy, Politics, and Society*, 2nd ser., Peter Laslett and W. G. Runciman, eds. (Oxford, 1963), chap. III, for a further discussion. I have attempted to compress here much that was derived from several years of conversations with William D. Burns.

has no alternative but to obey fully or to withdraw his allegiance altogether. Law,[9] after all, *is* the basic medium with which the state confronts the individual; one does not obey or disobey the state per se, but certain of its laws. To call a state "moral" or "immoral," therefore, is to characterize and evaluate its body of laws and policies and the way in which its citizens are treated. By the same token, we frequently use these characterizations to refer to *specific* laws and regulations. One of the things we presumably mean by the term "bad (or immoral) laws" is that (in some ideal way and to an extent not fully specified) such laws are not worthy of the obedience of the state's citizens. To deny the entitlement of a regime itself to political obedience would be equivalent to saying that the preponderance, if not all, of its laws was immoral. But it would be impossible to make such a judgment until the immorality of a great many individual laws was experienced. The view that political obligation is discharged by obeying the state *per se* rather than specific laws predicates the logical impossibility of violating *some* laws but not all of them as a means of fulfilling a diminished obligation to the state. The effective distinction between the civil disobedient (to say nothing of the resister) and the revolutionary thus disappears: one either obeys his state (and therefore its laws) or he does not; the number and kinds of laws he violates and how he does so become irrelevant. It follows that the behavior known as civil disobedience becomes meaningless.

While this is a *logically* tenable position, it is generally useless except perhaps as a club over the heads of dissidents—or the justification behind such a club. Moreover, I think this claim is incorrect. Political obligation, as Margaret MacDonald observed, is not merely an abstract matter of allegiance in general. It is at least equally a problem that expresses itself in

9. I am using "law" quite broadly here to include not only enactments of the government but also its policies and the orders of its officials.

concrete situations when individuals ask, "Should I obey *this* law *now?*" and "Why?"[10] When one disobeys a law, he is, to be sure, disobeying the regime that issued or enforces that law, but he is not necessarily rejecting that regime or questioning its entitlements to pass or make laws. In fact, considerations of one's *general* obligation to his state will always enter into and usually weigh against a calculation of whether or not to disobey a particular law. Once again, there appears to be an unavoidable and probably unconscious presumption in favor of the acceptability of a regime as a whole, which permits one to maintain his essential loyalty even though he questions and perhaps rejects and disobeys some laws. Thus, the insistence that political systems and not laws are to be obeyed ignores the reality of acts of political disobedience as well as the way in which feelings of obligation are built up or diminished. What is more, to assert that the state's hold over its citizens is so total and unexceptionable flies in the face of some of the most significant bases of democracy. The inability of this interpretation to contain or account for civil disobedience—let alone resistance—reveals the irrelevance and wrong-headedness of its rigidity.

The preceding have all been essentially *moral* arguments, stemming from the concept of political obligation, that have attempted to explain why civil disobedients are not necessarily required to pay the penalty for breaking the law as an act of protest. There is a more *political* consideration from which the same conclusion can be extracted: the state may be abusing the very process of prosecution and punishment and using it to accomplish political ends rather than to provide justice. The trials of Dr. Spock and his co-defendants, the Catonsville Nine, the Milwaukee Fourteen, and the Chicago "Conspiracy" all revealed the near impossibility of using the

10. Margaret MacDonald, "The Language of Political Theory," in *Logic and Language*, 1st ser., Antony Flew, ed. (Oxford, 1952), chap. IX.

judicial process in the United States to establish rational discourse and open an honest consideration of the issues where the core of the government's policy is under attack. "Repression" is a strong word, but it does not seem inappropriate when applied to these trials. However much one might wish to condemn the antics of the Chicago "Conspiracy" and their disdain for the sacred judicial tribunal and its procedures, it is becoming evident that their behavior was the only option open to them in the face of the contemptuous conduct of Judge Hoffman and the government attorneys. Only by responding as they did were the defendants able to keep the actual issues alive and before the public (even if they were not appreciated in the courtroom) and to drive home to a wide audience the idea that the government itself was perverting justice while claiming and hiding behind the protective cover of legality. Despite the formal indictments, the points at issue in the Chicago trial were not whether these eight individuals had crossed state lines with "intent" to cause a riot in violation of a federal statute (of questionable constitutionality) or whether they had "conspired" to cause a riot. The real questions were why so many "youths" are "turned off" by the government of the United States, why so many persons should have felt it was necessary to come to Chicago to demonstrate at the 1968 Democratic National Convention, and why they were deprived of their constitutionally protected rights of assembly and dissent. It was these questions that Judge Hoffman kept the defendants from raising overtly, and he did so by a series of acts that added significantly to the radical contention that the entire political process in the United States is a sham!

A great many people have found it difficult and uncomfortable to accept the actions of the Chicago defendants as a form of protest. Their behavior has not been judged from this perspective, for the courtroom and its trappings are sacrosanct, probably among the most widely accepted symbols of political legitimacy in the United States. But that is precisely what they are, *symbols* of legitimacy, which need not change in outward appearance even after legitimacy itself has disappeared. (Of course, symbols also create and strengthen legitimacy, as well as represent it, by fostering positive feelings toward a regime or political system; there are psychological senses in which symbols are indistinguishable from both the regime that uses them and the legitimacy they stand for or are intended to instill.) These particular symbols also play an extremely important substantive role in the preservation of legitimacy, for their practical function is to provide presumably neutral procedures through which grievances may be fairly and equitably redressed. In theory, the courtroom comes closer than any other institution to being the arena within which rational and open discourse can occur. The judicial process, unlike legislative debates or executive decision-making, necessarily includes the citizen. And the rational and "fair" deliberation that we like to believe is characteristic of our courtrooms is fundamentally identical to the spirit that should pervade democratic decision-making. All these factors undoubtedly combine to create popular reverence for the judiciary and help to blur the distinction between substance and symbol. When the judicial procedure has been corrupted or subverted and has lost its hold on the loyalty of citizens, much more has been lost than a deliberative and adjudicating apparatus.

The courtroom behavior of the "Conspirators" suggests their feelings that the judicial procedure was indeed being abused by the government and by the judge himself. (We often forget that judges and courts are governmental instrumentalities despite their role of deciding conflicts between individuals and the state. The symbolic function of the judiciary contributes to this forgetfulness.) Rather than the substantive furthering of the democratic process, the Chicago trial was an instance of the manipulation of symbols by the government. It was a grand show that purported to demonstrate that the channels of lawful decision-making were still open but which actually illustrated how easily those forms can be used to accomplish ends that are antithetical to their very purposes! Although they were not faced by the utter madness of a Julius Hoffman, the Spock-Coffin, Catonsville, and Milwaukee groups were not better served by their trials. The difference, however, is that they went along with the game, and the subversion of justice in their cases remains relatively obscured and unknown. (I do not mean to suggest that the Catonsville and Milwaukee groups had not broken the law or that there was no *legal* entitlement to punish them, but their conduct was part of a rational protest, and the reasons why they destroyed draft records were not properly considered in their trials. They were tried and convicted simply for the destruction of government property.)

Even if one objects to my characterization of recent trials in the United States, the use of the judicial process to achieve political ends is hardly unknown.[11] Where this practice exists or where there is reasonable belief that it does, the arguments for paying the penalty for illegal acts of rational protest are considerably weakened. One of the most important reasons for actually submitting to a trial and possible punishment is to increase the chances of getting a hearing and thereby winning converts. But when the state has virtually eliminated this possibility or has so increased the penalties as to make it

11. See Otto Kirscheimer, *Political Justice: The Use of Legal Procedures for Political Ends* (Princeton, 1961). On recent American trials see Jessica Mitford, *The Trial of Dr. Spock* (New York, 1969); Francine du Plessix Gray, *Divine Disobedience: Profiles in Catholic Radicalism* (New York, 1970), pp. 134-228; Daniel Berrigan, *The Trial of the Catonsville Nine* (Boston, 1970); and J. Anthony Lukas, *The Barnyard Epithet and Other Obscenities: Notes on the Chicago Conspiracy Trial* (New York, 1970).

a very unattractive alternative, there are hardly any prudential justifications for standing trial and certainly no moral
ones! This response by the state has interesting implications
for the theory of political protest and disobedience. The
penalty need not be regarded as simply the application of a
sanction and the legal consequence of breaking the law (as
Hans Kelsen, for instance, would view it),[12] but can be looked
upon as a law or policy in its own right that is unjustifiable
and can or should be violated on much the same grounds that
the initial law was broken. So conceived, resistance becomes a
further instance of civil disobedience. One important difference, however, is that in traditionally conceived civil disobedience, one knows what law he is violating, but resisting
the penalty (unless one literally flees the courtroom or
"jumps bail" on appeal) is, in effect, a prediction that the
punishment will be excessive or that the trial will be a
political persecution rather than a fair and rational hearing.

Kelsen's insistence upon the inescapable relation between
the positive requirements of a law and the sanctions applied
for violating it suggests a further potential support for resistance, which can only be mentioned here and not fully
pursued. A person who believes that he is entitled to disobey
a law ought on the same grounds to feel justified in refusing
to pay the penalty, for the punishment is actually a further
aspect of that very law. The disobedient has already rejected
his putative *legal* obligation to obey that particular law. Since
the obligation to pay the penalty is equally legal and cannot
logically be separated from the law, the sanction is no more
obliging than the law itself. Such a claim would probably not
meet with Professor Kelsen's approval, for his pure theory

12. Kelsen's conception of the relationship of the sanction to the positive re-
quirements of the law can be found in all his legal writings. See, most recently,
Kelsen, *The Pure Theory of Law,* trans. by Max Knight (Berkeley and Los
Angeles, 1967), esp. pp. 108-21.

recognizes no relevant considerations other than legal ones, but I think that the *logic* of this position is consistent with his views.

This same position can be given a slightly normative twist that has nothing to do with Kelsen but is a further variation of the political argument in favor of resistance. If the imposed penalty is or is felt to be inseparable from the violated law and if paying that penalty would defeat the purpose of having broken the law, there are reasons for resisting. This is especially important if one has based his civil disobedience upon moral or political claims (rather than legal-constitutional ones) to begin with, for he has already committed himself to the *legal* right of the system to adopt the objectionable law and is using civil disobedience to gain moral and political leverage over the law-making process. In conservation and ecological issues, this is particularly significant, for there are few legal bars to many of the objectionable practices that the government either engages in or sanctions. In this respect, submitting to the penalty would be too strong an acceptance of the notion that the political order is entitled to pass whatever laws it wishes so long as it stays within the letter of legality. In the final analysis, this is undoubtedly a correct view of democratic politics and of the way in which political choices are made among competing public values. However, if accepting the punishment becomes nothing more than an expression of one's right to differ with the political system, and if this acceptance would weaken the civil disobedient's case, he might be better advised on tactical and prudential grounds to resist.

Prudential and practical considerations, on the other hand, provide some of the strongest arguments *against* resistance. To understand this, we must keep in mind that civil disobedience begins as a form of protest and that its initial aim is to bring about change by eliciting the support of others.

Accordingly, publicity is very important, for it calls attention to the civil disobedient and to his objections. The same factors that dictate that civil disobedience be public—and virtually all commentators agree that this is one of the essential characteristics of civil disobedience—thus provide reasons for submitting to trial and punishment, assuming, of course, that the trial is actually an open hearing and that the punishment is not so great as to outweigh the advantages of accepting it. Also, many people may be inclined to accept the principles about commitment to the state and showing of good faith and sincerity that I have criticized. Such people might therefore be more willing to adopt the views of the persons they believe were principled, nonrevolutionary, and committed to their objectives. While it may not be a valid sign, the willingness of people to endure hardships for their convictions is often interpreted as a measure of the sincerity and worthiness of those positions. Paying the penalty has a significant degree of persuasive power.

At some point this position would logically have to be abandoned, for it would eventually lead to the absurd notion that those who are most willing to suffer have the best principles and the highest dedication and, accordingly, are entitled to the greatest support from others. This tendency to equate virtue with sacrifice and hardship goes considerably beyond the presumed relationship of punishment to civil disobedience and is undoubtedly a component of bourgeois ideology. The notion has no moral or logical validity; it nonetheless exists, and the would-be reformer who wishes to attract followers but forgets or ignores the prevalence of this belief does so to the peril of his objectives.

What this means, in short, is that despite the limited validity of the arguments that are usually advanced for taking the penalty, there are strong and potentially overriding political reasons for submitting. Thus, a civil disobedient who intends to engage in resistance has a morally compelling obligation to justify himself and to evince his loyalty to the system. He ought to be equally prepared, for tactical and political reasons, to state concisely and intelligently why he feels entitled to reject the established procedures and to refuse to submit to the penalty that may be imposed upon him for disobeying. But in order to defend his position, a disobedient individual must have access to the media that would make his claims known to the public at large. No political system can possess the publicity advantage the United States government now has over dissidents without violating an important part of the entire rational, democratic process. Where such a condition exists, civil disobedience, resistance, and other more extreme forms of protest are bound to occur. And they will be politically and morally justifiable because of the objective political situation.

Three
THE RESPONSIBILITIES OF PHILOSOPHERS

Introduction

At the present time in the United States urgent calls to action are addressed to citizens in general: to bring the Indochina war to a rapid end, to promote justice and peace in race relations, to eradicate poverty, to save the cities from decay, to perform many other urgent social tasks.

The general urgency of these concerns does not answer for individuals and institutions the question what *they* should do about them. Moreover, since these crises are in areas where government has been wrong or insufficient, the question is not being answered by a government-directed mobilization, as it would be for example, in a war which found general support.

These concerns have been especially vividly felt in professional and intellectual circles. They have touched off a great debate about the social and political responsibilities of scholars, intellectuals, and professionals generally, and of institutions such as universities and professional societies.

Is there *philosophical* work which the philosopher can do which is relevant to public issues? The concern of many philosophers in the past with the good state and society would suggest an affirmative answer. But the 'analytic' philosophy which has prevailed in American universities in recent years usually goes with an apparently narrower definition of the philosopher's task, restricting him to the analysis of concepts and of language, and sometimes excluding from philosophy substantive commitments in matters of value.

In the context provided by his radically critical view of American power and the intentions with which it is wielded,[1] Noam Chomsky suggests below that philosophers with this analytic training can do useful work in analyzing and criticizing the ideologies of power. He clearly intends not to accept the exclusion of moral judgment from philosophy. Though not without sympathy for it, he also rejects the widely advanced view that *as such* a professional has no social or political obligations.

A related part of 'liberal orthodoxy' attacked in recent years by radicals is the view that universities and other such institutions ought to be politically neutral. Robert Simon finds below that this view can still, with qualifications, be defended.

Lewis Schwartz analyzes in some detail the whole question of neutrality and public responsibility in the academic world. He deprecates the importance of the defined roles of individuals and institutions, and argues that they should assess their responsibilities directly, on the merits of the issues. For Schwartz, this argument works against neutrality and toward activism.

Stuart Hampshire finds in the political attitudes of Bertrand Russell in his old age a starting point for a discussion of the underlying ideologies and conceptions of rationality of the apologists for and radical opponents of the Vietnam war. He takes up again the issues in moral philosophy at stake in the discussions of Part I, introducing a new opposition, that between 'utilitarian' and 'natural law' conceptions of practical reason.

1. This view is developed at length in his *American Power and the New Mandarins* (New York: Pantheon, 1969).

8

Philosophers and Public Policy[1]

NOAM CHOMSKY

For a number of reasons, I have found it extraordinarily difficult to write about this topic. Perhaps it would help set the stage for a discussion if I were to begin by mentioning some of these, even though to do so, I will have to digress somewhat. The first problem is that I am approaching the topic of the symposium from several premises which themselves require argument and justification, although this is not the place to elaborate them. My response to this topic must naturally be based on a certain interpretation of the context in which questions of public policy arise in the United States at this particular historical moment, an interpretation which obviously cannot fail to be controversial but which, within

From *Ethics,* vol. 79 (October 1968). Copyright 1968 by the University of Chicago. Reprinted by permission of the author and publisher.
1. This paper was read at the May, 1968, meetings of the Western Division of the American Philosophical Association, in a symposium on this topic. It was not originally intended for publication and therefore incorporates some material from other writings that are now in press, in a collection of essays entitled *American Power and the New Mandarins* (New York: Pantheon Books.) [Published in 1969—eds.]

   When the paper was given, I had no specific model in mind of the work that a philosopher might do, entirely within the framework of his professional activities, on issues of the sort discussed here. One has since appeared, namely, the very thoughtful essay by Ronald Dworkin on "Civil Disobedience," *New York Review of Books,* June 6, 1968.

the framework of this symposium, I cannot develop but can only formulate as a basis for my own discussion of the topic. One premise is that the country faces a serious crisis and that, because of our international role, our crisis is a world crisis as well. Increasingly, the United States has become both the agent of repression and—to use Howard Zinn's phrase—"the white-gloved financier of counter-revolution" throughout the world.[2] It is, by any objective standard that I can imagine, the most aggressive country in the world, the greatest threat to world peace, and without parallel as a source of violence. In part, this violence is quite overt—I need say little about our behavior in Vietnam. In part it is more subtle, the violence of the status quo, the muted endless terror that we have imposed on vast areas that are under our control or susceptible to our influence. Americans are no more likely to accept such a judgment than were citizens of Japan or Germany thirty years ago. However, an objective analysis seems to me to permit no other evaluation. If we consider governments maintained in power by force or overthrown through subversion or intrigue, or the willingness to use the most awesome killing machine in history to enforce our rule, or the means employed—saturation bombing, free-strike zones, napalm and anti-personnel weapons, chemical warfare—there seems to me no other conclusion: we are simply without a rival today as an agent of international criminal violence.

There is, furthermore, a serious domestic crisis. Again, I need not speak of the problems of racism and poverty, which are all too obvious. What deserves some comment, however, is the callousness with which we react to the misery we impose. This is perhaps most evident in the growing opposition to the war in Vietnam. It is no secret to anyone that the war is highly unpopular. It is also no secret that the opposition to the war is based primarily on its cost. It is a "pragmatic op-

2. *Vietnam: The Logic of Withdrawal* (Boston: Beacon Press, 1967), p. 50.

position," motivated by calculations of cost and utility. Many of those who are now most vociferous in expressing their opposition to the war announce—in fact proclaim—that their opposition would cease if our effort to control and organize Vietnamese society were to prove successful. In that case, in the words of one such spokesman, we would "all be saluting the wisdom and statesmanship of the American government" (Arthur Schlesinger), even though, as he is the first to point out, we are turning Vietnam into "a land of ruin and wreck."[3] This pragmatic opposition holds that we should "take our stand" where the prospects for success are greater, that Vietnam is a lost cause, and, *for this reason,* that our efforts there should be modified or abandoned.

I do not want to debate the issue here but only to formulate a second premise from which my discussion of the topic of this meeting will begin: namely, that this quite pervasive pragmatic attitude toward the war in Vietnam is a sign of moral degeneration so severe that talk of using the normal channels of protest and dissent becomes meaningless and that various forms of resistance provide the most significant course of political action open to a concerned citizen.

Nothing supports this judgment more clearly, in my opinion, than the recent change in the domestic political climate, dramatized by the President's announcement that he will not seek reelection. The political commentators would have it that this event demonstrates that our political system is, after all, healthy and functioning. Confronted with the collapse of its war plans, an international economic crisis, and threatening internal conflicts, the Administration has, in effect, resigned—to put it in parliamentary terms. This shows the health of our democratic system. By such standards, an even more viable democratic system was that of Fascist Japan

3. Arthur M. Schlesinger, Jr., *The Bitter Heritage* (Boston: Houghton Mifflin, 1967), pp. 34, 47.

thirty years ago, where more than a dozen cabinets fell under not-dissimilar circumstances. What would have demonstrated the health of our system would have been a change of policy based on the realization that the policy was wrong, not that it was failing—a realization that success in such a policy would have been a tragedy. Nothing could be more remote from the American political consciousness. It is held, rather, that it is the peculiar genius of the American politics of accommodation to exclude moral considerations. How natural, then, and how good that only pragmatic considerations of cost and utility should determine whether we devastate another country, drive its people from their villages, and carry out the experiments with "material and human resources control" that so delight the "pacification theorist."

Three times in a generation American technology has laid waste a helpless Asian country. This fact should be seared into the consciousness of every American. A person who is not obsessed with this realization is living in a world of fantasy. But we have not, as a nation, learned to face this central fact of contemporary history. The systematic destruction of a virtually defenseless Japan was carried out with a sense of moral rectitude that was then, and remains today, unchallenged—or nearly so. In fact, Secretary of War Henry Stimson said at the time that there was something wrong with a nation that could listen with such equanimity to the reports of the terror bombing of Japanese cities. There were few voices to echo his doubts—which were expressed before the two atom bombs, before the grand finale requested by General Arnold and approved in Washington, a one thousand plane raid on central Japan launched after the surrender had been announced but before it had been officially received, a raid in which, according to the report of victims, the bombs were interspersed with leaflets announcing that Japan had surrendered. In Korea, the process was repeated, with only a few qualms. It is the amazing resistance of the Vietnamese that has forced us to ask: What have we done? There is little doubt that, were this resistance to collapse, the domestic furor over the war would disappear along with it.

Such facts as these—and endless details can all too easily be supplied—raise the question whether what is needed in the United States today is dissent or denazification. The question is a debatable one. Reasonable men may differ. The fact that the question is even debatable is a tragedy. I believe myself that what is needed is a kind of denazification. There is, of course, no more powerful force that can call us to account. The change will have to come from within. The fate of millions of poor and oppressed people throughout the world will be determined by our ability to carry out a profound "cultural revolution" in the United States.

It might be argued that it is naïve to discuss political and moral consciousness as if they were other than a surface manifestation of social institutions and the power structure and that, no matter what individual Americans may think and feel and believe, the American system will continue to try to dominate the earth by force. The inductive argument for the latter thesis is substantial. The Vietnam war is hardly without precedent in our history. It is, for example, distressingly like our colonial venture in the Philippines seventy years ago. What is more, it is remarkably similar to other episodes in the history of colonialism, for example, the Japanese attempt to defend the independence of Manchukuo from the "Communist threat" posed by Russia and the "Chinese bandits." Nevertheless, it is difficult to believe that American society will collapse from its own "internal contradictions" if it does not proceed to dominate the world. The belief that "the American system could survive in America only if it became a world system"—to quote President Truman in 1947—has, indeed, guided our international policy for many years, as has the belief, enunciated by liberal and conservative alike, that access to ever expanding markets and opportunities for investment is necessary for the survival of the American Way of Life. There is, no doubt, a large component of myth in this ideology. In any event, the question is somewhat academic. Whether we aim for reform or revolution, the early steps must be the same: an attempt to modify political and moral consciousness and to construct alternative institutional forms that reflect and support this development. Personally, I believe that our present crisis is in some measure, moral and intellectual rather than institutional and that reason and resistance can go a certain way, perhaps a long way, toward ameliorating it.

Considerations such as these—which I have not tried to justify but only to formulate—seem to me to provide the framework within which an American should ask himself what is his responsibility as a citizen. About this question there is a great deal to be said, and still more to be done. It is not, however, the question to which this session is addressed, and this is the central fact that causes my difficulty, noted at the outset, in trying to discuss the narrower topic of philosophers and public policy. At a time when we are waging a war of indescribable savagery against Vietnam—in the interests of the Vietnamese, of course, as the Japanese were merely trying to create an earthly paradise in Manchukuo—at a time when we are preparing for and in part already conducting other "limited wars" at home and abroad, at a time when thousands of young men, many of them our students, are facing jail or political exile because of their conscientious refusal to be agents of criminal violence, at a time when we are once again edging the world toward nuclear war, at such a time it is difficult to restrict oneself to the narrower question: What is one's responsibility *as a philosopher?* Nevertheless, I will try to do so.

I think it is possible to construct a reasonable argument to the effect that one has no particular responsibility, as a philosopher, to take a stand on questions of public policy, whatever one's duties may be as a citizen. The argument might proceed as follows. To hold that philosophers have some special responsibility in this regard suggests either that they have some unique competence to deal with the problems we face or that others—say biologists or mathematicians—are somehow more free to put these problems aside. But neither conclusion is correct. There is no specific competence that one attains through his professional training as a philosopher to deal with the problems of international or domestic repression, or, in general, with critique and implementation of public policy. Similarly, it is absurd to claim that biologists or mathematicians may freely dismiss these problems on the grounds that others have the technical expertise and moral responsibility to confront them. As a professional, one has only the duty of doing his work with integrity. Integrity, both personal and scholarly, demands that we face the questions that arise internally in some particular domain of study, that are on the border of research, and that promise to move the search for truth and understanding forward. It would be a sacrifice of such integrity to allow external factors to determine the course of research. This would represent a kind of "subversion of scholarship." The most meaningful contribution that an individual can make toward a more decent society is to base his life's work on an authentic commitment to important values, such as those that underlie serious scholarly or scientific work, in any field. But this demands that, as a professional, he stick to his last.

I think this argument has a good deal of force. I do not doubt that those who pursued their work at the Goethe Institute, in the shadow of Dachau, justified themselves by such considerations as these. Two or three years ago, I would have accepted this line of argument as correct, and it still seems to be persuasive.

There is, of course, an apparent counterargument: namely, that in a time of crisis one should abandon, or at least restrict, professional concerns and activities that do not adapt themselves in a natural way toward the resolution of this crisis. This argument is actually consistent with the first; and it can, I think, be maintained that this is all there is to the matter.

I think that for many professionals this may well be all that there is to the matter. I do not, for example, see any way to make my work as a linguist relevant, in any serious sense, to the problems of domestic or international society. The only relevance is remote and indirect, through the insight that such work might provide into the nature of human intelligence. But to accept that connection as "relevance" would be hypocrisy. The only solution I can see, in this case, is a schizophrenic existence, which seems to me morally obligatory and not at all impossible, in practice.

Philosophers, however, may be in a somewhat more fortunate position. There is no profession that can claim with greater authenticity that its concern is the intellectual culture of the society or that it possesses the tools for the analysis of ideology and the critique of social knowledge and its use. If it is correct to regard the American and world crisis as in part a cultural one, then philosophical analysis may have a definite contribution to make. Let me consider a few cases in point.

Our society stands in awe of "technical expertise" and gives great prestige and considerable latitude of action to the person who lays claim to it. In fact, it is widely maintained that we are becoming the first "post-industrial society," a society in which the dominant figure will be not the entrepreneur but the technical expert or even the scientist, those who create and apply the knowledge that is, for the first time in history,

the major motive force for social progress. According to this view, the university and the research institution will be the "creative eye," the central institutions of this new society, and the academic specialist will be the "new man" whose values will become dominant and who will himself be at or near the center of power.

There are many who look forward to this prospect with great hope. I am not one of them. It seems to me a prospect that is not appealing and that has many dangers. For one thing, the assumption that the state can be the source of effective social action is highly dubious. Furthermore, what reason is there to believe that those whose claim to power is based on knowledge and technique—or at least the claim to knowledge and technique—will be more humane and just in the exercise of power than those whose claim is based on wealth or aristocratic privilege? On the contrary, one might expect such a person to be arrogant, inflexible, incapable of admitting or adjusting to failure, since failure undermines his claim to power. To take just the most obvious instance, consider the Vietnam war, which was in large measure designed by the new breed of "action intellectuals" and which manifests all of these characteristics.

What is more, it is natural to expect that any group with access to power will construct an ideology that justifies its dominance on grounds of the general welfare. When it is the intelligentsia who aspire to power, the danger is even greater than before, since they can capitalize on the prestige of science and technology while, at the same time, now drawn into the mechanism of control, they lose their role as social critics. Perhaps the most important role of the intellectual since the enlightenment has been that of unmasking ideology, exposing the injustice and repression that exists in every society that we know, and seeking the way to a new and higher form of social life that will extend the possibilities for a free and creative life. We can confidently expect this role to be abandoned as the intellectual becomes the administrator of a new society.

These observations are hardly novel. I am simply paraphrasing a classical anarchist critique, of which typical expressions are the following:

Commenting on Marxian doctrine, Bakunin had this to say:

> According to the theory of Mr. Marx, the people not only must not destroy [the state] but must strengthen it and place it at the complete disposal of their benefactors, guardians, and teachers—the leaders of the Communist party, namely Mr. Marx and his friends, who will proceed to liberate [mankind] in their own way. They will concentrate the reins of government in a strong hand, because the ignorant people require an exceedingly firm guardianship; they will establish a single state bank, concentrating in its hands all commercial, industrial, agricultural and even scientific production, and then divide the masses into two armies—industrial and agricultural—under the direct command of the state engineers, who will constitute a new privileged scientific-political estate.[4]

Or compare the more general remarks by the anarchist historian Rudolf Rocker:

> Political rights do not originate in parliaments; they are rather forced upon them from without. And even their enactment into law has for a long time been no guarantee of their security. They do not exist because they have been legally set down on a piece of paper, but only when they have become the ingrown habit of a people, and when any

---

4. "Statehood and Anarchy," 1873; cited in P. Avrich, *The Russian Anarchists* (Princeton, N.J.: Princeton University Press, 1967), pp. 93-94.

attempt to impair them will meet with the violent resistance of the populace. Where this is not the case, there is no help in any parliamentary opposition or any Platonic appeals to the constitution. One compels respect from others when one knows how to defend one's dignity as a human being. This is not only true in private life; it has always been the same in political life as well.[5]

History has shown the accuracy of this analysis, both with respect to the role of an intellectual elite and with respect to the nature of political rights, whoever may rule. I see little reason to expect the future to show otherwise.

If it is true that the new, "post-industrial" society will be marked by the access to power of an intellectual elite, basing its claim to power on a presumably "value free" technology of social management, then the importance of the social critic becomes more crucial than ever before. This critic must be capable of analyzing the content of the claimed "expertise," its empirical justification, and its social use. These are typical questions of philosophy. The same analytical approach that seeks to explore the nature of scientific theories in general or the structure of some particular domain of knowledge or to investigate the concept of a human action can be turned to the study of the technology of control and manipulation that goes under the name of "behavioral science" and that serves as the basis for the ideology of the "new mandarins." Furthermore, this task will be of greater human significance, for the foreseeable future, than the investigation of the foundations of physics or the possibility of reducing mental states to brain states—questions that I do not, incidentally, mean to disparage—I hope that is clear.

I think it would be important for the university to provide

5. "Anarchism and Anarchosyndicalism," in *European Ideologies* (New York: Philosophical Library); reprinted in P. Eltzbacher (ed.), *Anarchism* (London: Freedom Press, 1960), p. 257.

the framework for critical work of this sort. The matter goes well beyond politics in a narrow sense. There are inherent dangers in professionalization that are not sufficiently recognized in university structure. There is a tendency, as a field becomes truly professionalized, for its problems to be determined less by considerations of intrinsic interest and more by the availability of certain tools that have been developed as the subject matures. Philosophy is not free from this tendency, of course. In part, this is of course not only unavoidable but even essential for scientific progress. But it is important to find a way, in teaching even more than in research, to place the work that is feasible and productive at a certain moment against the background of the general concerns that make some questions, but not others, worth pursuing. It is easy to give examples to show how certain fields have been seriously distorted by a failure to maintain this perspective. For example, I think it is possible to show that certain simple and very useful experimental ideas in the psychology of learning have for many psychologists taken on the status of conditions that define the subject matter of learning theory, much to the detriment of the field, in the long run. I think that in most academic fields a graduate student would benefit greatly from the experience, rarely offered in any academic program, of defending the significance of the field of work in which he is engaged and facing the challenge of a point of view and a critique that does not automatically accept the premises and limitations of scope that are to be found in any discipline. I am putting this too abstractly, but I think the point is clear, and I think that it indicates a defect of much of university education.

In the specific case of social and behavioral science in a "post-industrial society" with the university as a central institution of innovation and authority, the defect may become a disaster. To put it succinctly, the university requires a conscience, free from the controls that are implicit in any association with the organs of power, from any role in the formation and implementation of public policy. I think that any serious university should be thinking about how it might institute a program of radical social inquiry that would examine the premises of public policy and attempt a critical analysis of the prevailing ideology. Ideally, such a program should, perhaps, not even have separate faculty associated with it but should, rather, seek to involve as wide a segment of the university community as possible in far-reaching social criticism. A program of this sort would be a natural and valuable outgrowth of the philosopher's concern for conceptual analysis.

Again, I would like to stress that the issue is not one of politics in a narrow sense. I think that the applications of behavioral science in education or therapy, to mention just two examples, are as much in need of critical analysis as the applications to counterinsurgency. And the assumptions and values that lie behind the poverty program or urban renewal deserve the same serious analysis as those that lie behind the manipulative diplomacy of the postwar era. A dozen other examples could easily be cited. In the kind of liberal technocracy that we are likely to evolve, repression may be somewhat more masked and the technique of control more "sophisticated." A new coercive ideology, professing both humane values and "the scientific ethic," might easily become the intellectual property of the technical intelligentsia, which is based in the university but moves fairly freely to government and foundations. The fragmentation and professionalization that accompanies the decline of the "free-floating intellectual" who, we are told, is a relic from an earlier stage of society, can itself contribute to new forms of social control and intellectual impoverishment. This is not a necessary development, but it is also not an unlikely one. And it is one that we must find a way to resist, as much as we must find ways to resist other less subtle forms of barbarism. It would be entirely within the tradition of philosophy if it were to regard this task as its own.

More specific problems might be mentioned. Let me bring up just one. We all know that thousands of young men may be found guilty of "civil disobedience" for following the dictates of their conscience in the next few months and may suffer severe penalties for their willingness to live by the values that many of us profess. It would be a serious error to regard this as merely a matter of enforcement of law. The substantive content of the law is determined, to a significant extent, by the level of intellectual culture and moral perception of the society in general. If philosophers feel that these matters are part of their concern, then they must contribute to shaping the principles and understanding that determine what the interpretation of the law will be in concrete instances. To mention simply the most obvious question: Why is it not "civil disobedience" for the President to violate domestic and international law by the use of force in Vietnam, while it is civil disobedience for young men to refuse to serve as agents of criminal acts? The answer to this question has little to do with the law, and much to do with the distribution of force in our society. The courts are not capable of deciding that it is illegal to send an American expeditionary force to crush a rebellion in some foreign land, because of the social consequences that would ensue from that decision. When a powerful executive carries out criminal acts with impunity, the concept "government of laws" erodes beyond recognition, and the entire framework of law disintegrates. Those who would like to believe that their commitment is to truth, not power, cannot remain silent in the face of this travesty. It is too late to create a climate of opinion that will enable the judiciary to function, thus saving men from imprisonment for conscientious resistance to a demand that they be war criminals. It is not too late to work for a reconstruction of values and for the creation of a more healthy intellectual community to which these men can return as welcome and honored members. Surely the university faces no more urgent task, in the coming years, than to regenerate itself as a community worthy of men who make this sacrifice out of a commitment to the moral and intellectual values that the university pretends to honor. And I think it requires no elaborate argument to show that the faculty of philosophy might well be at the forefront of this effort.

The temptation is overwhelming, in a discussion of this issue, to quote Marx's famous marginal comment on Feuerbach, that "the philosophers have only interpreted the world differently; the point, however, is to change it." I will not try to resist the temptation; the task that faces the responsible *citizen* is to work to change the world. But we should not overlook the fact that the interpretation and analysis provided by the philosopher, by the intellectual more generally, are essential ingredients in any serious attempt to change the world. If student radicalism often turns to an anti-intellectual direction, the fault in part lies in the deficiencies of scholarship, of our intellectual culture, of the disciplines—such as philosophy—and the institutions—such as the university—that exist only to interpret and advance and defend this culture. Senator Fulbright, in a recent and extremely important speech on the Senate floor, stated that the universities have betrayed a public trust by associating themselves with the government and the corporate system in a military-industrial-academic complex. They have, as he rightly said, largely abandoned the function that they should serve in a free society and have forfeited their right to public support, to a substantial degree, by this retreat—one might say, by this treachery. Only a hypocrite can preach the virtues of non-violence to the Vietnamese or to the black community in the United States, while continuing to tolerate the incomparably greater violence to which they are subjected by the society to which he belongs. Similarly, only a hypocrite can condemn the anti-intellectualism of student activists, while tolerating the subversion of scholarship, the impoverishment of intellect, let us be honest—the downright immorality of the academic profession as they support American violence and repression by contributing to weaponry and counterinsurgency, by permitting the social sciences to develop as a technology of control and manipulation, or, more subtly, by helping to create and uphold the system of values that permits us to applaud the progmatic and responsible attitude shown by those who now oppose the war in Vietnam on grounds of tactics and cost effectiveness. To restore the integrity of intellectual life and cultural values is the most urgent, most crucial task that faces the universities and the professions. Philosophers might take the lead in this effort. If they do not, then they too will have betrayed a responsibility that should be theirs.

9

The Concept of a Politically Neutral University

ROBERT L. SIMON

At a time of increasing social concern, controversy exists over the role universities should play in political affairs. Advocates of institutional neutrality believe that universities ought not to engage in political action. While often encouraging political participation by individual students and faculty members, defenders of neutrality deny that educational institutions should take part in politics.[1] On the other hand, opponents of such neutrality maintain that political involvement by academic institutions is highly desirable.[2]

This paper is an attempt to clarify some of the issues involved in the debate over institutional neutrality. A rational resolution to this controversy would appear less unlikely if the various strands of the argument are disentangled.

One thing that is not always noticed is that debate over

1. There is a great difference between an individual student or teacher adopting a political position and a college or university doing so. Logically, this distinction holds even if every member of a university community defends the same political position. To say that an institution has engaged in political activity is at least to say that its officers have acted politically in their *role* or *capacity* as officers of the institution. No such consequence follows from the fact that the very same individuals have acted *as* individuals.

2. See, for example, the debate "On Institutional Neutrality" between Donald N. Koster and Winton U. Solberg, *American Association of University Professors Bulletin*, vol. 56, no. 1 (March 1970), pp. 11-13.

whether universities *ought* to be neutral is of significance
only if universities *can* be neutral in the first place. If politically neutral universities are an impossibility, argument
over whether universities should be neutral is surely point-
less.

Indeed, if it were impossible for universities to be politically neutral, important consequences would follow. If there
were no alternative to involvement, it could be plausibly
argued that universities ought consciously to promote political goals. For if universities are necessarily political, it might
well seem senseless to direct university policy without regard
for the political implications which might ensue. Planned political involvement by universities might seem to be a requirement of common sense if neutrality is actually impossible.

Accordingly, two separate issues should be distinguished
in the debate over institutional neutrality:

Can universities be politically neutral?
Should universities be politically neutral?

As already noted, the second issue is of practical concern
only if an affirmative answer to the former is presupposed.

I. CAN UNIVERSITIES BE POLITICALLY NEUTRAL?

In this section, I will consider two arguments for the view
that universities cannot be politically neutral. The first of
these maintains that the educational process is intrinsically
value-laden. The second emphasizes the extent of university
involvement in nonacademic enterprises. Although I am undoubtedly omitting other important arguments from consideration, the two cited seem to me to be significant. Each
is to be found in the rather sparse literature on the subject

and both are frequently employed in informal discussion and debate.

Neutrality Is Impossible Because the Educational Process Is Itself Value-Laden

Universities are often conceived of as open marketplaces of ideas. No positions are banned and different viewpoints compete for the allegiance of students and faculty alike. Research and classroom discussion are free from institutional censorship. Although individuals may advocate particular positions, no official orthodoxy of opinion is imposed by the institution itself.

It can be argued, however, that this very commitment to free inquiry is sufficient to preclude political neutrality. Thus in his book, *The Ideal of the University,* Robert Paul Wolff maintains that

> by permitting all voices to be heard, the university systematically undermines all those doctrines which claim exclusive possession of the truth and seek therefore to silence opposed voices. . . . American intellectuals cannot perceive that their own commitment to free debate is also a substantive political act, no more neutral than the prohibition of dissent in religiously or politically authoritarian countries.[3]

Wolff's claim here is that the allegiance of the university to free speech and open inquiry constitutes a value commitment that is political in nature. On this view, there can be no politically neutral universities since educational policy itself embodies political values.

Even if we grant Wolff's claim that commitment to free inquiry precludes political neutrality, we must be clear as to the extent to which neutrality is ruled out. Neutrality within

3. Robert Paul Wolff, *The Ideal of the University* (Boston: Beacon Press, 1969), p. 73.

the context of free speech should be distinguished from neutrality concerning the desirability of free speech. Let us grant that universities, in that they permit open discourse, are not politically neutral. It still may be possible for the university to be neutral in honoring this commitment. Lack of neutrality involved in *adherence* to free speech does not preclude genuine neutrality in the *application* of the free speech doctrine. Thus, in a free academic environment, proponents of censorship will not be allowed to act on their beliefs but nevertheless will be given the opportunity to advocate their views in open discourse.

Accordingly, one weakness of Wolff's argument is that it confuses two levels of neutrality. Lack of neutrality inherent in the commitment to free inquiry is not distinguished from neutrality in the practice of free inquiry. When properly understood, then, Wolff's argument does not show that the latter sort of neutrality is impossible.

Wolff's argument is open to still another objection, which further restricts the applicability of his conclusion. Wolff has concluded that a politically neutral university is impossible because universities, by their very nature, make substantive value judgments. However, this argument fails to distinguish value judgments that are part of the educational process from those that are extrinsic to it.

Thus, even if we acknowledge that academic allegiance to free speech is of political significance, such allegiance may not commit the university to a political stand on other issues. Commitment to free speech does not imply, for example, that universities cannot be neutral with respect to the debate on Vietnam.

Wolff has not distinguished values that are intrinsic to education from those that are extrinsic to it. As referred to here, values intrinsic to education are those that are logically constitutive of the educational process. Accordingly, it is true that no university can be neutral with respect to educationally intrinsic values. Since educationally intrinsic values are defined as those constitutive of the educational process, it is (logically) impossible for educational institutions to avoid such value commitments.[4]

It may also be the case that some policies must be employed as *means* for the realization of intrinsic values simply because, as a matter of fact, there are no other alternatives. This type of necessity is not logical in character. For example, in a society which does not know of the printing press, the lecture system may as a matter of fact be the only means of imparting information to large numbers of people. Although other alternatives are logically possible, they are not actually available. In such a society, given that the imparting of information is intrinsic to education, the lecture system must be employed if great numbers of people are to be educated.

Accordingly, neutrality is indeed impossible with respect both to intrinsic educational values and to the means necessary for the attainment of those values. It does not follow, however, that neutrality is impossible with respect to values which do not fall into either of the above categories. The impossibility with respect to some values does not imply the impossibility of neutrality with respect to all values.

This is not to deny that commitment to educationally intrinsic values often has political consequences. This is surely

4. Different accounts of the nature of education may disagree as to which values are educationally intrinsic. For example, one who counts free inquiry as such a value may deny that 'universities' run on totalitarian principles are really universities at all. Such disputes over the nature of education need not be merely verbal ones which can be settled simply by pointing out that the disputants are using the word 'education' differently. Presumably, each thinks his definition captures something more important than do the others' definitions. Such disputes may be neither factual nor verbal but, rather, evaluational.

so in totalitarian countries where free inquiry may be subversive of the existing authoritarian order. There are also political implications in societies where academic freedom is respected.

For example, it is frequently argued that secret research and military training are antithetical to the ideal of a free university community. In addition, university condemnation of outside interference with academic freedom can be justified by appeal to the university's commitment to free inquiry. This does not mean, however, that commitment to intrinsic educational values necessitates taking a political stand on unrelated issues.

The argument from the value-laden nature of education does not show that institutional neutrality is impossible in disputes where intrinsic educational values are not at issue. It may be the case, however, that the impossibility of political neutrality in such controversies can be established by another argument. It is to such an argument that we now turn.

Neutrality Is Impossible Because of University Involvement in Nonacademic Affairs

Proponents of this argument maintain that neutrality is impossible even with respect to values that are not educationally intrinsic. On their view, university involvement in other social institutions is so great that political repercussions cannot be avoided. Two versions of the argument can be distinguished. The first is conceptual in character, while the second rests largely upon empirical considerations.

Professor Wolff provides us with an example of the first version. It is a truth of elementary ethics, he tells us, that one can be as responsible for failure to act in crucial situations as one is for actions proper.[5] Given the financial and social power of the universities, their inaction on any issue

5. Wolff, op. cit., p. 71.

involves them in the political process quite as much as would any positive policy. In this regard, Wolff argues that

> in public life, when a man who has power refrains from using it, we all agree he acted politically. . . . Hence, acquiescence in governmental acts, under the guise of impartiality, actually strengthens the established forces and makes successful opposition all the harder.[6]

Professor Wolff does not offer a full analysis of neutrality. However, the quotation indicates that, on Wolff's view, possession of political power can preclude neutrality. Let us call the kind of neutrality with which Wolff seems to be concerned 'covert neutrality,' since failure to be neutral in this sense does not imply that overt political action has been taken. Covert neutrality can be defined as follows:

> X is covertly neutral with respect to a political dispute d if and only if X either has no power to affect d or is unaware of having the power to affect d.

On this account, if a university is able to affect some dispute, then the decision not to employ its power is as political as a decision to take positive action. Of course, such a university can fail to be covertly neutral only if it is aware of its power. We would hardly want to count decisions made in ignorance of political implications as evidence of political partiality.

Now, it is surely true that most colleges and universities have the power to influence many political disputes, and are often quite aware of having such power. It follows that such institutions fail to be covertly neutral.

Although this argument seems sound, its import is far from clear. As we will see, the meaning of 'neutrality' has been stretched so far that conclusions based upon it may be irrelevant to disputes in which 'neutrality' is employed in a more restricted sense.

6. Ibid.

The assertion that universities cannot be covertly neutral is as much a sociological claim about the status of universities in our society as it is about neutrality. A university can be covertly neutral only if it is politically powerless or unaware of its power. Thus, one need not examine a university's actions and policies to see if it is covertly neutral. One need only investigate the extent of its power and self-awareness.

It should now be clear why politically knowledgeable and influential colleges and universities cannot be covertly neutral. For to be covertly neutral, they must *by definition* be politically uninfluential or ignorant of their political capacities. Since Wolff's claim holds in virtue of its meaning, its truth must be granted. Its significance, however, is open to challenge.

Thus, the impossibility of covert neutrality does not establish the impossibility of other kinds of neutrality. Certainly it does not imply that universities are or must be active parties to political disputes. One might as well argue that America could not have stayed out of the First World War because Americans knew they had the power to influence the war.

Wolff's argument blurs the distinction between covert and overt neutrality. Overt neutrality can be defined as follows:

> X is overtly neutral with respect to a political dispute *d* if and only if X is able to aid some party to *d*, X does not act to aid any party to *d*, and X's motivation for not acting does not involve a desire to aid any party to *d* through his inaction.

Overt neutrality is a weaker notion than covert neutrality since failure to be neutral in the latter sense does not imply failure in the former sense as well.

For example, consider the following case. A and B are fighting. C, who is very powerful, and knows it, passes by but takes no part in the altercation. C clearly fails to be covertly neutral. However if his inaction is not motivated by a preference for either A or B, C is overtly neutral with respect to the dispute. This is so even if his refusal to fight aids A, who is badly trouncing B.

Similarly, universities can be overtly neutral, even with respect to such political controversies as that over the legitimacy of the Vietnam war. All that is required is that universities refrain from acting to support either the government or the critics, and that such inaction not arise from a preference for either side. Thus, universities may take no political action with respect to the war simply because they believe it desirable to remain overtly neutral in the dispute.

Wolff's argument fails because the impossibility of covert neutrality does not imply the impossibility of overt neutrality. The substantive issue of whether universities *should be* overtly neutral has not been eliminated.

However, another interpretation of the argument from involvement is possible. According to this second version, the claim that universities can be politically neutral is not conceptually incoherent but empirically false. Neutrality is unattainable, on this view, not as a matter of definition, but because of the financial dependency of universities on other institutions of a political character. Acceptance of government support and of returns on corporate investments are frequently cited as examples of such outside entanglements.[7]

It is surely true that most colleges and universities must invest in corporations in order to remain financially viable. This does not imply, however, that universities cannot be overtly neutral with respect to political disputes involving those very same corporations.

7. Koster, op. cit., p. 12.

In order to see this, we must distinguish between acts *to* do a certain thing and acts *which* do a certain thing. Thus, it is one thing to act (in order) to injure someone but quite another to perform some action which results in personal injury as an unintended by-product.

Given this distinction, it is possible for a university to act to invest in a given company, an act which aids that company in a political dispute, without the university acting to aid that company. We can distinguish, for example, between investors who invest in a certain corporation in order to show support for its politically controversial policies and other investors who invest solely to maximize profit. The latter group, but not the former, would be willing to shift its investments if better financial returns could be found elsewhere.[8]

Overt neutrality requires that no action be taken *to* aid a party to a political dispute, and that failure to take such action not be motivated by a preference for either side. These conditions are satisfied if the investments are made on financial grounds, even if the act of investing is one *which* aids a party to a political dispute. Of course, some investments may be morally suspect. What this shows, however, is that it is sometimes *wrong* to be neutral, not that neutrality is impossible.

Acceptance of certain forms of government assistance is also compatible with neutrality. This is not true of all forms of government support, however. Contracts to construct counter-insurgency programs, to develop weapons systems, and the like involve the universities directly in political action. Moreover, such programs, if they involve classified research, may conflict with such intrinsic educational values

8. That this latter group acted only to raise money is as empirically verifiable as is the claim 'They would be willing to shift their investment if better returns could be found elsewhere.'

as free access to information. However, it is surely possible for universities to reject contracts such as these.

On the other hand, the kind of aid which is indispensable for support of intrinsic educational values need not be subversive of overt neutrality; e.g. scholarship aid or funds for building construction. In reply, it might be argued that once it becomes a candidate for government assistance, the university is competing with other groups and individuals for a share of the legislative pie. As budget priorities are among the most important of political issues, it may be held that such competition involves universities in political battles.

However, this argument fails to distinguish between a university (i) reporting that it needs so much in funds to carry on its educational program, and (ii) assigning a priority to its needs relative to those of other groups and individuals. Now, to hold that one's own needs have a certain priority relative to those of others *is* to be a party to the political dispute over proper allocation of resources. As such, it is incompatible with neutrality. On the other hand, reports of needs do not include such evaluatory political content.

Accordingly, once *actions to* are distinguished from *actions which,* and once reports of needs are distinguished from assignments of priorities, overt neutrality turns out to be compatible with certain kinds of university involvement in government and business.[9]

One last point merits consideration in this context. Might

9. In light of university commitment to intrinsic educational values, it may seem *desirable* to take stronger action than the mere reporting of needs in order to preserve the financial support for those values. For example, it is sometimes maintained that universities ought to speak out against the Vietnam war since the war diverts funds away from education and educational values.

Such a claim, however, does not contradict my defense of the possibility of neutrality. My point is that there is a genuine option between such a course of action and overt neutrality. There may well be reasons for abandoning neutrality, but one such reason is not that neutrality is impossible to begin with.

it not be the case that even financial support of a nonpolitical variety would be distributed according to the political preferences of the donor? Indeed, recent cuts imposed by state legislatures on the academic budgets of many universities have been widely interpreted as punishment for campus political protests. Through such means, criteria of political acceptability imposed by external groups could come to encompass even curricular matters and the hiring and firing of individual faculty members.

Such external pressures surely constitute a grave threat to university autonomy, let alone neutrality. It is one thing to point this out, however, and quite another to argue that such pressures are irresistible, making neutrality impossible. Moreover, even if the latter conclusion could be adequately supported, its relevance here is far from clear. The argument of this paper has been that political neutrality is precluded neither by the nature of the university nor by the university's unavoidable financial entanglements with other institutions. Whether neutrality is possible in the face of severe political repression is another point entirely. But even *if* universities are unable to resist such severe external pressure, it does not follow that they are really political animals disguised in neutral clothing, even when such repression is absent.

In summary, those who believe that there can be no politically neutral university have made two points. They have shown both that it is impossible for universities to be covertly neutral and that it is impossible for universities to be neutral where intrinsic educational values are concerned. On the other hand, there seem to be areas where institutional neutrality is possible. Overt neutrality and neutrality with respect to educationally extrinsic values are at least logical possibilities. Although as a matter of fact, many universities are closely tied to government and industry, such relationships are compatible with overt neutrality under some conditions.

In view of our conclusion that some kinds of neutrality are at least logical possibilities, and perhaps practical ones as well, the issue of whether universities *ought* to be neutral is now of concern.

II. SHOULD UNIVERSITIES BE POLITICALLY NEUTRAL?

Given that it is possible for universities to be politically neutral in the ways specified, it still may be argued that they ought not to be neutral. If universities can promote some worthy political cause, then perhaps they should become involved.

In some cases, such a view may be correct. If the values at stake in a particular political controversy are so momentous as to outweigh educational values, then the latter ought surely to be sacrificed. It is not clear, however, that such is generally the case. Whether neutrality should be dispensed with depends, then, on the moral significance of the particular political question at issue.

One general point can be made nevertheless. If it can be shown that there are strong arguments for political neutrality, then a prima facie case would exist in its favor. That is, when there are no stronger countervailing factors, the arguments for neutrality become decisive. In this section, I will try to develop such a prima facie case for neutrality.

The Argument from Free Inquiry

This argument is based on the conception of the university as a center of free inquiry. No views are prohibited and all views are to be evaluated by the impartial criteria which govern the field in question. Reasoned investigation is to be regarded as the means for attainment of knowledge.

If educational institutions were to take partisan political positions, conflicts between educational and political goals might develop. In such a case, would the university take the politically profitable course of action or the educationally sound one? If political ends were to receive the higher priority, then educational efficiency would suffer. For one thing, faculty members who disagree with the university's politics, or who resent it taking a political role at all, might leave. Indeed, it might be politically advantageous to make them leave. Moreover, politicization of the university can only encourage counter-pressure from opposing political groups outside the university. Of course, political actions by individuals also elicit such a response. It is surely reasonable to believe, however, that the response would be more repressive if universities not only defended the right of dissent (which is required by allegiance to intrinsic educational values) but also officially endorsed the views of the dissenters. In view of these considerations, the university is likely to remain a center of free inquiry to the extent that, as an institution, it remains free of overt political involvement.

Accordingly, the freedom of the university from internal and external pressures to conform is the very condition which enables teachers and students to examine the political orthodoxies of the moment from diverse points of view. This Argument from Free Inquiry rests upon the model of the university as an open marketplace of ideas. Political neutrality is defended as necessary for free inquiry. However, the picture of the university as an open marketplace of ideas is itself not free from challenge.[10]

Critics deny that all ideas and all points of view are given a hearing by the academic community. Thus, there are no departments of astrology and alchemists are not invited to

10. For example, see Robert Paul Wolff, *The Poverty of Liberalism* (Boston: Beacon Press, 1968), p. 16.

address scientific meetings. Scientology is not taught by philosophy departments and historians pay no attention when attempts are made to explain some great event as due to the influence of gremlins. In other words, certain types of work are rejected a priori without consideration of the individual case at hand.

What critics often fail to notice is that such limitations need not conflict with the model of the university as a center of unrestricted inquiry. Although this point deserves fuller treatment than can be given here, at least the following can be said. One reason for valuing open inquiry is that it provides a forum for testing hypotheses. That some positions fail such a test is not sufficient to show that free inquiry does not exist. To think otherwise is to turn a condition of the success of open investigation into a criterion of its absence. Thus, there is no conflict with free inquiry if those who engage in it limit their investigations as required by the results of past inquiries. This is altogether different from refusing to consider a proposal in advance of adequate evaluation, especially if such refusal is motivated by ideological or other non-epistemic factors. Of course, if further inquiry is limited by past results, those previous findings must be publicly accessible, so as to be open to check by interested parties.

There is also a distinction between limitations on debate *within* a field and limitations on debate *about* it. Scientists, for example, are likely to deny not only that astrologists are good scientists but that they are scientists at all. However, investigation of the nature of science, an activity that is not part of science but about it, subjects just such distinctions to critical examination.

Free inquiry is compatible with limitations on debate within a field, then, so long as such limitations are (i) epistemically justifiable by appeal to the publicly accessible results of free inquiry, (ii) proportional in force to the degree of their justifiability, and (iii) subject to meta-examination where appropriate. These conditions are rational in allowing investigators to concentrate on areas of investigation which appear fruitful, while also containing checks against dogmatism and censorship.

The Argument from Free Inquiry establishes the prima facie desirability of a politically neutral university. Neutrality is defended as a means for the promotion of rational investigation. Therefore, commitment to the latter supports commitment to the former as well.

The Argument from Respect for Persons

Part of respecting a person is to respect his autonomy as an individual. Except in the case of children and the mentally handicapped, it is normally a sign of disrespect to attempt to make another person's decisions for him. It is part of the liberal democratic tradition that each individual has the right to decide his own destiny insofar as this is compatible with respect for the rights of others.

Universities are concerned with development of potential for rational, informed decision. To the extent that politicization conflicts with such a goal by inhibiting free inquiry, then to that extent does it involve disrespect for persons by limiting their opportunities for rational development. It is surely an abridgment of a person's rights to inhibit his capacity to make rational decisions based on knowledge of a wide range of alternatives.

Accordingly, neutrality can be defended by appeal to respect for persons and the notion of individual rights implied by such respect. If this argument has force, politicization violates the rights of every member of the academic community.

In spite of these last remarks, this paper should not be read as a blanket endorsement of neutrality. Rather, one of its conclusions is that the case for neutrality is prima facie only. However, an argument against neutrality must be a strong one, for there are always powerful considerations on the other side.

Accordingly, the discussion of university involvement in politics must take place at the level of individual cases. Moreover, it must also involve evaluative considerations. The charge that academic institutions are necessarily participants in politics need not be of concern. Anti-neutralist claims may sometimes be justifiable. However, the justification must consist of moral arguments and specific fact rather than appeal to the alleged impossibility of a neutral university.[11]

11. I would like to thank my colleagues Betty Ring, Russell Blackwood, and Norman Bowie for their helpful comments on an earlier draft. I am also grateful to Charles Parsons for his suggestions, and particularly for his help in clarifying the distinction between overt and covert neutrality.

10

The Responsibilities of Universities

LEWIS M. SCHWARTZ

In a recent essay on the responsibilities of philosophers, William Earle states that

> the responsibilities of a professional philosopher exhaust themselves in his profession; his political responsibilities are therefore nil. His political responsibilities as a citizen are identical with those of every other citizen, where, as a philosopher, he occupies neither a higher nor a lower place.[1]

This thesis, suitably expanded to include other areas of academic specialization, constitutes what I take to be an accurate characterization of the dominant attitudes of university faculty. It is a view which has frequently been expressed in terms of the notion of competence. Thus, for example, it is maintained that it is not part of the competence of faculty to make judgments about the justifiability of U.S. participation in the war in Southeast Asia. (I take it that "competence" is here used with its legal or moral connotation of authority or responsibility, rather than its more usual interpretation of capability. Those who defend Earle's

1. William Earle, "The Political Responsibilities of Philosophers," *Ethics*, vol. 79 (October 1968), p. 10.

thesis do not deny the competence of faculty to engage in political activity as citizens.) Further, this same thesis, suitably modified, constitutes an accurate characterization of the prevailing attitudes toward the political role of universities themselves, insofar as it is thought proper to distinguish between a university and the individuals who comprise it. Thus, not infrequently one hears expressed the view that universities ought not to make political judgments or engage in political activities, on the ground that their competence is academic only. Universities ought, in other words, to confine themselves to actions which are academic in nature or to actions which relate directly to the well-being of academic institutions.

Formulation of any of these theses is usually followed by a discussion of the nature of the academic field in question, or by a discussion of the nature of universities. Thus, Earle:

> A profession comprises an area of verifiable and teachable knowledge; the professional's competence extends so far and only so far. But does not every aspect of life fall under some area of teachable knowledge? Could there not be a profession eventually of everything, perhaps even called "philosophy," with our identifiable subject matter? No, not unless every problem is a problem in knowledge to which there is a theoretical solution. But it is immediately clear that there is one area where the problem is not what shall I think, but rather what shall I do, an area which is sometimes called "life" or "existence" and which comprises decisions which I make for my own personal life and those we collectively make in politics.[2]

And, thus, Chomsky:

> Philosophers, however, may be in a somewhat more fortunate position. There is no profession that can claim with

2. Earle, op. cit., p. 10.

greater authenticity that its concern is the intellectual culture of the society or that it possesses the tools for the analysis of ideology and the critique of social knowledge and its
use. If it is correct to regard the American and world crisis
as in part a cultural one, then philosophical analysis may
have a definite contribution to make.[3]

One contention of this paper is that by structuring the debate in this way, the crucial issues upon which determination of the responsibilities of universities and faculty depend
have been misplaced. I shall argue, on the contrary,

1. that the issues of academic responsibility do not rest
upon determination of the proper limits of philosophical investigation, or on determination of the proper limits of academic investigation generally. These are properly academic
questions which do not necessarily admit of answers that are
identical to the answers to questions concerning what constitutes appropriate university activity; and

2. that proper principles of academic responsibility yield
the conclusion that social and political, and therefore moral,
factors are relevant to determinations of curricula, that is, to
determinations of what may properly be researched and
taught.[4]

I

Those who hold the general view that the responsibilities of
universities and faculty are exclusively academic may be presumed to admit (1) that universities do sometimes engage in
political and social actions and (2) that, in any case, there

3. Noam Chomsky, "Philosophers and Public Policy," this volume, p. 208.
4. Throughout this essay I shall use the term "intrinsic university activity" to
refer to research and teaching. I shall use "extrinsic university activity" to
refer to other activities of universities; for example, making investments, hiring nonacademic personnel, purchasing land, etc.

are political and social consequences to the intrinsic university activities, i.e. research and teaching.

1. With respect to the first, it is clear that universities often engage in political and social activities. For example, universities frequently petition social and governmental agencies for the adoption of policies which it is thought will be beneficial to the university or to academic institutions generally, or for the change of policies which are thought to be inimical to them. Public universities might, for example, petition for certain changes in programs of admissions, in salary structures, and in policies regarding privileged behavior on campus. Universities engage in all sorts of business activities, from hiring nonacademic personnel to running commercial enterprises, patents and stocks, and lobbying for various policies.

Proponents of the view we are examining are likely to answer that universities may properly engage in such activities (a) to the extent that they may reasonably be construed as necessary or useful means to enable the university to engage in its primary, i.e. intrinsic, activities, or (b) to the extent that the university exercises its expertise with respect to the consequences of governmental, etc., actions on universities themselves. In other words, universities may properly engage in extrinsic activities to the extent that they may reasonably be construed as conducive to the well-being of universities.

Such a defense appeals presumably to the principle that institutional action is either amoral, i.e. not subject to moral criticism, or subject to moral criticism only to the extent that the actions of the institution conflict with what may be called the defining purposes or interests of the institution. Put somewhat differently, we may construe this principle as asserting that decision-makers for institutions can act immorally only to the extent that they base decisions upon factors other than those relevant to the stated or implied institutional purposes. This is, of course, not to rule out the possibility of imprudent decisions.

This principle is a favorite of businessmen and heads of state. Thus, for example: as a member of the board of directors, I am morally bound not to make decisions on moral grounds, but rather to make them solely on the grounds of their effects on this business. For, after all, people have invested in this business in order to make money, and I am therefore morally bound to take all and only those actions which will contribute to that end.

I shall not take the time to criticize this principle in detail. It is, I think, obviously unsatisfactory. What I am concerned to do, however, is to show that this principle is no less unsatisfactory when applied to universities. Thus, to take a somewhat trivial example, such a principle legitimizes the making of a petition by a university to end the war in Southeast Asia so long as the grounds for the petition are limited to the effects of the continuation of the war on universities, e.g. that the prosecution of the war is inimical to the proper pursuit of research or teaching. On the other hand, it forbids a petition by the university to end the war just on the grounds that the war is morally intolerable. It is, I suggest, a curious rule of behavior which permits self-interested action but which rules out, as a violation of one's academic responsibilities, actions which, though perhaps contrary to the interests of an academic institution, are nevertheless otherwise imperative.

Defenders of the view that we are examining may be expected to reply that special considerations arise in determining the responsibilities of universities (and faculty) which do not arise—or might not arise—when considering the responsibilities of businesses or governments. They may be expected to argue that there are at least some institutions, most notably the judiciary, to which this general principle properly applies, and that, roughly speaking, universities by nature are more like these institutions than like private enterprise. The ground of their reply is as follows: The goal of inquiry is truth; but inquiry may be perverted if extraneous factors are permitted to influence the processes of reasoning and data-gathering. Like law, inquiry must, in some sense, be disinterested. Thus, the consequences for everyone would be better if universities were apolitical than if universities did take political and social factors into account in making decisions. We shall postpone our examination of this general principle. For the moment, I want to consider in what sense it may be correct to say that universities have interests.

With respect to this question, it is important to see that analogy with the judiciary is likely to be misleading. The judiciary cannot, whereas an academic institution can, have interests of its own. The judiciary exists only to settle disputes that arise among individuals or institutions that do have interests of their own. Nor will it do to say that the judiciary does indeed have its own interest, namely, fairly to settle the competing claims of other individuals or institutions. For, as we shall see, any such argument involves a kind of fallacy of types.

The use of an analogy might help to explain this point.[5] The practical—as opposed to the theoretical—function of a person's reasoning faculty is, we might say, to organize and arrange the competing interests of the individual, or, in other words, to determine, given his competing interests, what arrangement of his time and resources will provide him with the greatest satisfactions. But one can hardly infer from this that, aside from these interests, the individual has consequently a new interest, namely an interest in organizing and arranging his activities so as to yield maximum satis-

5. I shall develop this analogy throughout the essay. It is, I think, of interest in its own right.

factions, and that this interest must compete with his other interests for his resources. Insofar as we properly talk of such interests, they are interests of a different logical type from those interests which compete for the individual's time and resources. One might, of course, develop an interest of this first type in learning how practical reason operates, that is, in formulating the principles of the operation of practical reason, but that is clearly an instance of reasoning theoretically about the nature of practical reason and not an instance of practical reasoning.

So, too, at the societal level, we may properly construe law as concerned with ordering and arranging the interests of individuals taken as wholes, i.e. as concerned with interpersonal rather than intrapersonal conflicts of interest. There are, of course, differences in the operating principles of practical reason and of law. For whereas practical reason operates, we might say, on the principle of the maximization of the sum total of individual satisfactions, and thus must presumably seek to settle conflicts among competing interests on this principle, law does not, or does not in any obvious way, operate (solely) on the principle of maximizing the sum total of well-being. Thus, for example, although it might be true that in a given case society would be better off if a given decision were made, it ought nevertheless not to be made, because the consequences would be unfair to a given individual. On the other hand, it would make only metaphorical sense to say that although a given individual would maximize his own satisfactions if he did a given thing, he ought nevertheless not to do so, because the consequences would be unfair, let us say, to his interest in food. In any case, the point is the same: the operation of law, like the operation of practical reason, cannot properly be construed as an interest of the same type as the interests among which it mediates.

If we take this analogy one step further, we can see that among the practical functions of reason must be included the allocation of the individual's resources with respect to the development of his theoretical reasoning capacity. It takes time, energy, etc., to develop that capacity. But here we must be careful. For the development of theoretical reason might (1) be relevant to the optimum operation of practical reason itself, insofar as it provides the information, etc., relevant to the satisfaction of competing interests. But (2) the development of the individual's theoretical reason might itself be (or become) one of the competing interests, for an individual might be (or become) intrinsically interested in attaining knowledge, irrespective of its uses. That is, an individual might be interested not only in having food, shelter, clothing, etc., but also in learning for its own sake.

Roughly speaking, with respect to the first function, practical reason ought only to allocate the individual's resources for the development of knowledge that is likely to be relevant to satisfying the individual's other interests, and then only to the extent that, in so doing, conflicts are not created with respect to the satisfaction of the individual's other interests; that is, only to the extent that in so allocating resources maximization of satisfactions is not prevented. With respect to the second, practical reason ought to allocate the individual's resources on precisely the same principles that it allocates all resources. In other words, the development of theoretical reason ought to be viewed as only one among a number of competing interests.

So, too, at the societal level. We may speak of the university as the institutional analogue of the theoretical function of the individual. Insofar as we construe academic activity as fundamentally one among a number of competing interests, i.e. as analogous to the interest that an individual might have in learning for its own sake, then the resources of society ought presumably to be allocated to it in accordance with the principles of the fair allocation of resources to competing interests. But insofar as we construe it as relevant also to the satisfaction of all other interests, i.e. as analogous to the role of theoretical reason in developing the means, etc., for the satisfaction of the individual's other interests, then, rationally speaking, resources ought to be allocated to universities not only in accordance with the principles of the fair allocation of resources, but also in accordance with the economic considerations of maximizing the satisfactions of all interests.

It is, I think, a thoroughly uninteresting question whether it is more desirable to restrict the use of the term "academic" to the pursuit of knowledge for its own sake than it is to incorporate under that term everything (or pretty much everything) that corresponds to the theoretical function of reason. The crucial questions concern the allocation of resources. Perhaps the most convenient use of the term "academic" would include all and only that research and teaching which, for various reasons, is most desirably pursued organizationally apart from the other institutions of society. That would be to make the term "academic" basically a social, or political, concept.

2. It is evident that what goes on at universities does frequently have consequences for society, sometimes profound and immediate, sometimes more subtle and long-range. Thus, even were we to accept Earle's thesis that in doing philosophy, i.e. in teaching or doing research in philosophy, one is doing something which is itself apolitical, we could not justifiably conclude, on that ground alone, that philosophers are not subject to criticism with respect to political responsibilities. It is, or should be, clear, in other words, that although one might choose to engage in an activity which is itself nonpolitical, one might nevertheless be subject to competing

responsibilities which might arise outside of that nonpolitical activity. Nonpolitical activities might, and frequently do, have consequences of a political and social nature, as a musician who continues to play the "Blue Danube" during a barroom brawl well knows.

Thus, even if we accept Earle's thesis, there remain questions of political responsibilities. Baldly put, from this point of view these questions concern whether an individual ought (or is obligated) to alter his research or his teaching in response to political and social needs, and therefore whether there are times when an individual ought (or is obligated) to stop doing altogether what he has been doing, in preference for engaging in some other activity. They are, in other words, questions about when, if at all, an individual's responsibilities as a citizen require alteration or abandonment of his obligations as a philosopher, or more generally, as a member of the faculty of a university.

Doing philosophy is presumably one way in which an individual may fulfill his responsibilities as a citizen. Thus, for instance, if we suppose that it is a responsibility of a citizen to contribute to the common good and that doing philosophy contributes to the common good, then doing philosophy is a way in which a citizen might fulfill this responsibility. But if, on the other hand, doing philosophy in fact does harm—either directly or as a consequence of a failure thereby to do other things, then it might be an individual's responsibility not to do philosophy. One may not plead that he was engaged in philosophical reflections as a justification for failing to help people from the burning building next door, though one might justifiably plead that he was engaged in performing open-heart surgery.

From an institutional point of view, the relevant questions are very much the same: when, if at all, is it proper for an institution to expand or restrict the subjects taught and the research engaged in? But further, as we have seen, we must also include questions about whether and to what extent it is justifiable for institutions to expand or restrict the extrinsic activities in which they normally engage; for example, when, if at all, is it justifiable for academic institutions to speak out on issues which are not directly related to their primary activities?

The usual response to this second line of argument is to point out that although what is done at universities might have significant political or social consequences for society, nevertheless the overall advantages to society which result from politically neutral universities, i.e. from universities which do not take political factors into account in deciding upon what university activities are permissible, whether extrinsic or intrinsic, outweigh the advantages that will likely result if universities sometimes participate in political matters. This is a familiar sort of argument. Its paradigm application, perhaps, is with respect to the alleged political independence of the judiciary. Thus, for example, the desirable consequences, let us say, of finding a public menace guilty of some crime despite the lack of evidence against him, and thus of introducing political factors into the making of such decisions, are outweighed by the disadvantages of a system of justice which permits such a practice. Similarly, it is held that the advantages of apolitical universities outweigh—except in extreme cases—the advantages of universities which engage in political activities or which take political factors into account in deciding what is to be researched and what is to be taught.

In what follows, I shall argue that this thesis is mistaken.[6]

---

6. I am not sure where Chomsky stands on this matter. I am inclined to believe that he accepts the above thesis, but supposes that the moral and intellectual crisis which Americans face at the moment constitutes one of the extreme cases which would justify altering the apolitical nature of universities.

Before we turn to a direct examination of it, however, it will be useful to continue with our exposition and criticism of the traditional view, according to which determinations of what is to be researched and what is to be taught are academic issues, i.e. that the sole relevant grounds for making such decisions are academic grounds. I shall, on the contrary, argue that they are more appropriately thought of as political or social issues, which raise directly the important question of academic responsibility.

II

Earle contends that there is a distinction between the question "What shall I think?" and the question "What shall I do?" which warrants classifying considerations relevant to the former as appropriate for university activity and to the latter as inappropriate. This contention rests upon a mistaken view of the distinction between practical and theoretical reason. It rests upon a view, formulated perhaps most clearly by Hume, which supposes that reason is exercised essentially only with respect to matters that are either true or false; that is, reason is exercised only with respect to matters of fact and matters of language. On this view, reason is properly understood to be relevant to rational action only insofar as the agent might exercise reason to determine those matters of fact relevant to the fulfillment of his wants, needs, desires, etc. Specifically, reason's role with respect to action is limited to the determination of the means for the fulfillment of desires.

On the other hand, talk about what ought to be done, whether it is talk about what an individual ought to do or what an institution ought to do, is not a matter for reason, and thus such talk has no place in a university, presumably either as a matter of classroom discussion or as a matter of research. On this view, ought-sentences are understood to be neither true nor false; they are, rather, best understood as expressions of attitudes, and therefore, as "existential" matters which cannot be rationally grounded. One must choose what to do; one cannot demonstrate that it is (morally) right to do it.

But is this distinction satisfactory?[7] Earle has, I think, confused determinations of what ought to be done with decisions to do. The questions "What shall I do?" and "What shall we do?" do admit of answers. They admit of answers of the form: "*It is the case* that so-and-so ought to do such-and-such." Answers to practical questions are properly formulated in ought-language; they are ought-judgments. But they are nonetheless assertions which are either true or false. This is not, of course, to say that to determine that a given course of action is the one that ought to be taken is to choose (or decide, or will) to take that course of action. People do not always do, or for that matter decide, choose, or will to do, either what they ought to do or what they believe that they ought to do.

In seeking to determine what ought to be done, we look for justificatory reasons for doing one or another thing. A justificatory reason for doing something is a reason for believing that it ought to be done. But an individual is not thereby moved to do the act in question. More importantly, the question of whether a given fact (or belief) is or is not a reason for doing something is itself not a matter of choice, will, or preference, whether individual or collective. It is not an "existential matter": it is a matter for critical examination and rational determination.

There is, of course, a distinction to be drawn between the judgment that something is the case and the judgment that

7. Clearly, full treatment of this question cannot be accomplished here. It is a matter to be relegated to professional journals.

something ought to be done, i.e. that someone ought to do something. But the distinction rests primarily on the sorts of things that can be justificatory reasons, on the one hand for believing something, and on the other hand for doing something. In particular, the fact that my believing that something is the case will make me happier (etc.) than my not believing that it is the case, cannot be a reason for my believing that it is the case. But the fact that my doing a given act will make me happier than my not doing that act, is a reason—though not necessarily a conclusive reason—for my doing that thing. Believing is in crucial respects not like performing an action. Teleological considerations are relevant to doing, but teleological considerations are not relevant to justifiable believing about what is the case. We answer the question "What ought so-and-so to do?" by sentences of the form "It is the case that so-and-so ought to do such-and-such." For in saying that we are saying that there are reasons for believing something, and in the determination that there are reasons for believing teleological considerations are not relevant; but of course beliefs *about* such considerations are relevant. One does not choose whether there are reasons for doing something or not; and insofar as we may properly speak of deciding whether there are reasons, we use the term "decide" in just the same way as we use it when we speak of deciding whether something is the case.

In terms of our earlier analogy, we may say that practical reason might properly assign to theoretical reason the task of understanding the way it (practical reason) operates, in order that it may function more effectively. So, too, we may suppose that it is reasonable for a society to allocate resources for the study of the allocation processes themselves—as well as for the study of particular allocations—so that it may function more effectively and, in this case, more fairly. It is in this sense, then, that we may correctly conclude that the careful study of what ought to be done may properly be an academic function.

I do not, of course, suggest that by itself this is sufficient to show that Earle is wrong in his view about what constitutes appropriate curriculum or appropriate research. To show that his thesis is not supported by the fact–value distinction is not to show that it is supported by nothing. Nor do I suggest that what I have said is sufficient to show that Earle is wrong in his thesis about the responsibilities of philosophers. Nevertheless, it does support the contention that matters of the justification of public policies, as much as questions of their history and probable consequences, may properly be dealt with academically, indeed, even within the classroom. More precisely, it supports the contention that if the one is justifiable academically, so is the other.

Nor does participation in such investigations necessarily diminish one's capacity to remain "academically dispassionate." Academic lawyers are able to retain their neutrality though they engage in criticism and analysis of actual courtroom decisions and procedures, and though they engage—as some do—in discussions concerning the legal justification for our conduct in Southeast Asia. And philosophers, by the same token, can retain their academic dispassion though they might argue, as professional philosophers, that our conduct in Southeast Asia has been morally wrong. And finally, if, as some have maintained, the government is entitled to the best advice it can get on matters of fact, then it is entitled—though it may prefer not to have it—to the best advice it can get on matters of justification, including moral justification.

Further, in examining Earle's view, we should consider the alternative principle(s) that would be available were political and social considerations determined to be entirely irrelevant to decisions concerning what is and what is not to be researched and taught. Indeed, Earle himself makes reference to what we may call the "purist" view of the university, though admittedly only in the context of classroom activity. He says:

> The much cherished freedom of the classroom is, of course, hardly the freedom to use it for any purpose whatsoever. It is its freedom from pressure originating outside of the logic of the course itself. These pressures can be from the administration, the community, and also from the existential options of the professor teaching it. *It is the freedom of thought to follow its own proper logic, a logic which could in fact be perverted by any influence outside that logic.*[8] [Italics added.]

The principle suggested here may without difficulty be expanded to incorporate all academic work. We shall construe it as a principle which determines what is to be researched and taught at the university in terms of the internal logic of the various fields of inquiry, which are themselves reflections of prevailing beliefs about the structure of human thought.

On this view, much of the research now countenanced on university campuses would properly be adjudged to be illegitimate, i.e. nonacademic. The direction and motivation for much of what is now countenanced on college campuses have been determined largely by the pressures of social and political problems. Among the influencing factors may be included the competition—among both universities and individuals—for grants from governmental and social agencies for research into particular problems only tangentially related to

8. Earle, op. cit., p. 11. It should be noted that a defense of the sanctity of the classroom may be constructed by appeal to the principle discussed above, namely, that organizational activity ought to be limited to the defining purposes of the organization, plus activities which may reasonably be construed as means to the fulfillment of those activities. Such a defense would, of course, be subject to the same criticisms that would be applicable to any appeal to that principle, though, since the particulars are different, determination of actual responsibilities might differ.

the internal development of the various fields of inquiry; the desire among faculty members to develop sufficient expertise in some of the problem areas so as to become valuable, so to speak, to these nonacademic agencies; and finally the motive to do research into marginally academic areas, e.g. into current political and social problems, for the sake of being of help in their solution. Much of the present research, for example, carried out under the name of sociology is motivated by this latter interest. Many of the experiments done in ghetto areas can hardly be said to constitute experimentation for the purpose of verifying or falsifying hypotheses of general interest to sociological theory. Nor need we single out sociology for such criticism. Much of the technology which has found its way into the university, much of the experimental work done even in the "hard sciences," and much of the work done in so-called area studies, find their moving force outside the logic of the development of human knowledge.

This more rigid criterion of permissible university activity corresponds much more closely to what, on the individual level, we characterized as the interest in developing theoretical reason for its own sake. I suspect that historically the expansion of the university curriculum into its present form is explainable in terms which refer primarily to the development of a complex society requiring both general and specialized training which could most conveniently be carried out apart from the other institutions of society. Though one might seek to provide justification for this expansion in terms of one's understanding of the notion of the academic, by seeking to determine the significant characteristics shared by centrally academic subjects, it seems to me that what are fundamentally operative are social pressures to provide this necessary kind of training in the most economical fashion. Thus the activities to be properly pursued at a university are fundamentally determined by the desirability of engaging in certain inquiries organizationally apart from other institutions of society. And if we insist on identifying the notion of the academic with that which is properly pursued at the university, then we shall be forced to conclude that the term "academic" is determined by social and political considerations, i.e. that it is fundamentally a term of social or political classification.

Now it might be thought that in rejecting the distinction between permissible and forbidden university work in terms of the fact–value (i.e. practical reason–theoretical reason) distinction, I am arguing in favor of more work being done along the lines that Chomsky deems appropriate; for example, philosophical analysis of ideology. However, I am not so arguing, or rather I am not so arguing on what may be called academic grounds. For I think that the questions of the responsibilities of universities and their faculties, including the question of what sort of research they ought to do, are not to be settled by determining what is and what is not properly considered to be academic work. Thus, even were there to exist universal agreement that casuistical investigation about, for example, the justification of the behavior of the United States in Southeast Asia, ought to be countenanced within the academic rubric, it could hardly be maintained that such investigations are as far-reaching philosophically as the fundamental questions with which philosophers normally deal. And although it may be true that philosophers will be led to recognize crucial distinctions as a consequence of turning their attention to the analysis of current issues, political and social, there is good reason to suppose that they are more likely to enhance their understanding of central philosophical issues by means of the artificial examples that they are wont to use.

If, then, in response to external pressures, one is moved to alter the direction of his research and teaching toward public policy questions of general interest, one has, in an important way, ceased to be directed by one's understanding of the internal logic of his discipline. If this is justifiable, it requires justification. If this is the philosopher's responsibility, it must be shown to be his responsibility. But one thing is clear: any such justification will have to make reference to those responsibilities which arise outside of academic life.

On the other hand, it might be thought that I am arguing for the purer view of what sorts of things are acceptable areas of research and teaching. It is true that many of the moral problems which plague universities and their faculties would be significantly lessened were such a criterion strictly applied. Nevertheless, I am not arguing for this conclusion, for, again, I do not think that the issue lies here. Determination of appropriate activity for a university does not rest on determination of the criteria for something properly to be identified as academic.

III

My thesis, in general, is that the decisions concerning what is and what is not a proper university activity are, at bottom, social decisions, and are therefore subject to moral criticism. They are not properly understood as academic decisions, though in making such decisions the well-being, so to speak, of academic studies must certainly be taken into account. The view that I am defending is readily understandable as the institutional analogue of rational decision-making by individuals. Among the factors that properly count as reasons for an individual to do something is included, for example, the fact that his doing that thing will enhance his own well-being. The fact that someone enjoys doing something is a reason for him to do that thing. In like fashion, we shall say that the fact that a given (institutional) act will enhance the well-being of academic institutions is a reason for a university to perform that act. But, just as the fact that my doing something will harm another is a reason for me not to do that act, so the fact that by doing something a university will harm others is a reason for it not to do that act.

Thus, for example, there is good reason to suppose that much of the technical training and much of the research into political and social problems which are now part of university curricula are either necessary or desirable if an advanced, technocratic society is to operate successfully. Such research and training can perhaps be carried on most fruitfully and economically at universities. These are, I suggest, good reasons for universities to incorporate such activities into their curricula. They are thus reasons for modifying curricula away from the strict criterion discussed above. Of course, to suggest that there are reasons for so modifying curricula is not to suggest that there are no reasons for refusing or deciding not to cooperate with the other institutions of society. Thus, for example, included in the weighing of reasons must be such factors as the effect of such curriculum changes on the thoroughness of the intellectual training provided by the university.

More importantly, it follows from this thesis that universities may, in appropriate circumstances, restrict or prohibit certain activities which have heretofore been allowed to operate within the university. If it is permissible, for other than strict academic reasons, for universities to cooperate with other institutions of society, then it may become obligatory, for other nonacademic reasons, for universities to refuse to cooperate. The most obvious examples arise when the activity in question is judged to contribute significantly to immoral policies.

Consider, for example, the case of ROTC. A number of universities have recently limited the scope of ROTC operation on their campuses. Some universities have sought to remove it altogether from the curriculum. For the most part, the justification that has been offered makes reference solely to the academic qualifications of ROTC training. What was at one time judged to be academically satisfactory is now seen to be unjustifiable. My own view of the matter, on the other hand, is that such justifications are at best misleading. For example, one is hard put to see just how ROTC training can be found to be academically unjustifiable while teacher education, including classroom practice, is not only accepted, but is, in some cases, required. What is operating here under the mask of an academic judgment is a political judgment, and it ought to be recognized as such. Under usual circumstances, there are good reasons for universities to cooperate with the military. But some universities have judged, correctly in my opinion, that to continue to cooperate at this time would be significantly to contribute to an immoral governmental policy, namely, the war in Southeast Asia.

Finally, having formulated this view, and having briefly examined some of its consequences, let us return to the issue raised at the end of section I: that except in extreme cases the advantages to society to be realized from academic institutions removed entirely from political considerations are greater than the advantages of academic institutions which do take such considerations into account in making their policy decisions, both intrinsic and extrinsic. Put slightly differently, the thesis holds that, while there are indeed political consequences to academic activities, and while there might indeed be instances when, should the university refrain from taking political considerations into account, it would fail to perform actions that are socially more desirable than what it would

otherwise do, nevertheless the overall consequences of politically neutral universities are to be preferred.

In order to examine this view, we shall return to the analogy developed earlier. We have seen that practical reason
functions to distribute the resources of the individual in accordance with the principle of maximizing satisfactions. We
have seen, further, that in order to do this properly, practical
reason ought to distribute resources for the development of
the individual's theoretical reasoning capacity both (1) in
case the individual is intrinsically interested in learning and
(2) in case and to the extent that such development is a condition of maximizing the satisfactions to be derived from the
individual's other interests. At the societal level, as we have
seen, resources ought to be allocated to universities (1) to
the extent that such allocation is fair with respect to the
competing intrinsic interests of the individual members of the
society, and (2) to the extent that the development of universities is a condition of maximizing the satisfactions of members of society. These issues of allocation are, as such, straightforward political, social, and moral questions.

What then leads some to suppose that universities ought to
be apolitical? In terms of our analogy, we may represent their
reasoning as follows: among the factors that must be taken
into account in deciding how to allocate resources are (a) the
extent to which the recipient interests in question are in need
of (require) resources and (b) the extent to which these
interests will be negatively affected, i.e. unable to satisfy
themselves or serve their function of providing the necessary
means for the satisfaction of other interests, if they engage
themselves in the processes of distribution. With respect to
the first factor, it is not difficult to see that the distribution of
resources is not necessarily fair or optimal if it proceeds without consideration of the quantity of resources needed to
achieve fulfillment.

But with respect to the second, so the argument runs, the excessive influence of some interests may pervert the capacity of reason, i.e. of inquiry, to come to a successful conclusion, namely, knowledge, and thus may pervert both the intrinsic interest of individuals in achieving knowledge and the capacity of universities to serve the needs of other institutions. Psychologically speaking, as we have seen, the fact that an individual will enjoy doing something is a reason for him to do that thing. But an individual might be led, by virtue of the fact that he will enjoy doing something, or by virtue of the fact that he believes that he will enjoy doing something, to hope, want, wish, or desire, and thus believe that certain things are the case, for example, that the means are available for him to do that thing. So, too, he might be led to believe that there are no overriding reasons for him not to do that thing. But none of this has the slightest tendency to show that in fact the means are available for doing the thing in question or that in fact there are no overriding reasons. In other words, desiring that something is the case might play a role in determining (causing) the individual to believe that it is the case, though his desiring that it is the case can never be a justificatory reason for his believing that it is the case.

Similarly at the societal level. The fact that the society (collectively) wants to accomplish something, for example, the domination of another country, may lead it to desire that certain things are the case; for example, that the other society is weak, corrupt, immoral, dominated by others, etc. This desire might indeed become a cause of some people believing these things to be the case, though it can never be a justificatory reason for so believing. It might further lead them to demand that people believe (or at least say that they believe or act as though they believe) that these things are the case. Fundamentally, the societal analogue of the psychological phenomenon of believing what one wishes to believe is, on the one hand, censorship, and, on the other, propaganda. Clearly those responsible for providing the theoretical knowledge necessary for the satisfaction of other interests must not be party to such influences. It is therefore concluded that universities ought, as much as possible, to be insulated from the political and social pressures that may tend to pervert them.

But none of these considerations, it seems to me, goes anywhere toward showing that determinations of what is to be researched and what is to be taught ought to be made in isolation from political and social considerations. One can hardly suppose it to be rational to isolate one's intellect from one's needs, despite the fact that there is risk of perverting the intellect. Deciding to inquire is a matter of practical reason, that is, it is a matter for the proper allocation of resources. But inquiry itself is a matter for theoretical reason, and ought indeed to be isolated as much as possible from perverting influences. What must be isolated is inquiry itself, not the decisions concerning what inquiries to make. There is nothing in the above arguments to show that allowing social and political, and therefore moral, factors to play a role in determinations of curricula would create conditions that must, or would even be likely, to result in the perversion of inquiry itself.

11

Russell, Radicalism, and Reason

A Review of *The Autobiogaaphy of Bertrand Russell,* Volume III

STUART HAMPSHIRE

The last volume of Bertrand Russell's autobiography received little attention when it appeared, not long before his death. Yet it raises a number of questions and doubts which are relevant to the thinking of radicals and liberals in the United States and in Western Europe today.

Covering the years 1944-1969, this third volume was principally a record of Russell's various crusades on behalf of nuclear disarmament and civil liberties, and of his embittered opposition to American imperialism. His platform appearances on behalf of nuclear disarmament, the battles in committees, and the founding of his Peace Foundation sometimes make for dull reading now, even though they are the heroic expression of an unquiet old age. The quoted correspondence clearly shows that in this last, wholly political phase of his various life, Russell was driven forward, not only by his sympathy with suffering, but also, and increasingly, by anger: more than anger, by a generalized and philosophical rage about the human condition, and by a kind of Shakespearean disgust.

His rage was directed against the unvarying wickedness of governments and of their scientific, commercial, and bureaucratic accomplices, and, to a lesser degree, also against the docility and gullibility of a decent and deceived public. Starvation, tyranny, and wars could even now be avoided, if governments were less wickedly intent upon magnifying their own powers, and if their subjects would attend to simple arguments. If these conditions are not fulfilled, mankind will destroy itself, and will continue to suffer even worse disasters on the road to a final destruction soon to become unavoidable. These were Russell's final beliefs, which took the place of the confident, even gay, radicalism of his middle years.

This despairing attitude of the aged Russell is one paradigm of the intellectual radical in politics: only the energy and intellectual authority were unique. Particularly exemplary are the righteous anger and the accompanying conviction that those who have power, the government and the establishment, are peculiarly corrupt in virtue of having this power; the governed, cozened and bemused, may still be open to rational persuasion from the radicals' platforms, because they are not committed to destructive policies by purely selfish interests.

From the standpoint of this kind of intellectual radicalism, there is a natural division between the victims and their deceivers, and the shepherds always prey upon the flock, whether they be capitalist entrepreneurs and managers or commissars and party hacks. In fact the secretaries of defense and chiefs of staff of the superpowers, who are nominally enemies, are more and more united in a preconscious conspiracy to sustain their deadly international game of competitive armament and subsidized guerrilla warfare. They suppress in their own territories any radical criticism of the assumptions that justify this game, and thereby justify their personal preeminence and the exercise of their skills. They will have a common interest in suppressing dissent, student protest, the potentially subversive freedom of writers and artists, and the demands of minorities for equal treatment.

This Russellian form of radicalism makes a very simple theory of contemporary politics; but it cannot be dismissed, as it usually is, on that ground alone, for it is certainly no vice in a theory that it is simple in relation to the complexity of the phenomena which it must explain. The first question is whether this very simple theory has yielded predictions that are more in accord with later experience than the predictions based upon rival theories.

Hardheaded liberals, who have for so long derided the simple-minded radicalism that Russell represented, would surely do well to be modest and cautious at this point. For the test is: Did their alternative theories yield predictions (say in 1965 and the two following years) which were more closely confirmed by events? Did they predict that the American government, continuously advised by university professors, would persist for several years in methods of warfare and of pacification that are criminal in international law and custom, and that are modeled on communist methods? Did they predict that the American government, in pursuit of its presumed strategic interests, would prop up, by firepower and money, any puppet, however repressive, provided only that he would not have dealings with Russia and China? Did they anticipate that the principles of the Nuremberg trials and pledges to international order would be brought into contempt so soon and by a democracy? Or did they rather predict that the phrase "American imperialism" would turn out to be a ridiculous misnomer? That the allegations of war crimes at the Stockholm Tribunals would be proved a farce, providing material only for cranks?

Having participated in, or observed, debates between radicals and liberals from 1963 onward, as an alien in the US,

I have a clear memory of the correct answers to these questions. The liberal theory always was that the Vietnam war was, at the worst, a mistake, a temporary aberration and miscalculation, rather like the Suez expedition of the British; the American government was not interested in strategic bases or a prolonged presence, and would withdraw if it became clear that a sustainable democratic government, with adequate local support, was not to be found; this is what I was told by the well informed. Only the radicals predicted, in 1965 and 1966, the cost-efficiency ruthlessness, now called "Vietnamization," the imitation of communist methods in the establishment of bases, the burning of villages, the gradual extension of the war to the whole area. I remember this balance of the argument surrounding the rhetorical phrase "American imperialism," because in 1965 I believed in the liberal theory of the war as a mistake: the theory that the Kennedy and Johnson administrations had walked into a trap, misled by their military staffs, and that, once they realized this, they would change both their policy and their military advisers.

But I gradually realized that the notion of mistake was soon playing the same role in the interpretation of American policy as that played by epicycles in Ptolemaic astronomy; as more and more "mistakes" accumulated the theory became untenable. The radicals of 1965 had been proved right. For liberals the prolonged aerial terrorism, the ever new burnt villages, the resettlement camps, the free-fire zones, and the Harvard professors calmly assessing their efficiency were a surprise, and seemed an inexplicable collapse in national decency. The radicals with whom I had argued, and who had not thought Russell, with his talk of "American imperialism," a mere crank, nor the Stockholm Tribunal a farce, could, and did, say—"I told you so: why would you not believe that the American government, with its academic and military advisers, is ready to match atrocity with atrocity indefinitely in defense of American influence in Asian countries, no matter what the cost to the local populations?"

There is an answer to this question, and the radical versus liberal argument is certainly not closed at this point. The word "imperialism," brandished by radicals and by Russell, has no more explanatory and predictive power than the theory of modern politics from which it originally derived its sense: the Marxist-Leninist theory, which yields predictions that have been discredited by events over and over again, more amply even than liberal theory. As used by Russellian radicals, the word "imperialism" serves only to summarize the facts and not to explain or interpret them, even in a minimal sense.

We have no tolerably precise and unrefuted theory of imperialism which points to the forces that now ensure that liberal expectations should be disappointed, and liberal principles trampled on, by successive US governments. Russell's own explanations, which impute the organized brutalities to the egoism and stupidity of politicians and generals, depend upon ignoring the fact that the politicians and generals can count upon support for these policies from a clear majority of the voters. Chauvinism and xenophobia are likely now to be the majority attitude in any country, socialist or capitalist, and the liberal and radical opposition to them is likely to be a self-conscious minority. I doubt that Russell ever adjusted his theories to this fact, or that he ever gave Tocqueville's predictions their due importance.

Unlike his predecessors and peers in public philosophy–Plato, Aristotle, Spinoza, Locke, Hume, Hegel–Russell did not apply to politics the analytical methods which he called for in the theory of knowledge. He made no solid contribution to political philosophy, although he thought continuously about politics from 1914 onward. Yet the foregoing names show that there is no historical and regular connection between being a great philosopher and also an intellectual of wide range, and ignoring, or despising, the peculiar difficulties of theoretical analysis which practical politics present. The connection was rather a peculiarity of Russell's temperament, partly an effect of that imperious rage which he first felt in 1914 and which is so vividly described in his autobiography: and perhaps partly the effect of an austere conception of reason, derived from mathematics, which stood in the way of his ever arriving at a theory of rationality in politics, or of practical reasoning in general. He therefore contributed to the modern stereotype of the intellectual in politics as always putting a simple moral disgust in the place of a slow analysis of changing possibilities.

But the fact remains that, in this last phase, he was more truly prophetic in his emotional attitudes and beliefs than either he or his liberal critics knew. A substantial minority of a new generation, particularly, but not only, in America, now shares exactly his moral disgust, and the accompanying impatience with conventional political analysis; and this post-Russell generation has made its rage, particularly in the United States, an effective political force. But, unlike Russell, they will need, and will look for, a method of political analysis—and, in this narrow sense, a theory—which is less unreliable, under contemporary conditions, than what is handed down to them either in the classics of liberalism or by Marxists. Where will this theory be found? Perhaps a dim outline can already be seen.

Their first step has been critical, rather than constructive, and has earned the label—quite mistakenly, as I think—of "irrationalism." "Reason" is a normative and not a neutral scientific term. What counts as reason, as opposed to thought of less constructive and useful kinds, is largely a matter of judgment, at least in practical and political contexts; and this judgment must refer to a sufficient, proved consistency in obtaining results in the relevant field, results which are permanently accepted as correct, and which are obtained by constant habits of thought. The academic and near-academic experts on foreign policy, who have advised the Kennedy, Johnson, and Nixon governments, provide an interesting counterfeit model of rationality, with all the traditional external marks of reason, without the underlying substance; this same model of rationality was paraded by Mr. McNamara and his defense advisers.

The model is not only operative in Washington, but also in universities, where strategic studies are encouraged and potential political experts are trained. It is this simulacrum of rationality in politics that students have intelligently rejected, judging it by consistency in result: and they see that unprofitable outrages and a gross political insensitiveness flow from these habits of thought, which ought not therefore to be given the honorific title of reason. The method of thought is evidently not appropriate to its material.

This established model of reason can be characterized as a coarse, quantitative, calculative Benthamism, refined by game theory, which adds and subtracts incentives and disincentives, volumes of firepower, and amounts of social services, and then arrives by computation at probable human responses distributed in a total population: which calculates the cost-effectiveness of alternative policies by the number of American lives to be lost and the amount of American wealth to be dissipated in securing the sufficient compliance of foreigners to dominant American interests. The model bears the label of rationality, not because it has proved successful in political practice, but because it has the look of a human technology and of market research and profit-loss calculations, all of which are used in the great commercial corporations; and these corporations are now the institutional models of rational planning.

Within the last few centuries, it has been conventional to contrast reason both with sentiment and with intuition, that is, with any sense of confidence that a judgment is correct which is not defended and maintained by reference to a regular method of computation. Therefore those, and particularly students, who are now expressing their disgust at computational politics are dismissed as sentimentalists trying to turn the clock back to a prerational phase, when modern technology and industry were unknown. They are political Luddites.

But their challenge to the computational model of reason in politics may be philosophically defensible; and the parallel between political decision and correct solutions in the applied sciences may be largely fallacious. The survival of the species, and of any individual nation, may now, and for the first time, depend on an altogether different method of political reasoning. The ineptitude of the Harvard professors, and of the other Presidential and military advisers, has been shown to reside precisely in the apparent cleverness and the advertised coolness of their calculations, in the contemptuous "realism" of which they boasted in arguments with radicals in 1965, 1966, and the succeeding years.

Their "realistic" calculations were a failure, at least partly because of a lack of self-consciousness; they did not realize soon enough that their habits of calculation, which had earned them success under American conditions, would earn no respect or response in the scattered populations which they were manipulating. Their recommended methods of warfare and of propaganda, which are an exportation of the planning methods of commerical corporations selling a product, produce only disloyalty and a revulsion against the civilization that finds these methods reasonable and natural. The vulgarity of mind that shows through the calculations, and in the terms in which they are expressed, defeats itself; it also seems to many students to justify a repudiation of some of the forms of life which have produced it.

It is not reasonable, after contrasting calculative reason with mere sentiment, to use methods of warfare and of persuasion that are repugnant to the normal human sentiments of the aliens affected by them. In commerce the costs of failure are quantitatively calculable and limited; and in Machiavelli's Italian cities the costs of violence and deceit were calculable and limited also, because millions of unknown men were not simultaneously involved in every political event, nor was the risk of failure ever the risk of total destruction. Critical university students have therefore now arrived at Russell's moral disgust, but with at least one important difference: they cannot share the illusion of his traditional, 1914-style radicalism, which attributed war policies to the interests of a ruling class or group, and which pictured the working mass of the population as deluded victims. They know that they are a minority, and they believe on good evidence that the social structure which has produced the new technology of limited warfare also has its proper expression in a nervous mass chauvinism and in widespread contempt for alien forms of life. But this belief is a mere observation of fact, and they know that they still lack any tested theory which plausibly explains these connections.

If the liberal and radical intelligentsia, which includes perhaps one-third of a university age group, knows itself to be a minority in the country as a whole; if it also knows that similar, though less numerous and powerful, liberal and radical minorities exist in other industrialized countries, capitalist and communist alike; if it also knows that it still has no sufficiently precise social theory which can be made the basis of predictions and of an organized party: what forms will its political action most naturally and reasonably take?

First, it will form a unifying consciousness of itself as a

pressure group, able to disrupt spasmodically, but effectively, the smooth pseudo-rational calculations of the policy-makers. Secondly, it will represent itself to itself as a movement of resistance to prevailing standards of rationality, not only in policy planning, but in social organization generally, and particularly in universities and schools. Thirdly, it will try to engender by example forms of life and moral attitudes which invert the dominant national models, and which are not only potentially international but are also unlike those forms of life that have both supported and depended on technological success in the West. They will measure the reasonableness of their actions and attitudes by independent criteria, the criteria of a minority, which is conscious of itself as being a minority.

The amended criterion of practical reasonableness will be a denial of the computational model of reason in politics, and it will single out for support those policies which are intrinsically reasonable, relative to standard and permanent common interests and sentiments. Those who adopt such a criterion will therefore reinvent for themselves a secular version of practical reason as it was conceived by theorists of natural law, which prescribed limits to the justification of inhuman policies by reference to their desirable consequences in particular cases; and these limits are to be discerned by a reasonable reflection on the intrinsic nature and quality of the actions which the policy involves. This retrogressive step now looks revolutionary.

A minority can reasonably be self-sufficient and experimental in manners and morals if it is a voluntary association of peers performing its experiments only upon itself and expecting to change the way of life of a majority only by infection, if at all; and if it is not calculating a remote change in the balance of power at the center. One can see this strategy as an extension to public life of the idea of a moratorium, which is the mode of experience of a student at a university, who naturally sees himself as enjoying a moratorium in his development.

But it will be asked—how can this moratorium and withdrawal from the computational politics of confrontation be effective in face of the totalitarian powers? Is it not unreasonable, by any criterion, to suppose that disunited and unmobilized populations will survive? This question may first be answered in its own terms, by a computation of consequences. The superior rationality of the radicals, as it seems to me, resides in the elements which, unlike the pragmatic liberals, they include in their computations of a probable future. They will include in their sums not only the interests and armaments of the opposing decision-makers, but also the limited capacities of mind and the fixed habits of thought of these men; and they will not omit themselves, the dissident minority, from the calculations. As Russell always argued, the question at issue is whether the species can survive for a long time, with any tolerable form of life, given the capacities of mind of the probable decision-makers and the nature of contemporary and future armaments.

Suppose that the development of the means of production and of destruction accelerates in a more or less deterministic pattern, and concurrently the skills, interests, loyalties, and habits of thought appropriate to these means of production and destruction are by the ordinary mechanisms reinforced and spread in whole populations: then majority support for the computational politics of confrontation between fully mobilized populations is so far assured. The radicals' idea of a moratorium is the belief that the only point of leverage immune to these deterministic connections is to be found in those who, being temporarily dissociated from the productive and destructive process by their own interests and circumstances as students, may choose to prolong this dissociation together with the experimental habit of thought that it permits.

The contradiction in the present system of national mobilization of resources, capitalist and communist alike, may reside in the facts, first, that a large university-trained minority is needed if technology and planning are to be continuously developed, and, second, that a sufficient minority of this minority will, during its time out, see the necessity of arresting the mobilization and of interrupting its apparent deterministic connections. If one calculates that the habits of thought and the mental capacities of communist and capitalist decision-makers, together with their armaments, provide a high risk of total destruction within a generation or two, as smaller nations join the race; and if one calculates that this is a mounting risk over many generations, it becomes rational to support the moratorium policy of dissociation and to build a continuing movement around this dissociation. This is the familiar consequentialist, or utilitarian, defense of the rationality of the moratorium, one that is conditional upon a disputable calculation. This is a version of Russell's argument, who, faithful to Mill, was always a consequentialist: his empiricist principles in philosophy would not allow him to use "reason" in any looser, non-computational sense. He therefore never arrived at a moral philosophy which would match and inform his emotions.

There is a different argument, which is reasonable, judged by the other, looser criterion of reason. If it did not arouse prejudice, it could be called the Aristotelian sense of reason. This argument appeals to certain very general facts about standard, recurring human needs and sentiments, but it does not depend on any precise computation of remote consequences. Some policies can be dismissed as contrary to reason, in spite of the consequential advantages that they may seem to bring in particular circumstances, because their successful execution would involve too great a coarsening of the sensibilities of their agents, and for this reason would make their lives subhuman, wretched, and shameful to themselves. There is a limit, set by the innate and normal structure of human feelings and interests, to the tolerable postponement of natural impulses of gentleness or generosity or justice for the sake of a future safety or advantage. The Southeast Asian policies of the US government under three Presidents, with popular support and the advice of business managers and academic experts, have been contrary to reason in this looser sense. The chosen means are manifestly incoherent with the chosen ends.

When inhuman and brutalizing means are used in resisting communist power the outcome will be a demoralized and divided population, not only despised by others, but also despising itself. This internal demoralization is not to be counted, within the theory, as a compatible and separate consequence of the policy, but rather as an intrinsic feature of the policy itself; for the original decision was to match communist methods of guerrilla warfare and pacification with an anticommunist version, and this required the adoption by the executants of the same mentality, of the same brutality in calculation; this mentality was chosen.

This is now familiar and evident. From the standpoint of the students, the significant fact is that when the free-fire zones and bombing and resettlement policies were adopted, the protests against these policies as contrary to tolerable principles of conduct did not come principally from intellectual leaders in Washington or from the academic advisers of the President or even, at first, from an obvious majority of university professors. On the contrary, I remember many members of these groups congratulating themselves on their adult and rational computation of consequences in contrast with the childish moralizing of radical students. That a large minority of students should in consequence distrust these official habits of thought, and the standards of rationality implied, and the academic authority associated with them, does not prove that they are enemies of reason. They naturally call for a rethinking, in philosophical terms, of what constitutes reasonable judgment in politics.

Beneath the opposition between the two standards of reason there is probably a deeper difference between contemporary radicals and their older liberal critics: a difference that is not easily formulated because a less than fully conscious thought is involved. It concerns the imagined time scale against which the effects of policies are calculated. A classical liberal, like Macaulay or Arnold before him, looks at contemporary institutions and habits of thought as persisting through vicissitudes in successive generations and sees the lives of only one generation, including his own life, as a phase or incident of a long process, in which some of the past is transmitted to his decendants and some is replaced in his own time. An individual's experience of social and political change, and his own contribution to it, has often been pictured by analogy with his more primitive experience of the continuing family into which he was born. He sees his own possible forms of life as limited on two sides, by his inheritance and by his need to transmit at least some of this inheritance to his children and to their descendants. He is a station on a permanent social way.

There are probable conditions under which this intimate sense of continuity, of one's own activities as constituting a phase, or incident, in an extending social process may be weakened, or lost, by many converging changes: by the spread of liberal ideas themselves, which deny an older stress upon inheritance; by mobility and also social mobility; by the spread of higher education, which loosens family connections; by accelerating technology, which makes the imagined future seem wholly unlike the past; also by the new image of a final catastrophe in a future war.

It is possible to picture the span of one's own life and family and that of one's friends, not as phases in a continuing social process, but as properly to be judged in isolation and for their wholly intrinsic qualities. One sees one's own life as the recurrence of a standard and permanent type, and not as a small contribution to a larger whole. This is an alternative picture, in itself neither more nor less reasonable than the picture that it may replace.

The judgment of a form of life for its intrinsic qualities, apart from its contribution to a phase of social change or of social stability, was quite normal in the West in those periods when religious belief in personal survival was usual, and when a wholly secular morality was the exception. These were the periods in which morality was conventionally based upon a doctrine of natural law which prescribed some absolute rules of conduct, valid for a recurring type of situation in a recurring form of life.

When critical intelligence has undermined the general belief in the supernatural sanctions behind an individual's normal judgments, the gap is usually filled by the idea of social utility in the long run; and the appeal to natural law is then dismissed from the prevailing liberal morality; for social change ensures that circumstances are always new.

But this liberal ethics presupposes both that the future of humanity is relatively secure, and also that social progress could be definitely identified as an accompaniment of general intellectual enlightenment. These two assumptions are quite explicit in Mill, and in Russell's earlier, more jaunty radical writings on morals and politics, before the age of anger and disappointment. But many reasonable persons cannot now make these assumptions. Therefore the signs of a rejection of the criterion of long-term social utility and social contribution are not to be counted as signs of a revolt against reason, in all its known senses: they are rather signs of a return to an earlier notion of practical reasoning, which has again become plausible because of changed expectations and a changed background of assumptions.

The new moral individualism would no doubt be unreasonable in Israel or in the new African and ex-colonial states, or wherever mobilization for an emergency is the condition of the survival of a new social order. But at least in the overdeveloped countries, in the United States, the Soviet Union and its satellites, and in Western Europe, it is not unreasonable to measure one's activities while still young against a shorter time span and to reject the seemingly perpetual mobilization which the politics of confrontation requires. To surrender the ambitions that any individual may have for his own adequate private life, as being the recurrence of an ideal type, may seem an unneeded compromise with the determinism of technology and national power. The race for supreme national power is just as likely to destroy the social order in nuclear war, or in destruction of the environment, as to preserve it in stalemate.

Those who are intelligent and young are likely therefore to follow their experimental moral reasoning, having a different time scale in mind and seeing their own immediate inheritance as principally an inheritance of war, the arms race, and repression. Only a moratorium, time out from the use of accelerating technology as new national power, will seem to them to offer recurrence of typical experience on a recognizably human scale for their children. The so-called generation gap is, I think, principally this absence of a hitherto normal sense of being able to transmit to children an inherited moral culture which has at least been proved to be safe and to preserve normal life. Because their parents seem to have provided no safety for grandchildren, they refuse the normal process of imagining themselves occupying their parents' positions.

The symbolism of the moratoria and mass meetings of these last few years seems to me now in retrospect very clear. The break evidently came with the realization that professors and deans of great universities, with their panoply of educated reason, could dismiss the critics of the Vietnam war as adolescent sentimentalists. The relation between reason and sentiment in politics and the nature of adult judgment in modern politics had to be rethought, because it seemed that the official reasoning was the computation of strained and stunted men, who to their younger critics had the look of overgrown schoolboys in Machiavellian dress.

The active, critical minority of students has been, on the whole, right in their judgment of events in the years 1965-70; and, in default of a comprehensive social theory, it has been reasonable also for them to build their movement of protest on the idea of a moratorium, of a period of confusion and arrest and redefinition, before it is too late. From their standpoint on the time scale, they may have no reasonable alternative.

Notes on Contributors

Hugo Adam Bedau, Jr., born in 1926, is Austin Fletcher Professor of Philosophy at Tufts University. He is the author of articles on justice, equality, human rights, civil disobedience, and other topics in social, political, and legal philosophy. He has edited *The Death Penalty in America* (2d ed. 1967), *Civil Disobedience: Theory and Practice* (1969), and *Justice and Equality* (1971).

Peter Caws, born in England in 1931, is Professor of Philosophy at Hunter College of the City University of New York. He has published *The Philosophy of Science: A Systematic Account* (1965) and *Science and the Theory of Value* (1967), as well as articles on the philosophy of science, structuralism, and educational policy. He reviews regularly for the *New Republic*.

Noam Chomsky, born in 1928, is Ferrari P. Ward Professor of Modern Languages and Linguistics at Massachusetts Institute of Technology. His work in linguistics has had a powerful impact not only on that field but also on psychology and philosophy. Since 1965 he has been a national leader of opposition to the American war effort in Vietnam and to

American imperialism generally. He is the author of *Syntactic Structures* (1957), *Current Issues in Linguistic Theory* (1964), *Aspects of the Theory of Syntax* (1965), *Cartesian Linguistics* (1966), *Topics in the Theory of Generative Grammar* (1966), *The Sound Pattern of English* (with Morris Halle, 1968), *Language and Mind* (1968), *American Power and the New Mandarins* (1969), and *At War with Asia* (1970).

Sidney Gendin, born in 1934, is Associate Professor of Philosophy at Eastern Michigan University. His main interests are in theory of knowledge and contemporary ethics. His articles on ethics have appeared in the *Australasian Journal of Philosophy, Mind, Philosophy and Phenomenological Research*, and other journals.

Stuart Hampshire, born in 1914, is Warden of Wadham College, Oxford. From 1963 to 1970 he was Professor of Philosophy at Princeton University. He is the author of *Spinoza* (1951), *Thought and Action* (1959), *Freedom of the Individual* (1965), and of articles in philosophy and related areas, some of which are collected in *Modern Writers and Other Essays* (1970) and *Freedom of Mind and Other Essays* (1971).

Virginia Held is Assistant Professor of Philosophy at Hunter College of the City University of New York. She has also taught at Barnard and worked as a reporter. She is the author of *The Public Interest and Individual Interests* (1970) and of articles on social and political philosophy, game theory, ethics, and public policy, in *The Journal of Philosophy, The Public Interest, Ethics,* and other publications.

Joseph Margolis, born in 1924, is Professor of Philosophy at Temple University. He is the author of *The Language of Art and Art Criticism* (1965), *Psychotherapy and Morality*

(1966), *Values and Conduct* (1971), and *Philosophical Problems* (to appear in 1972). He has also edited the following: *Philosophy Looks at the Arts* (1962), *Contemporary Ethical Theory* (1966), *An Introduction to Philosophical Inquiry* (1967), and *Fact and Existence* (1970).

Kai Nielsen, born in 1926, is Professor of Philosophy at the University of Calgary. Formerly he taught at New York University and at Amherst College. He is an editor of the *Canadian Journal of Philosophy*. He has written *Reason and Practice* (1971), *Contemporary Critiques of Religion* (1971), and many articles in a wide range of philosophical journals.

Charles Parsons, born in 1933, is Professor of Philosophy at Columbia University and an editor of *The Journal of Philosophy*. He has published articles and reviews on mathematical logic, the philosophy of mathematics, and Kant.

Gordon J. Schochet was born in 1937. He is Associate Professor of Political Science at Livingston College, Rutgers University, where he teaches social and political philosophy. He has written articles on civil disobedience and the political thought of Hobbes and Locke, and *Patriarchalism in Political Thought* (to appear in 1972).

Lewis M. Schwartz, born in 1939, is Assistant Professor of Philosophy at Lehman College of the City University of New York. He is the author of *Ethical Theory* (1971).

Robert L. Simon, born in 1941, is Assistant Professor of Philosophy at Hamilton College. He has contributed to philosophical journals in the areas of political philosophy and ethics.

Index

Airplanes, hijacking and seizure, 56, 57
Algeria, 28, 56
Allende, Salvador, 88
American Revolution, 25-26, 28, 42, 84-87
Amsterdam, riot in, 57
Angola, 49
Arendt, Hannah, 128
Argentina, 48, 56
Aristotle, 76, 83, 269
Arnold, Gen. H. H., 204
Auer, Ignaz, 113
Austria, 113

Baier, Kurt, 45
Bakunin, Mikhail A., 210
Bedau, Hugo Adam, 108, 129
Belgium, general strike, 114
Berlin, Isaiah, 32
Bernstein, Eduard, 18, 113
Berrigan, Rev. Daniel J., 57
Blum, Leon, 114
Brazil, 48, 58
Brown, Harrison, 118

A Call to Resist Illegitimate Authority, 4-5
Cambodia, 109
Catonsville Nine, 189, 192

Caws, Peter, 15, 72
Charles I, King, 84, 85
Chartists, 113
Chicago Democratic Convention, violence and trials, 189-92
Chile, Marxist government, 88
China, revolution, 25, 30, 85, 86
Chomsky, Noam, 11n., 38n., 40n., 50n., 200, 201, 235-36, 244n., 251
Civil disobedience, 5, 6n., 108, 123, 160-74, 214
    defiance of law and, 161-69
    government toleration of, 160-74
    moral judgment and, 165-68, 176-77, 186-89
    punishment and, 160-63, 175-96
    resistance to punishment and, 175-96
    strikes and, 123, 125-28
Civil War, U.S., 96, 129, 158
Columbia University, 9n.
Condorcet, Marquis de, 21
Conscientious objectors, 169
    exemption for, 154-56
Courts, trials of protesters, 189-93
Cox, Archibald, 164n.
Cuba, 149-50
    revolution, 25, 26, 30, 86

Dahl, Robert E., 121
Dahrendorf, Ralf, 19n., 32

Declaration of Independence, 89
Douglas, William O., 86-87
Draft Law, 129-32, 157-59
  conscientious objectors exempt, 154-56
  Supreme Court decisions on, 130, 142n.-143n., 145
Draft resistance, see Military service
Dworkin, Ronald, 167-68

Earle, William, 234-35, 242-43, 245-46, 248-49
Ellin, Joseph, 180
Engels, Friedrich, 77-78
English revolutions, see Great Britain

Fanon, Frantz, 26
Fascism, 46, 83
Foot, P. R., 45
Fortas, Abe, 164n., 172n.
France: conscription in, 145
  disorders in 1968, 88, 114, 116n.
  general strikes, 113-14
  Revolution, 25, 42, 43, 52-53, 80, 83-85
Friedrich, Carl J., 27
Fulbright, William, 215

Gendin, Sidney, 108, 160
George III, King, 84, 86-87
Germany, Revisionist debates, 113
Germany, West, 23-24, 39
Gompers, Samuel, 114
Government: civil disobedience and, 160-74
  as corporation, 117-19
  legitimacy and illegitimacy of, 5, 6n., 190-91
  moral obligation to serve, 138-41; see also Military service
Great Britain: Chartists, 113
  general strike, 113
  Puritan Revolution, 83-84
  Reform Bill of 1867, 113
  revolutionary situation in, 39
  revolutions, 25, 42, 43, 83-86, 96-97
Griswold, Erwin, 161

Habermas, Jürgen, 32
Hamilton, Alexander, 98-99
Hampshire, Stuart, 200, 258
Hegel, Georg Wilhelm Friedrich, 21, 92-93, 104
Held, Virginia, 108, 109
Hershey, Lewis B., 131
Hitler, Adolf, 50, 170
Hobbes, Thomas, 179
Hoffman, Julius, Judge, 190, 192
Hook, Sidney, 161
Hume, David, 245

India, 56
Indians, American, 57
Institutions, professional, 8-10
Israel, 56, 149

Jackson State College, 55, 109
Japan, 203-4
  in Manchukuo, 205, 206
  in World War II, 204
Jefferson, Thomas, 79, 88-89
Johnson, Lyndon B., 130, 203
Jordan, 57

Kaplan, Abraham, 125n.
Kaufman, Arnold, 112
Kautsky, Karl, 18, 26
Kelsen, Hans, 193-94
Kent State University, 55, 109
Kerensky, Alexander F., 86
King, Martin Luther, 97, 172-73
Kojève, Alexandre, 92-93
Korea, 204

Labor strikes, 110-17, 120-22, 127
Laslett, Peter, 83
Lasswell, Harold D., 125n.
Law, defiance of, and civil disobedience, 161-69
Lenin, Nikolai, 18, 87-88
Leopold III, King, 114
Liddell-Hart, B. H., 145
Lincoln, Abraham, 129
Lindblom, Charles E., 121
Locke, John, 83, 89-90, 150-51
Louis XVI, King, 84, 85
Luxemburg, Rosa, 18, 49

MacDonald, Margaret, 188-89
MacIntyre, Alasdair, 32, 45-46, 187n.
McNamara, Robert, 264
McPherson, C. B., 27-28
Manchester, England, riot in, 58
Manchukuo, 205, 206
Marcuse, Herbert, 27-28, 32-33, 96
   on violence, 36-37, 40-46, 48-49
Margolis, Joseph, 16, 52
Marx, Karl, 21, 33, 210, 215
   on philosophy, 72-73, 103
   revolution, theory of, 76-78, 81, 87-88
Melman, Seymour, 117
Military-industrial complex, 117-18
   labor and, 114
   student protests against, 110
Military service, 129-59
   conscientious objectors, exemption for, 154-56
   draft law, 129-32, 157-59
   legal obligation of, 129-33, 135-36, 158-59
   moral obligation of, 129-59
   resistance to, 135, 169, 181n., 214, 254
   Supreme Court decisions on, 130, 142n.-143n., 145
   voluntary, 137-39, 146
Mill, John Stuart, 154, 269, 272
Milwaukee Fourteen, 189, 192
Minneapolis, explosion in, 58
Moral judgment, civil disobedience and, 165-68, 176-77, 186-89
Moral obligation, military service and, 129-59
Mozambique, 49

Nazism, 46, 50
Nicholas II, Tsar, 84
Nielsen, Kai, 15, 17, 22n., 45n.
Nixon, Richard M., 131
Nonviolence: civil disobedience and, 170
   demonstrations, 97-98, 123

O'Brien, Conor Cruise, 40
Omaha, explosion in, 58

Parsons, Charles, 3
Philippines, 205
Philosopher-kings, 99-101, 103
Philosophers: education and, 101-2
   influence of, 10-11
   political action and, 72-74, 103-4, 199-200
   public policy and, 201-16
   responsibilities of, 199-200, 206-16, 234-36, 242-43
Plato, 33, 72-73, 92, 94, 102, 104, 107
   on philosopher-kings, 99-101, 103
Political strikes, 109-28
Popper, Karl, 24, 32
   on violence, 33-47
Protest: civil disobedience and, 168-69
   nonviolent, 97-98, 123
   strikes as, 109-28
   trials of protesters, 189-92
   violence in, 55-60, 96-98
   see also Vietnam war, protests and opposition
Punishment: civil disobediance and, 160-63, 175-96
   resistance to, 175-96

Rawls, John, 45, 140n.-142n., 161
Reagan, Ronald, 50
Reform: definition of, 21-23
   radical, 28-32
   revolution and, 17-51, 72-104
   strikes and, 112-15
Reich, Charles, 116n.
Revel, Jean-François, 81
Revolution: conversion and, 91-92
   cultural, 116n.
   definition of, 23
   epochal, 76-82, 90
   Marxian theory of, 76-78, 81, 87-88
   reform and, 17-51, 72-104
   socio-political, 23-28, 37-38, 75-85, 90
   in U.S., outlook for, 39-40, 48, 81-82
   violence in, 33-47, 94-97
Rocker, Rudolf, 210-11
ROTC, 254
Russell, Bertrand, 10, 200, 258-74
Russia, revolution, 25, 52-53, 83-86

San Rafael, Calif., courtroom killing,
    58
Schlesinger, Arthur, Jr., 203
Schochet, Gordon, 108, 175
Schwartz, Lewis M., 11n., 200, 234
Scientists, responsibility of, 9-10
Selective Service Act, 129-32, 154,
    157-59
Simon, Robert L., 8, 200, 217
Skolnick, Jerome H., 112
Society, transformation of, 18-21, 47-
    51
Sociopolitical revolutions, 24-28, 37-
    38, 75-85, 90
Socrates, 103, 107, 186
Soledad brothers, 58
Sorel, Georges, 113
South Africa, 49
Spock, Benjamin, 189, 192
Stimson, Henry, 204
Strikes: civil disobedience and, 123,
    125-28
  general, 113-14
  labor, 110-17, 120-22, 127
  political, 109-28
  student, 109-11, 115
  violence in, 120-21
Student strikes and protests, 109-11,
    115, 270-71, 274
Supreme Court, 173
  draft law decisions, 130, 142n.-143n.,
    145
Sweden, 113

Thoreau, Henry David, 144, 171
Truman, Harry S., 205

United States: American Revolution,
    25-26, 28, 42, 84-87
  Civil War, 96, 129, 158
  government as corporation, 117-19
  reforms in, 96-98
  reforms, hypothetical examples of,
    28-31
  revolutionary change, outlook for,
    39-40, 48, 81-82, 86-87, 89, 96-
    97
  strikes in, 114-16

Vietnam war policy, 201-16, 260-
    62, 270-71
  violence and riots in, 55-59, 95-97
Universities: political neutrality of,
    8, 11, 217-33, 243-45
  responsibility of, 211-16, 234-57
  student protests against war, 270-
    71, 274
  student strikes, 109-11, 115
  West German, reform of, 23-24
University of Chicago, Conference on
    the Draft, 130
University of Wisconsin, bombing,
    56-57
Uruguay, 56
Utopianism, 33-36

Vietnam, South, 49
Vietnam war: military service in, as
    obligation, 130-31
  protests and opposition, 4-5, 98,
    109, 201-16, 254, 260-64, 270-71,
    274
Violence: ethical defense of, 52-71
  examples of, 55-58
  Marcuse's ideas on, 36-37, 40-46,
    48-49
  Popper's ideas on, 33-47
  as protest, 55-60, 96-98
  in revolutions, 33-47, 94-97
  in strikes, 120-21
  see also Nonviolence
von Wright, G. H., 45

Walzer, Michael, 122
Warnock, G., 45
Wilson, Woodrow, 138
Winch, Peter, 45
Wittgenstein, Ludwig, 30
Wolff, Robert Paul, 219-20, 222-25
Women, strikes by, 115-16
Women Strike for Peace, 109
World War I, draft in, 129-30, 138,
    146, 158
World War II: draft in, 158-59
  Japan in, 204

Zinn, Howard, 202